Liverpool Studies in European Regional Cultures 2

Landscape, Heritage and Identity:
Case Studies in Irish Ethnography

LANDSCAPE, HERITAGE AND IDENTITY

Case Studies in Irish Ethnography

edited by

ULLRICH KOCKEL

*Published on behalf of the
Culture and Tourism Research Unit
at the Institute of Irish Studies,
University of Liverpool*

LIVERPOOL UNIVERSITY PRESS
1995

First published 1995 by
Liverpool University Press
Senate House
Liverpool
L69 3BX

British Library Cataloguing-in-Publication Data
A British Library CIP Record is available

0-85323-500-7

Printed and bound in the European Union by
Bell & Bain Limited, Glasgow

Preface

Ethnography, together with history, is enjoying something of a popular revival in recent years, and this is most evident in what has been described as the 'heritage boom'. One of the great socio-cultural trends in the final decades of the twentieth century seems to be an increased awareness of, and interest in historico-cultural questions, and especially in people's ethnic 'roots'. This has now almost reached a point where, at the level of popular culture, heritage is appreciated mainly for its entertainment value.

At the level of academic research, an increasing number of young scholars are also becoming interested in cultural issues, and this growing interest is reflected in the present volume, which includes a number of first contributions from researchers at the beginning of their career. A first publication is always an exciting experience, and we hope that the book will be well received.

As the series editors, we would like to thank Robin Bloxsidge of Liverpool University Press, who has been most supportive of the project, and has also lent a helping hand with the cover design. Once again, special thanks are due to Sarah Stamper for 'tidying up' the manuscripts which, as usual, arrived in different formats and styles. We would also like to acknowledge the support of Professor Patrick Buckland and the Institute of Irish Studies at the University of Liverpool, which provides the home for our research unit, and resources to produce this series.

Ullrich Kockel
Máiréad Nic Craith
(Series Editors)

Contents

List of Illustrations

Figures

Tables

Contributors

Mary Cosgrove   Department of Art and Design,
                           University of Ulster at Belfast

Sharron FitzGerald   Department of Geography & European
                           Studies, University College Cork

Heather Hegarty   Department of Geography & European
                           Studies, University College Cork

Mary Kells   Department of Social Anthropology,
                           London School of Economics and
                           Political Sciences

Moya Kneafsey   Culture & Tourism Research Unit,
                           Department of Geography, University
                           of Liverpool

Ullrich Kockel   Culture & Tourism Research Unit,
                           Institute of Irish Studies, University
                           of Liverpool

Janet Leyland   Culture & Tourism Research Unit,
                           Institute of Irish Studies, University
                           of Liverpool

Karin Molde   Seminar für Anglistik und
                           Amerikanistik, Universität Bremen

Máiréad Nic Craith   Culture & Tourism Research Unit,
                           Institute of Irish Studies, University of
                           Liverpool

Hermann Rasche   Department of German, University
                           College Galway

Introduction

ULLRICH KOCKEL

The overall perspective of the LIVERPOOL STUDIES IN EUROPEAN REGIONAL CULTURES is that of 'European ethnology' a discipline which emerged in the 1960s, following Bausinger's (1961) deconstruction of the *Volkskunde*-approach to cultural studies (*cf.* Greverus 1978; Kockel 1993; Jeggle 1994). Bausinger postulated an empirical cultural science concerned not with an idea of timeless meanings that are nowhere realised, but with the actual spiritual and material world of ordinary folk:

> *nicht eine nirgends realisierte Idee zeitloser Gehalte, sondern die wirkliche geistige und materielle Welt des "einfachen Volkes".*

He called for a greater historicisation of *Volkskunde* within a social historical perspective, and emphasised the spatial, temporal and social horizons of culture—in other words, the wider context of cultural contents and activities.

European ethnology investigates the relationship between culture and society in a European context. 'Culture' here encompasses the totality of lifestyles, forms and experiences, moral concepts and values—actions, norms and representations, to quote Czech scholars Holy and Stuchlik (1983)—of different social groups. It includes individual and collective 'life-worlds' and modes of environmental

Ullrich Kockel (ed.), *Landscape, Heritage and Identity: Case Studies in Irish Ethnography*, Liverpool University Press 1995, 1-10.

appropriation as expressed in language, social relations, and patterns of work and leisure. 'Culture' in this broad sense is visible in everyday rituals, in stories, tastes and routine acts, all with their own culturally conditioned logic. European ethnology examines these diverse forms of everyday culture from a comparative perspective, where 'comparative' does not necessarily mean that individual case studies must be far apart in space and/or time. Rather, the emphasis is on appropriate contextualisation of the case material, a process in which geographical and historical cross-referencing forms only the first, albeit decisive step (*cf.* Kockel and Ruane 1992).

Analysis in European ethnology is based mainly on ethnographic case studies. In the English-speaking world, the term 'ethnography' has acquired certain connotations over the past generation or so. It is widely used to designate qualitative research methods, in particular participant observation and oral history, and a specific style of writing which is commonly associated more with literature, or even journalism, than with social science. The colloquial understanding of ethnography is, therefore, quite narrow, essentially denoting a 'soft' approach to research, and a 'popular' style of writing about it. Research users and funding councils, however, have long recognised the merit of the approach in specific circumstances, and ethnography is now slowly, but surely, gaining ground even in 'hard' social science departments.

In European ethnology, and especially in France, Germany and Scandinavia, ethnography is more broadly defined as the rigorous, scientific (*wissenschaftliche*) description of culture in all its aspects, and it is this broader sense in which the term is used in the present volume. On examining the large body of work produced in the field of European ethnology over the past three decades, one is struck by the methodological pluralism that seems to prevail, ranging from literary criticism to mathematical modelling. Similarly, presentation styles are now much more varied than the traditional narrative account supplemented by a few photographs, maps and location sketches. Needless to say, European ethnology is also quite eclectic in its use of sources. Much of what is now part and parcel of undergraduate training was simply 'not done' when most of today's lecturers were themselves undergraduates. This transformation has greatly stimulated intellectual development within a discipline which is still expanding, as a major textbook (Brednich 1994) demonstrates. Since the first edition of his *Grundriss der Volkskunde* in 1988, the editor had to add several chapters to take account of newly-established key research areas, such as *Bildforschung* (picture research; see below). Having come through a school system which, by and large, prepares them for certainties and clear-cut boundaries between the academic disciplines, undergraduates on my introductory ethnography course are understandably surprised when they are told that the appropriate sources, methods, and forms of representation used in any project are determined primarily by the research questions asked, and not by any disciplinary canon.

The 1960s were also some kind of water-shed in Irish ethnography (*cf.* Wilson 1984), where a similar development took place. Whereas European ethnology emerged from an exchange of ideas between different national traditions of cultural studies in mainland Europe, the parallel process in Irish ethnography was very much dominated by theoretical debates in American cultural anthropology and, to a lesser extent, British social anthropology. In mainland European countries, the study of one's own culture has a long tradition and evolved independently alongside anthropology, producing its own methodologies and theoretical frameworks (Jacobeit 1986; Hartmann 1994; Sievers 1994). In the English-speaking world, it is of much more recent origin, and has grown primarily out of an anthropology concerned with 'exotic' cultures. The specific problems generated by this history have prompted considerable theoretical debate (*cf.* Jackson 1987; Cohen 1990). Ireland is a particularly interesting case in this respect, since it was regarded as sufficiently 'exotic' to merit anthropological study at a time when anthropology was still firmly trapped in its essentially colonialist paradigm. The early anthropological studies of Ireland informed much of subsequent research, keeping the focus of Irish ethnography on kinship and life-cycle patterns. This type of research was largely the domain of American and, at a later stage, British scholars. Indigenous ethnographic work, not unusually for a young nation state, consisted almost exclusively in the collection of folklore, in which Scandinavian ethnographers in particular took an active interest. The research of Estyn Evans is exceptional in this period. Under the influence of the *Landschaft* and *Kulturraum* paradigms in geography, Evans (1942; 1957) pioneered what may well be described as an early Irish approach to European ethnology with its methodological pluralism.

Since the 1960s, Irish ethnography has moved on considerably from its traditional focus on kinship and life-cycle, and from the paradigm of community studies (Wilson 1984), now encompassing a broader spectrum of issues, and employing a much wider range of methods. Recent research is more concerned with political and contextual questions, and with problems like gender relations or economic development, as the essays in Curtin and Wilson's (1989) *Ireland from Below* demonstrate. Partly as a reaction against the largely ahistorical stance of traditional anthropological research, and partly as a reflection of the contemporary rediscovery of history at the level of popular culture, there is now also a growing body of work in historical ethnography (*cf.* Silverman and Gulliver 1992), sharing the methodological and theoretical concerns of European ethnology as outlined by Kaschuba (1986).

Both contemporary and historical research are characterised by a broadening of the agenda, the incorporation of a larger variety of methods, and greater attention to different types of sources. French thinkers like Bourdieu and Foucault have been especially influential in recent years, and there is even a noticeable trace of Feyerabend in Irish ethnography (although by no means as pronounced there as it is in European ethnology on the mainland).

The essays in the present volume reflect this 'new' turn in Irish ethnography, conducted in the spirit of European ethnology. Only two of the authors hold any formal qualifications in anthropology, and this is indicative of the changing nature of Irish ethnography. The common, unifying feature of the ten essays is their concern with the rigorous, scientific description of culture, both historical and contemporary.

European ethnology has always emphasised the environment as an important concern in the study of culture, and this has been well recognised in Irish ethnography since Evans' work in the 1940s. The historical landscape, what we do in it and with it, and what it means for us and the way we relate to others, is a theme for most of the contributors to this volume.

Through processes of environmental appropriation, we turn the landscape into part of our heritage. However, 'heritage' is much wider than this, including not only the built environment and other aspects of material culture, folklore, traditional customs and rituals, but also—and perhaps most importantly—language, both as a vital part of our heritage, and as the primary means of transmitting this heritage to others across space and time. Thus it is appropriate that linguistic heritage receives particular attention in this collection of essays; it is the main topic of two contributions, and a subsidiary theme in two others.

At the heart of all contributions is the issue that has occupied many of the finest brains world-wide ever since the postmodernists entered the stage more than a decade ago—the question of identity. Along with 'culture', 'everyday life' and 'historicity', 'identity' has become a key concern of European ethnology as American cultural hegemony and the free movement of labour within the Common European Market, together with other factors, have made it appear increasingly problematic—that is, since about the 1960s. Volume 3 in this series, which is a study of ethnic frontiers in contemporary Europe, will address the obvious question of whether, and to what extent, European ethnology has been an intellectual reaction against a perceived 'internationalisation of culture' (*cf.* Bausinger 1961; Kaschuba 1986). For the time being, it shall suffice to note that the three countries in Europe which have been particularly exposed to American cultural hegemony—Britain, Germany and Ireland—are also the ones suffering the most serious identity 'crisis' which, in the case of Ireland, is potentially exacerbated by a history of mass migration. Consequently, Irish ethnography must not be restricted to the description of what happens in the island of Ireland, but ought to give due consideration to the situation of migrants in their new environment.

Much of the work presented in this volume is of an exploratory nature, dealing with issues that have to-date attracted little attention in Irish ethnography. The language question is addressed in the first two essays, both taking a historical perspective. An evaluation of the position of Irish in contemporary Northern Ireland, based on the most recent census returns, forms the background for Máiréad Nic Craith's review of the changing political and religious connotations of the language in this divided society. Janet Leyland takes a close look at two historical Gaelic island communities—the Great Blasket and St Kilda—in the societal and political context of their time, investigating the causes of language decline. Another Gaelic island community provides the backdrop for Mary Cosgrove's study of the artist Paul Henry, an iconographic-ethnological interpretation of the genesis of his art in the spirit of *Bildforschung* (Bringéus 1981; see above) which investigates the social environment and function, and possible literary and other inspirations of the work. The creative combination of different theoretical approaches to historical ethnography, especially the *Annales* school and the 'thick description' proposed by scholars like Clifford Geertz, is attempted by Sharron FitzGerald, whose reflective account of her experience 'in the field' exemplifies the tendency within the 'new' ethnography, to make the actual research process part of the inquiry. Moya Kneafsey's essay strikes a similar chord; her themes are the 'musealising tendency' (Assion 1986) of contemporary culture and the conflict between the technological capability of developers and the life-worlds of those whose heritage is being used as a resource, a problem which is of particular interest to peripheral regions, and which the smaller states in Central/Eastern Europe have long recognised (Hoffmann 1986).

The next four essays deal with migration, but their focus is rather unusual in the Irish context, as three of them are about immigration to the island. Very little work has to-date been done on this topic in any academic discipline, and for this reason alone the case studies are breaking new ground. Hermann Rasche considers the last major historical immigration, the Palatine settlements of the eighteenth century, drawing on a wide range of sources, and tracing the ethnic development of the settlers to the present day, when the 'heritage boom' has led to a raised ethnic awareness among their descendants. One of the main regions of immigration, West Cork, provides the geographical backdrop for Heather Hegarty's study of the lifestyles and socio-economic impact of immigrants; her findings offer an interesting contrast and regional addition to the only earlier work tackling these issues (Kockel 1989; 1991), based on the western seaboard from Kerry to Donegal. Germans have been, and still are, the largest immigrant group in the Republic of Ireland who have no ethnic roots in the island, and Karin Molde provides the first survey of contemporary German immigrants, their migration motives, and their perceptions of Irish everyday life. Although emigration is a salient fact of Irish life, research on Irish migrants abroad does not usually feature in Irish ethnography, perhaps because ethnographers tend to concentrate on people living in the island; Mary Kells has been researching the largest Irish migrant community in Europe, London, for many years, and her observations on the negotiation of Irish ethnicity offer important insights into inter-ethnic processes involving 'white' immigrants, a problematic that, in the European context, has so far been raised mainly for Finnish migrants in Sweden (*cf.* Jaakkola 1987). In the final essay, I attempt a review of the current debate on Irish ethnic identity and its markers, appropriate and otherwise, drawing together some of the issues raised by the other authors and considering research implications for the European ethnologist studying Ireland.

In putting together this collection of essays, the guiding principle was to afford the reader an insight into Irish ethnography in the context of European ethnology as it has been shaped over the past generation or so, addressing itself to new concerns, adopting and adapting fresh approaches to more traditional topics, and making the research more accessible to meaningful comparative analysis. The second objective was to present a selection of work on topics and in fields of inquiry which are relatively new to Irish ethnography. Thus the volume is not meant to provide a comprehensive overview of ethnographic research on Ireland and the Irish, but rather to complement such excellent collections as Curtin and Wilson (1989), or Silverman and Gulliver (1992), by emphasising a new dimension. Intended primarily as a reader for undergraduate and postgraduate courses, it is hoped that the volume will also be of interest to researchers interested in developing the study of Irish culture from the perspective of European ethnology.

REFERENCES

Assion, P
1986 Historismus, Traditionalismus, Folklorismus—Zur musealisierenden Tendenz der Gegenwartskultur. In Jeggle, U *et.al.* (eds), 351-62.
Bausinger, H
1961 *Volkskultur in der technischen Welt*, Stuttgart.
1971 *Volkskunde. Von der Altertumsforschung zur Kulturanalyse*, Darmstadt.
Bausinger, H, Jeggle, U, Korff, G, and Scharfe, M
1978 *Grundzüge der Volkskunde*, Darmstadt.
Brednich, R (ed.)
1994 *Grundriss der Volkskunde. Einführung in die Forschungsfelder der Europäischen Ethnologie*, 2nd rev. and ext. ed. of 1988, Berlin.
Bringéus, N
1981 *Bildlore—studiet av folkliga bildbudskap*, Stockholm.
Cohen, A
1990 Self and Other in the Tradition of British Anthropology, *Anthropological Journal on European Cultures* 1(1), 35-63.

Curtin, C and Wilson T (eds)
1989 *Ireland from Below: Social Change and Local Communities,* Galway.

Evans, E
1942 *Irish Heritage,* Dundalk.
1957 *Irish Folk Ways,* London.

Greverus, I
1978 *Kultur und Alltagswelt. Eine Einführung in Fragen der Kulturanthropologie,* München.

Hartmann, A
1994 Die Anfänge der Volkskunde. In Brednich, R (ed.), 9-30.

Hoffmann, T
1986 Alte Mauern—neue Museen? Konflikte zwischen visueller Revolution und Museologie. In Jeggle, U *et.al.* (eds), 391-6.

Holy, L and Stuchlik, M
1983 *Actions, Norms and Representations. Foundations of an Anthropological Inquiry,* Cambridge.

Jaakkola, M
1987 Informal Networks and Formal Associations of Finnish Immigrants in Sweden. In Rex, J, Joly, D and Wilpert, C (eds), *Immigrant Associations in Europe,* Aldershot.

Jackson, A.
1987 *Anthropology at Home,* Tavistock.

Jacobeit, W
1986 Weltbild im Wandel? Zur 'Volkskultur' zwischen Feudalismus und Kapitalismus. In Jeggle, U *et.al.* (eds), 25-36.

Jeggle, U
1994 Volkskunde im 20. Jahrhundert. In Brednich, R (ed.), 51-72.

Jeggle, U, Korff, G, Scharfe, M and Warneke, J (eds)
1986 *Volkskultur in der Moderne. Probleme und Perspektiven empirischer Kulturforschung,* Reinbek.

Kaschuba, W
1986 Mythos oder Eigen-Sinn. 'Volkskultur' zwischen Volkskunde und Sozialgeschichte. In Jeggle, U *et.al.* (eds.), 469-507.

Kockel, U

1989 Immigrants—Entrepreneurs of the Future? *Common Ground* 70, 6-8.

1991 Countercultural Migration in the West of Ireland. In King, R (ed.), *Contemporary Irish Migration*, Dublin, 70-82.

1993 *The Gentle Subversion. Informal Economy and Regional Development in the West of Ireland*, Bremen.

Kockel, U and Ruane, J

1992 Different Irelands: The Problem of Context in Irish Ethnography, *Anthropological Journal on European Cultures* 1(2), 7-35.

Kramer, D

1994 Museumswesen. In Brednich, R (ed.), 539-61.

Sievers, D

1994 Fragestellungen der Volkskunde im 19. Jahrhundert. In Brednich, R (ed.), 31-50.

Silverman, M and Gulliver, P (eds)

1992 *Approaching the Past. Historical Anthropology through Irish Case Studies*, New York.

Wilson, T

1984 From Clare to the Common Market: Perspectives in Irish Ethnography, *Anthropological Quarterly* 57(1), 1-15.

The Symbolism of Language in Northern Ireland

MÁIRÉAD NIC CRAITH

INTRODUCTION

This essay explores the evolution of the Irish language as a symbol of varying religious entities. My review will begin with a brief report of the position of Irish in Northern Ireland as demonstrated in the censuses of 1911 and 1991. In particular, attention will be paid to the link (if any) between one's religious denomination and one's knowledge of Irish. The aim of this initial section is to question the validity of the common assumption that if one speaks Irish, then one is Catholic and probably Nationalist.

The essay will then seek to trace the origins of this supposition and will focus on Protestant involvement with Irish in the past. The enthusiasm of many Protestant individuals for Irish in nineteenth century Ulster will be appraised. Catholic indifference towards the language during this specific period will also be assessed. The association of Irish with Protestant proselytism at the beginning of the nineteenth century will be suggested as a contributory factor to the decline of Irish among the Catholic population at this time.

The alleged link between Irish and Protestant proselytism did not endure throughout that century and the subsequent shift towards the association of Irish with the Catholic sentiment in the latter half of

Ullrich Kockel (ed.), *Landscape, Heritage and Identity: Case Studies in Irish Ethnography*, Liverpool University Press 1995, 11-46.

the nineteenth century will be assessed. This essay probes the accuracy of any of these suppositions and seeks to trace some of the events which may have aroused hostility by both Catholics and Protestants towards the language. In conclusion, some of the circumstances which may contribute today to the endurance of Irish as a separatist factor are analyzed and suggestions for remedial action are evaluated.

CENSUS STATISTICS

In 1921, the British Government withdrew the question concerning knowledge of Irish from the census form in Northern Ireland. This, in effect, was tantamount to a withdrawal of official recognition of the existence of this language in the United Kingdom. The removal of this question occurred despite the fact that the 1911 census had shown that in the first decade of the twentieth century, there were eight districts in Northern Ireland in which Irish had survived among 5% or more of the total population.

The 1911 Census

Three of these regions lay entirely within the new Northern Ireland state, and Irish-speakers made up over a third of their population. This inner core of the mid-Ulster Gaeltacht embraced the regions of the Sperrins, the Red Bay Gaeltacht in the Glens of Antrim and Rathlin Island off the north coast of Antrim. Furthermore, this new Northern Irish state had three areas along its border, in which between 5% and 20% of the population were Irish-speaking. These border regions were in South Armagh, West Tyrone and Southwest Fermanagh. Approximately 20% of the population of the Strabane area on the border were also Irish-speakers. The Irish spoken here was more probably the result of immigration of native Irish speakers from mid-Ulster and Donegal rather than the continuous survival of the language from one generation to the next. Finally, in the area around Trillick in Southwest Tyrone, about 5% of the population were Irish-speakers. It is clear, therefore, that there was a considerable minority of Irish-speakers in the new Northern Irish state at the time of the withdrawal of the language question in the census.

The 1991 Census

It was not until the last census in 1991, that the question of knowledge of Irish was re-inserted into the census form. The 1991 census queried whether each individual over the age of 3 in a household could speak, read, and/or write Irish. Those without a knowledge of Irish were also asked to indicate this. The result demonstrated that quite a sizeable proportion of the population of Northern Ireland had some knowledge of the language.

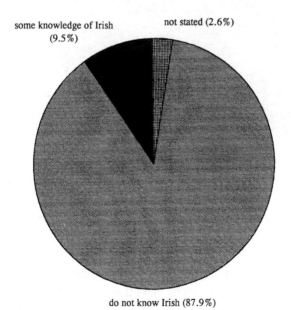

Figure 1   *Irish language competence in Northern Ireland, 1991 (Census of Population)*

The census related that of the total population of 1,502,385 people in Northern Ireland, 79,012 can speak, read, and write Irish. A further 45,338 can speak the language. In total, some 142,003 people—i.e., 9.5% of the population in Northern Ireland—claim to have at least some cognizance of Irish (Census of Population 1991). Details of the various levels of competency are given in Figure 1.

Moreover, the census report provided details regarding the various skills in the language possessed by the Irish-speakers. Figure 2 represents the varying degrees of skills involved.

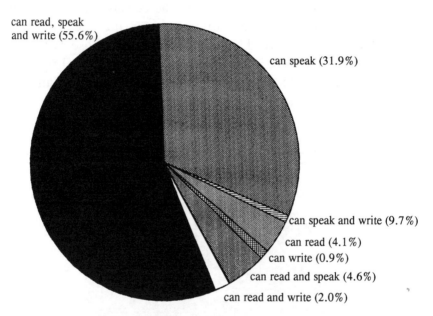

Figure 2   *Different degrees of language skill in Northern Ireland, 1991 (Census of Population)*

As is the case with any census question concerning language, there was no objective assessment of the accuracy of any of these statements regarding one's level of skills in Irish. One could question, therefore, the legitimacy of the statistics given in this census.

Many sociologists have debated the validity of self-assessment in census questions and query whether an individual can be sufficiently aware of his own language usage in order to report it validly on a census from. This was a problem noted by Garret Fitzgerald when conducting a study on the 1881 census of Ireland. He recognised that

> the question about Irish-speaking, unlike most census questions, is open to a degree of legitimate subjectivity in the answering. Individuals' concepts of the extent of the knowledge of a language that may justify a capacity to speak it can vary quite widely (Fitzgerald 1984).

This question remains unresolved, however. It is acknowledged by the eminent sociolinguist, Baetens Beardsmore, that even if the language question were restricted to asking merely which languages were spoken, the question would still be open to a degree of ambiguity (Beardsmore 1982).

A further factor which may distort the validity of language statistics is the possible existence of conscious or unconscious attitudes towards the language of investigation, which may interfere with the legitimacy of the self report. It is widely acknowledged, for example, that when the language question was first inserted into the census form in 1851 in Ireland, many people failed to reveal a knowledge of Irish, as it was suspected that the British government had some ulterior motive in asking the question. Joshua Fishman has scrutinised this difficulty at great length and he concluded that when respondents wished to provide accurate replies and when the questions asked were sufficiently simple, then the results of any language question in a census merited further specialised attention (Fishman and Terry 1971). It is clear, therefore, that unless there was an obvious resistance to the language question in the census form of 1991, or indeed an overly zealous welcome for it, then it is probable that the figures recorded present a more or less accurate account of the current vitality of Irish in Northern Ireland.

Of course the figures recorded in the 1991 census are not merely illustrative of the current vigour of Irish. When one investigates the percentage of Irish-speakers in each age group, and one places each age group in the context of their years of birth, then the statistics may used to present a picture of the vitality of Irish over a number of decades. Many Irish statisticians have employed this method. Adams (1974) was the first, however, to use it specifically to illustrate the strength of Irish in Ulster.

He examined the 1851 census and, by investigating the vigour of the language in various age groups, he was able to present a record of Irish-speaking in Ulster between the years 1761 and 1851. By following a similar method with the 1991 census, one can deduce the proportion of Irish-speakers in each decade in Northern Ireland since partition. These estimates are shown in Figure 3.

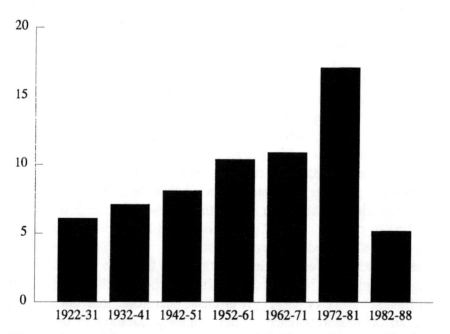

Figure 3   *Minimum percentage of Irish-speakers in Northern Ireland, 1921-88 (Census of Population, own calculations)*

Such a methodology is fraught with difficulties, however, especially as the calculations merely take account of the proportion of Irish-speakers in the youngest age group in any particular decade, that is, the level of Irish-speaking at the time when those recorded in the older age group were mere children. In very many cases, the method has, therefore, led to a gross underestimation of the proportion of Irish-speakers. In Figure 3, the results for 1972-81 probably reflect the impact of the 'Troubles' on cultural awareness in the Nationalist community, while the estimate for 1982-88 is rather low because it does not represent a complete cohort.

Language and Religious Denomination

For the purposes of this essay, the current vitality of Irish must be set in the context of religious denomination. This is important as for many people today, the Irish language is still associated with Catholicism and Nationalism. Meic Stephens (1976) writes that

> [t]he most important fact to be borne in mind about the language's position in Northern Ireland is that the vast majority of Irish-speakers in the region are Roman Catholics among whom the language has long been an essential part of their Republican consciousness. Only very rarely is it spoken or learned by Protestants, although there are notable exceptions, and almost never by Unionists for whom Irish is inextricably associated with Roman Catholicism and the Republican cause.

Happily, the Protestant perception of Irish has radically altered since that statement was written in 1976. Despite all the changes that have occurred, however, Irish is still very often associated today with Catholicism and Nationalism. The census report of 1991 contained a table which linked the question of one's religious affiliation with one's knowledge of Irish. In order to put the findings of the census in context, it is necessary first of all to provide a breakdown of the

17

current proportional strengths of religious denominations in Northern Ireland, as shown in Figure 4.

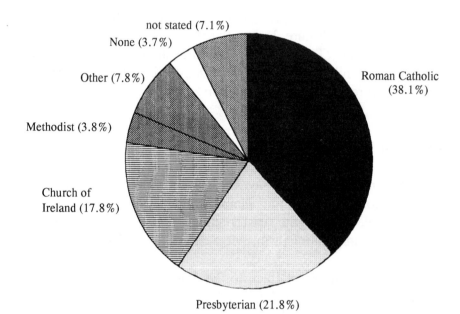

Presbyterian (21.8%)

Figure 4   *Religious denominations in Northern Ireland, 1991 (Census of Population)*

The proportion of each denomination with a knowledge of Irish is shown in Table 1. This table demonstrates clearly that the denominational group with the greatest knowledge of Irish was undoubtedly the Catholic, which probably explains to a certain degree why a knowledge of Irish is associated with that religion. However, of those with a knowledge of Irish in each denomination, the proportion with all three skills of speaking, reading and writing Irish is quite high (Figure 5).

Table 1   *Knowledge of Irish by religious group in Northern Ireland, 1991 (Census of Population)*

	Number of Irish-Speakers	Percentage of Religious Group
Roman Catholic	126,626	22.15%
Presbyterian	1,614	0.50%
Church of Ireland	2,012	0.75%
Methodist	296	0.52%
Other denominations	1,624	1.39%
None	2,615	4.69%
Not stated	7,216	6.72%

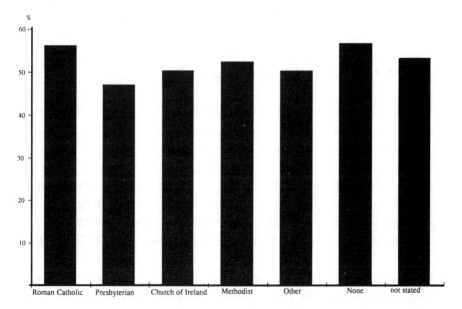

Figure 5   *Level of competency among Irish-speakers in each denominational group, 1991 (Census of Population)*

19

Máiréad Nic Craith

IRISH AND THE PROTESTANT TRADITION

Recent history, however, illustrates an active Protestant interest in the language, particularly in the first half of the last century. It is now common knowledge, that many of the Protestant colonists from Scotland were Gaelic-speakers, who conversed freely with the Irish speaking indigenous population. As late as 1819, the Reverend Stewart Dobbs noted that the Irish spoken in the parish of Ardclinis and Laid (near Cushendall) was more akin to Scots Gaelic than southern Irish (Mason 1816). Similarly in County Donegal, it was reported that the language spoken by the peasantry was 'a patois which is more nearly allied to (Scottish) Erse than to Irish' (*op.cit.*).

Parochial surveys at the beginning of the nineteenth century indicate that it was not uncommon for Protestants to have a knowledge of Irish. In Inver in County Donegal it was claimed that Irish was spoken by the Catholics and by most of the Protestants. In Antrim it was noted that everybody spoke English but the descendants of the first Scottish settlers spoke also a dialect of Celtic.

Protestant Personalities Speaking Irish

Even at the beginning of the nineteenth century, it was common for Presbyterian clergy in Ulster to evangelise in Irish. Pádraig Ó Snodaigh (1973) notes that

> native Irish-speaking followers of John Wesley—men like Charles Graham, Gideon Ouseley and Tomás Breatnach—evangelised in Irish. The Rev. William Laing, a native of Perth, preached in Irish in the Newry district from 1780-1816.

The Reverend William Neilson, who was born in County Down in 1774, learned Irish in his youth at the Rademon Academy which was run by his father. He was ordained as a Presbyterian minister in Dundalk in 1796 and was to minister in Irish there until 1818.

20

During these years, he paid frequent visits to the home of his childhood. In 1798, while delivering a sermon in Irish in Rademon, he was arrested by British soldiers and tried before a court. He reassured the court that the contents of his sermon were entirely religious in nature and was only released when he provided his adjudicators with an English language translation of the text. This arrest for the delivery of an Irish address did not deter him and in 1805, he conducted a tour throughout Ulster preaching in Irish. In 1818, he was appointed to the Belfast Academical Institution as Head of Classics and Professor of a variety of languages including Irish. He held Irish classes three times weekly there until his untimely death in 1818 at the age of forty-seven.

Samuel Bryson, who was a colleague of Neilson's, was born in Hollywood in 1776. A Presbyterian minister, he dedicated much of his life to the compilation and transcription of manuscripts. Between the years 1803 and 1810, he wrote eight manuscripts, which included a late version of the story of *Deirdre and the Sons of Uisneach* as well as many sagas, romances and songs. Until his death in 1853, he was involved in many societies including the Belfast Harp Society and the Literary Society.

James McKnight was born near Rathfriland in 1801 and was reared in an atmosphere conducive to a love of Irish, as his father was a fluent speaker of the language. Though he trained initially as a Presbyterian minister, he never actually became a clergyman and opted instead for journalism. As editor of the *Belfast News Letter* between the years 1830-1845, he frequently complained that despite his enthusiasm to conduct such evaluations, publishers of books in Irish failed to send him review copies on any regular basis. His appreciation of the language was demonstrated in his assessments of various books and manuscripts and it is clear that he regarded Irish as a common linguistic heritage which crossed the sectarian divide. He wrote that if the energy and zeal which are too frequently expended in teaching Irishmen how to hate each other most effectually, were employed in doing for our native language—and for millions who know no other ... how different in a little time would be our national condition (quoted in Blaney 1991).

A Unionist, he became involved with the question of rights for Irish tenant farmers and in 1850 he founded the Ulster Tenant Rights Movement. On his death bed in 1876, he requested his Catholic maid to recite the Lord's prayer in Irish for him and listened carefully, only interrupting to correct her pronunciation.

Robert McAdam, born in 1808, was one of the greatest Irish language enthusiasts in nineteenth century Belfast. An industrialist, he and his brother set up the Soho Foundry in Townsend Street, which at one stage employed in excess of two hundred and fifty workers. In his youth, he was appointed as secretary to the Ulster Gaelic Society. His interest in the language remained unabated during his lifetime and when Queen Victoria visited Belfast in 1849, he prepared mottoes in Irish to greet her which read (quoted in Ó Buachalla 1968):

Céad míle fáilte ar mhiliún don mBanríoghan
Go Cóigeadh Uladh na hÉire
Go mba mharthannach slán an urraim is a dtáin í
Le gean 's le grádh ó a géilltean

This has been translated as (McGimpsey 1992)

a hundred thousand welcomes a million times over to the Queen on her visit to the Ulster Province of Ireland; may their respect and popular support for her be unsullied and everlasting, with fondness and love from her subjects.

Two years later, McAdam was responsible for the inclusion of a question concerning a knowledge of Irish in the census form.

Though censuses had been taken in Ireland from 1821 onwards, there had been no inquiry regarding one's linguistic abilities until the persuasive efforts of McAdam convinced the administration that such was necessary. Throughout his lifetime, he acquired an enormous collection of manuscripts engaging scribes from all over the country. He was misfortunate in his later years, however. His business went bankrupt and his manuscripts were auctioned. He died shortly before the founding of the Gaelic League in Belfast.

Though Protestant involvement with Irish declined somewhat in the latter half of the nineteenth century, certain individuals maintained a high level of interest in the language. Earnest Blythe, who was later to become a cabinet minister in the government of the Republic of Ireland, was a native of Magheragall near Lisburn. Sir William MacArthur was born in Belmont in County Down in 1884, and as a student pursuing medicine in Queen's University, he partook in the founding of the Gaelic society—a club which is still in existence today.

Protestant Involvement with Gaelic Societies

At the level of clubs and societies, Protestants were also involved in the language movement in nineteenth century Belfast. Two Protestants, Edward Bunting and Dr James MacDonnell, a native of Antrim, founded the Irish Harp society in Belfast on St Patrick's Day in 1808. Though the primary aim of this society was to teach the harp to blind boys and girls, thereby proving them with a source of income in their adult years, the secondary aim of the society was to encourage a study of the Irish language.

In 1828, the Ulster Gaelic Society was founded by a number of Ulster Protestants. The aim of this society was to promote primary education through the medium of Irish to pupils residing in Irish-speaking parts of Ulster. Its president was the Third Marquis of Devonshire, a landlord with an estate of 100,000 acres. The chairperson was a medical doctor, James McDonnell, and the two secretaries were Robert S. McAdam and the Reverend R. J. Bryce. The success of this society was such that it encouraged many of the Belfast *literati* of the time, including Samuel Ferguson, Thomas O'Hagan, George Fox and others to learn Irish. This society was in effect a celebration of the success of the cultivation of Irish in Belfast over the previous forty years. It also led to the *Ulster Journal of Archaeology*. The later decline of this society and the death of Dr McDonnell in 1845 were the precursors of the end of the golden age of Irish in Belfast.

When the Gaelic League was founded in Belfast in 1895, Protestants formed the majority of the committee. One of the founders of this branch was Francis Joseph Bigger, who was born in Belfast in 1863, and was throughout his life an active member of the Church of Ireland. He encouraged the founding of Irish classes throughout Ulster and published works concerning the scholars Bryson and Neilson.

CATHOLIC INVOLVEMENT WITH THE LANGUAGE

It was about the time of increasing Protestant interest in the language that Catholics were deserting it with increasing rapidity. A variety of reports written at the beginning of the nineteenth century display the rapidity with which Ulster Catholics were actively learning the English language and forsaking their native tongue.

Catholic Apathy towards Irish

In 1744, W. Harris explained that Irish was principally spoken among the poorer Catholics only. Wealthier Catholics communicated through the medium of English. He wrote that the Irish tongue is in a manner banished among the common people, and what little of it is spoken can be heard only among the inferior ranks of Irish papists, and even that diminishes every day (Harris 1744).

At the beginning of the nineteenth century, Edward Wakefield, a British MP who was touring Ireland, wrote of the counties of Antrim, Armagh, Derry and Down that the Irish language was chiefly confined to people in mountainous districts. Reverend Dr Graves estimated that if Armagh and Down were considered together, then it appeared that the proportion of Irish- to English-speakers was two to five (Ó Duibhín 1991). In 1823, George Benn in a statistical survey of the parish of Belfast declared that

the English tongue is universally spoken in this parish, the few remaining inhabitants of the Irish stock being almost wholly unacquainted with the dialect of the ancestors (quoted in Ó Casaide 1930).

In western Antrim, it was reported in 1814 that the Catholics seldom spoke Irish except in the upper portions of the parish (Mason 1814). In Devenish, County Fermanagh, it was reported that Catholics could neither understand nor speak Irish (Mason 1816). On the northern border of the county, it was noted that though Catholics could speak Irish, they preferred to converse in English (Mason 1814).

Catholic Personalities using Irish

In common with the Protestant community however, certain Catholic personalities were making a distinctive contribution towards the fortunes of the language. In these days of the celebration of the Protestant contribution towards the language, the efforts of many Catholic individuals are left untold. One of these was Father Peter Lamb, a curate in County Armagh at the beginning of the nineteenth century, who was appointed as parish priest in Lower Creggan, Newtownhamilton in 1844. During his lifetime, this priest was responsible for the collection and preservation of many Irish songs and poems. In particular, he was friendly with an individual named Arthur Bennet, who had in his possession many of the works of the well known poet, Peadar Ó Doirnín. But for the pleading of Peter Lamb, Arthur Bennet would have retained these poems in his possession without allowing a single individual to look at them. It is entirely due to Peter Lamb that many of Peadar Ó Doirnín's poems survive to the present day (Ó Buachalla 1965).

Another Catholic individual who made a tremendous contribution to the Irish language was Séamus Mac Conamara, born in Newry in 1909, who will be remembered for his novel *An Coimhthíoch* which tells the story of a priest in South Armagh who was falsely accused and convicted of a crime. This novel was published after the author's untimely death in 1936.

Yet another individual of great renown in recent times was Cardinal Tomás Ó Fiaich, a native of Crossmaglen in Armagh, who was born in 1923. Between 1940 and 1944, Tomás Ó Fiaich was a student at Maynooth College. Owing to illness, however, he was transferred to the College of St Peter in Loch Gorman, and was ordained a priest there in 1948. Soon after, he was awarded an MA from University College, Dublin. He was awarded a PhD with distinction in 1953 from the University in Louvain. At this time, he was appointed to a position as history lecturer in the Seminary in Maynooth. Five years later, he was to become the Professor of History there. In 1974, he was established as President of the college. He was named as Archbishop of Armagh in 1977 and as Cardinal Primate of all Ireland in 1979.

During his lifetime, he worked ceaselessly to promote the language and frequently used the language to communicate. He offered assistance to many Irish language organisations and was nominated to various positions on Glór na Ngael, the Advisory Council for Irish, and the Government Commission for the revival of Irish. Whenever the opportunity afforded it, he communicated in Irish, and he was also a prolific writer in the language. Many of his essays have been published posthumously.

The Catholic Church's Embrace of the English Language

Few members of the Catholic Church were concerned with the Irish language at the beginning of the nineteenth century. Despite the efforts of an occasional priest or clergyman on behalf of Irish, the emergence of the English language at the beginning of the nineteenth century was forceful. English was quickly acquiring a status as the only language appropriate to commerce and administration. Conversely, Irish was being rapidly associated with ignorance and poverty. The Catholic clergy participated fully in this process of the elevation of English. As MacDonagh (1983) explains, it was not the case that the Catholic clergy actively conspired against the language. However, unlike their Protestant counterparts, they failed to give it any practical support (*op.cit.*):

> Catholic interest in the preservation or revival of Gaelic was comparatively slight until late in the nineteenth century. It was not that the Church was ever opposed to Gaelic as such ... But all this support was essentially utilitarian. Where the flock spoke only Gaelic, a priest must also do so if he were to be an effective pastor. It implied no effort to keep the people Gaelic-speaking, or to prize the indigenous tongue. On the contrary, the bulk of the clergy probably shared the peasant attitude that Gaelic was the badge of poverty and failure.

Many historians concur with the view that the Catholic clergy sustained and augmented the vitality of English (see, for example, Ó Tuathaigh 1972). Indeed, as Maureen Wall explains, they hardly had any other option. English was the language of administration in Maynooth college. This government-aided institution, which was founded in 1795, was the sole location for the training of the

Catholic clergy in Ireland. The English-speaking priests who emerged from this institution, frequently went to minister in the Irish-speaking districts. There were exceptions against this trend towards English, however, and it should be noted that Dr Crolly, the Catholic Bishop of the diocese of Down and Connor in the early nineteenth century, was favourably disposed towards the native language and was determined that the clergy leaving the seminary should have some knowledge of Irish.

Generally speaking, however, the Catholic Bishops throughout the country were largely uninterested in the fate of Irish. Ó Ríordáin (1990) writes:

> The bishops in the late eighteenth and early nineteenth centuries were confronted with a difficult choice—should Irish or English be chosen as the medium for handing on the faith. On the one hand, the traditional vehicle, Irish language and culture, was in decline, while English, the language of the newly emerging merchant class in the towns, and the language of an expanding empire, had the tide in its favour. Most of the bishops sailed with the tide, though not always without feelings of perplexity.

In Ulster, Robert McAdam noted that one of the major factors in the decline of Irish in the first half of the nineteenth century was the fact that the Catholic clergy failed to use the language when teaching the catechism or delivering sermons. This he said was despite the fact that the Irish language had offered protection to this religion during the previous three hundred years.

SUSPICIONS AND MISGIVINGS

As a response to the Catholic Church's use of English, this language gained considerable status among its congregation. Further events in

Ulster and indeed throughout Ireland as a whole, tended to increase Catholic scorn for the native language.

Catholic Apprehension and the Irish Society

In 1818, the Irish Society for Promoting the Education and Religious Instruction of the Native Irish through the medium of their own tongue was founded in Dublin (*cf.* Nic Craith 1993). A sub-branch of this, the Home Mission, was established by the synod of Ulster in 1836. The initial years of this society were very successful and it was not long before 150 teachers were working for the society in Ulster. In some parts of Ulster, this society suffered little or no opposition from the Catholic clergy. In the glens of Antrim, however, resistance to the society by the Catholic clergy was intense and the dispute was given public attention in the local media, in the daily Catholic journal the *Vindicator* and its Protestant counterpart, the *Banner of Ulster*.

In 1840, the Catholic bishop warned the Catholic congregation against the dangers of these Irish schools. Two years later, four Catholic teachers employed by the Home Mission declared in the *Vindicator* that though they were in receipt of a salary, they were not actually teaching any pupils. A denial was quickly dispatched to the *Banner*, however, in the form of a letter from the same four teachers, contradicting the contents of their first letter, and accompanied by a statement from an inspector employed by the Home Mission, Francis Brennan, declaring that he had personally examined the pupils taught by these four teachers. This was immediately followed by a further dispatch to the *Vindicator* by the same group of four denying the contents of their second letter. The third letter was accompanied by a statement from the local parish priest to the effect that there were no Home Mission schools in existence in his parish.

In 1842, the yearly report of the Home Mission asserted that they had established no less than twenty-seven Protestant Irish schools in the glens of Antrim and that some seven hundred pupils were attending these. A raging battle over the existence of these schools ensued which resulted in a growing distrust by the Catholic population of the motivations of these Protestant institutions and their Irish teachers. The kernel of the problem lay in the fact that these Irish teachers were availing of the Protestant bible in Irish as a means to teach the reading of the language, and the perception was that Irish was being used as an instrument of proselytism. As early as 1824, a London priest had outlined the dangers inherent in the availability of the Protestant Bible in Irish. The danger was reinforced by the lack of any Catholic version of it in the native tongue. He wrote:

> My reason for insinuating a supernatural assistance ... is their [the Protestants'; MNC] deep-laid plan of circulating the Bible in the Irish language among the poorer Catholicks [*sic*] of Ireland—for a more dangerous scheme could not be devised. Some may say there can be no danger to religion—that few people can read the Irish language but I shall say to the one—if there be even a possibility of danger to our religion as in the Veto—for instance—we should use our endeavours to guard against it ... We all know how fond Irishmen in general are of their own language—even such as cannot speak it—and this attachment is peculiarly discernable among the poorer classes—perhaps not having anything else literary to occupy their minds at leisure hours ... The bible in the native language is in greater circulation in Ireland than most people are aware of (Ms. 13,647, National Library, Ireland).

A particular enhancement of the status of English in Antrim during this dispute lay in the fact that the public battle that ensued between the Catholic clergy and the Home Mission, was conducted entirely in English. One Monsignor later commented that this battle in itself was entirely responsible for the decline of the Irish language along the Antrim coast.

One of the Protestant personalities in this proselytising movement was John McCambridge, the last Gaelic poet of the glens. He composed *Aird a' Chumhaing*, in which he imagined his distress as an exile in Kintyre looking back at the Antrim coast. On writing the poem, his grief was such that any thoughts he had previously entertained of leaving Ireland were quickly dispelled. He had a genuine interest in the language and according to Eoin McNeill

> My mother knew him well and says that on every possible occasion he tried to interest people in the Irish language, and would rather talk about it than anything else (quoted in MacPóilín n.d.)

Due to the suspicion aroused by the proselytising community in the glens of Antrim, McCambridge's attempts to halt the decline of the language failed. The language itself and the teaching of it had become tainted with mistrust.

John Murphy, who had actively participated in the activities of the Irish Society at an earlier stage in his life, described the fallacy of the teaching of Irish by this mission as follows:

> The teaching or learning of Irish is certainly, *in itself*, harmless, just as the teaching or learning of any other language is so. There can be no doubt of this. But why say it is unlawful and sinful? No one asserts that the teaching or learning of Irish is *in itself* unlawful and sinful; but an act in itself perfectly harmless and inculpable, can, in *certain circumstances*, so change its character as to become one of quite a different nature: for example, the eating of flesh meat is *in itself* a lawful act, but if the eating of it should be attended with some sinful circumstance, it (the eating) immediately becomes unlawful and sinful, in as much as the

31

sinful circumstance would not occur but for the eating... In like manner, if the teaching or learning of Irish, which is quite lawful *in itself,* as it has been observed, should be the cause of sin to the Teachers, the scholars or others, it instantly changes its nature, and from an innocent act that it was, becomes a sinful one. And does the teaching or learning of Irish, under any circumstances become the cause of sin? Who will deny that the teaching or learning of Irish, *in connection with the Irish society*, is not the cause of sin? Is not the *Irish Society* itself the prolific source of innumerable heinous sins?—And is there any thing more certain than that the *Irish Teachers and scholars are the cause of the existence of the Irish Society*? If the *Irish Society* had neither Teachers nor scholars how could it continue? *Of what use would it then be?* Should the Teachers and scholars withdraw from the Society—renounce all further connection with it, down would come the entire fabric tumbling to the ground (Murphy n.d.; orig. emphases).

Pamphlets and comments such as this were of little assistance to Irish and helped to further the cause of English in many regions.

Protestant Misgivings

In the second half of the nineteenth century, Protestant interest in the Irish language declined rapidly. There existed a basic mistrust of the language among the Protestant community in Belfast. The chair of Celtic in Queen's University, which had been established in 1849, was left vacant in 1862. Samuel Ferguson noted that one of the reasons for this was the fact that

all things Celtic are regarded by our educated classes as of questionable *ton* and an idea exists that it is inexpedient to encourage anything tending to foster Irish sentiment (quoted in Ó Buachalla 1968).

Furthermore, the great enlargement of the Catholic community in Belfast during the first half of the nineteenth century had sparked a fear of their increasing strength among the Protestant community. In 1800, the Catholic proportion of Belfast was small and Catholics formed a mere 8% of the town. Within twenty years this had increased dramatically and Catholics formed more than 32% of the population in 1830. During the years that followed, the Catholics maintained their proportional strength in Belfast, and in 1861 they numbered 41,237—some 34% of the city's population. The rift between the religious groups was enlarged with the unification of all classes of Protestants by the Orange Order.

Despite their suspicions, however, Unionists had not abandoned the language completely. At the Ulster Unionist convention held in the Botanic Park in June 1892, the motto displayed above the Irish harp read 'Érin go Bragh' (Ireland forever). This assembly was attended by 11,879 delegates. Apart from this notable exception however, little public attention was given to the Irish language in Belfast in the latter half of the nineteenth century until the founding of the Gaelic League there in 1895. The first branch of the League in Belfast was founded in the Naturalists Field Club which had been the location for a regular Irish class. Protestants formed the majority of the Committee on this occasion. However, this changed over the years, and it was not long before the League became the preserve of Catholics and nationalists. Many non-members viewed the learning of Irish by Gaelic Leaguers as a gesture of independence. This gesture would later be replaced by the Easter Rising of 1916. The situation is described by Cathail Ó'Byrne (1946):

With the advent of the Gaelic League ... [Irish] in Belfast came, at last partly, into its own. But the League was never considered quite "respectable"—that awful Belfast word—by the planters. To be a Gaelic Leaguer was to be suspect always. The League might shout at its loudest and longest that it was non-political and non-sectarian. The slogan did not impress Belfast. With the League's membership ninety-nine percent

Catholic, what could one expect? "Scratch a Gaelic Leaguer and you'll find a Fenian" was the formula in the old days.

Despite its inferred religious affiliation, the Gaelic League was extremely successful in its early days in Belfast. In 1898, its language classes were attended by fifty-eight people. Attendance had grown to 593 in 1904 (Maguire 1990). Furthermore, the Belfast branch established training colleges in order that teachers taking its classes would be fully trained. On a national basis also, the activities of the League were successful. It initiated a publishing scheme to advance and develop modern Irish literature and to generate textbooks for use in its classes. It succeeded in the introduction of a bilingual policy for schools in 1904 which validated the use of Irish as a medium of instruction in Gaeltacht. It later established Irish as a compulsory subject for matriculation in the National University of Ireland.

A particular concern of many Irish-speakers in Ulster at this time was the feeling that the Ulster dialect of the language was being neglected. In response to this concern, Comhaltas Uladh was established. This organisation, which was affiliated to the League, specifically aimed to protect the interests of Ulster Irish-speakers and succeeded in many ventures, including the establishment of summer colleges, particularly in the Donegal Gaeltacht.

IRISH AS A SYMBOL OF NATIONALISM

Certain events in the late nineteenth and early twentieth centuries led to an association between the Irish language movement and the struggle for Independence from Britain. The political movement which led to the establishment of the Irish free state in 1922, had a close association with the movement to restore the Irish language. In 1915, at its Ard Fheis in Dundalk, the Gaelic League declared that its activities had both a political and cultural significance. This led to increased suspicion of the language movement by many

Protestants and/or Unionists and its president, Dr Douglas Hyde, resigned. In the civil war which later ensued, both Michael Collins and his adversary, Éamon de Valera, stated that the restoration of the language was at least as important as political independence.

With regard to the political connotations of the language, Vincent McKee (1994) writes:

> It is significant that the Gaelic generation figured several leading Nationalists whose prominence in the separatist movement, 1912-22, and/or leadership of the infant Irish Free State (whether as Free Staters or Republicans) after 1922 lent high esteem to the Gaelic language and culture. They included the poet and executed 1916 Rising leader, Pádraig Pearse; the Antrim-born former British civil servant who converted to the Nationalist cause—executed by HMG in 1917—Roger Casement; another Antrim native, the historian, Professor Eoin MacNeill, who became education minister in the first Free State government; and Sinn Féin President 1918-1922, subsequently Fianna Fáil founder (1925) and Taoiseach/President thereafter, Eamon De Valera. To this school, nationalism meant more than simple political determination; it extended to a rediscovery of Ireland's Gaelic heritage in respect of language, literature, music and sports, with positive promotion to follow by future Irish governments.

In itself, the association of a language movement with a nationalist movement was not unusual. Many of the linguistic movements of the nineteenth and twentieth centuries were associated with nationalist movements. Consider the examples of Norway and Finland. In an article entitled 'The Irish Language and Nationalism' (1977), John MacNamara cites at least sixteen countries where linguistic and nationalist movements were closely associated, in the nineteenth and twentieth centuries. Be that as it may, one must not ignore the fact that Northern Unionists might still associate the Irish language with the freedom movement, and for them, this alone may deter them from becoming involved with the language.

The Current Situation

History has demonstrated that the Irish language is part of the common cultural heritage of the people of Northern Ireland. Despite the past, however, there is still a deep rooted suspicion of the language among many Unionists. In the Catholic community, it is assumed that linguistic, cultural and political allegiances are inextricably bound together. If a Protestant displays an interest in the language, it is frequently presumed that he has nationalist tendencies. McGimpsey (1992) explains it as follows:

> There are, on the other hand, some working-class loyalists who speak Irish. It is generally assumed that they learned the language in Long Kesh. This probably comes from the widely held belief that Gusty Spence is a fluent Irish speaker. When you meet someone who knows a smattering of Irish he was probably in jail for three or four years. If he is fluent then he is an ex-lifer.

There is not a total rejection of the language by Protestants however. The *Belfast Newsletter* of 29 July 1970 reported that a Belfast Orange Lodge had dedicated its new banner with a motto written in the Irish language. This was the report on the event:

> The history-making gesture was made by Ireland's Heritage L.O.L. No.1303 at its dinner in the Presbyterian Hostel on Saturday. There, the Rev. Martin Smyth, County Grand Master of Belfast, dedicated the banner which has the Gaelic motto 'Oidhreacht Éireann' (Ireland's heritage). The motto has been printed in Gaelic in order to exemplify the fact that members advocate a return to the real significance of Irish history. Mr. Smyth, after a dinner held to mark the occasion, said he

welcomed the idea as it was in a sense a re-affirmation of the Protestant faith ... Congratulating the Lodge on its acquisition of a new banner, Mr. Smyth said the emblem exemplified the movement's belief in the dignity of Irish history (quoted in Ó Glaisne 1981).

In some cases, Ulster Protestants today believe that not only is the Irish language part of their linguistic heritage, but that in fact it was pilfered from them by Catholics who subsequently attempted to deny the Protestant input. This argument was given publicity in the *Combat* magazine of 25 April 1974:

> The majority of Ulster Protestants equate Gaelic and Irish culture with Roman Catholicism and are of the opinion that no 'good Prod' would have anything to do with such Popish traditions. The truth of the matter is, Ulster Protestants have as much claim, if not more in some cases, to the Gaelic culture as the Roman Catholic population. Someone once said that the Irish language was stolen from the Protestant people by the Papists; it would be more correct to say that the Protestant people gave their culture away to the Roman Catholics (quoted in Ó Glaisne 1981).

Though many Catholics would be unhappy with the suggestion that the Irish language was part of a culture given away to them by their Protestant counterparts, many of them would welcome an increased Protestant involvement with Irish. Unfortunately, despite the fact that as we have earlier noted, much of the pioneering work on behalf of the language at the beginning of the nineteenth century was accomplished by Presbyterians, Irish is regarded by many outside the Catholic community with suspicion and is still largely associated with Catholicism and nationalism.

Differential Access in the Education System

Separatism is not confined to the religious sphere, however. At present, structural problems exist which restrict access to and the availability of Irish language in the educational system. In recent years, Northern Ireland has witnessed a new demand for Irish in education. This has resulted in the establishment of a number of all-Irish schools. At the time of writing, there are two grant-aided all-Irish primary schools located in West Belfast, Bunscoil Phobal Feirste and Gaelscoil na bhfál. Pupils in Derry are also taught through Irish at primary level. These three schools had a total enrolment of 648 pupils in September 1992. Two other Irish medium primary schools funded privately are located in the North. These are Bunscoil an Iúir in Newry and a school in the Twinbrook area of West Belfast. It appears unlikely that either of these schools will attain the quota of pupils required for a government grant. An enrolment of 200 pupils in an urban area and 100 pupils in a rural area is required before funding can be granted. It seems possible, however, that the Twinbrook school 'might qualify on the basis of being a satellite for the bunscoil in West Belfast' (CAJ 1993)

At second level, Northern Ireland is witnessing the emergence of education through Irish. As in the case of the primary schools, this is mainly as a result of the will of the people rather than any help given by the British government. Four years ago, Meánscoil Bhéal Feirste opened with just nine pupils. At the time of writing, there are a hundred children attending this school. Last September, a new second level school, Meánscoil Dhoire Cholm Cille, opened in Arás an Ghrianáin in Derry. Eleven pupils have registered in the first year and the £50,000 required for the running costs will have to be found from a source other than the Department of Education (*Anois*, 17/18 September 1994).

The demand for education through the medium of the native language is not a phenomenon exclusive to Northern Ireland. Throughout Ireland, there are now over ninety primary schools and twenty-three second level schools teaching through the medium of Irish. Despite a range of problems—including accommodation and funding, lack of official recognition, and not least a serious deficiency of resources (principally textbooks and equipment)— these schools are flourishing. In October 1993, the *Irish Times* published the following report on these schools:

> [They] are thriving in this often hostile and restrictive environment. Not only are they thriving, but recently published research carried out by the Department of Education shows that educational standards in gaelscoileanna are significantly higher than other schools with regard to English reading skills (*Irish Times*, 5 October 1993).

Many other marginalised language regions are also experiencing a similar growth in immersion type schools. Wales, for example, has witnessed an unprecedented growth in this type of school. The original Welsh language primary school in Cardiff opened in 1949 with eighteen pupils. By 1992, this had spawned six schools with a total of 1,400 pupils (Davies 1993).

In Catalonia, the Catalan language was banned from schools for nearly the whole of the Franco dictatorship. It was not until 1970/71 that a few hours of native languages were permitted. Catalan became obligatory in 1978, when a Royal Decree introduced the Catalan language into various syllabi. Many linguistic immersion schools have also developed, and over the course of the next few years, 76% of the primary schools will become Catalan unilingual schools (Lepretre 1992).

In the Basque country, the language was also officially banned from schools during the Franco dictatorship and was only taught in underground schools known as *ikastolas*. These schools were later given full official recognition under the statute of autonomy and were heavily subsidised by the state. Under state protection, these schools continued to have an emphasis on the Basque immersion. In more recent times, however, these schools have developed into public institutions, paid for by public funds. They have a continued emphasis on the Basque language with separate full immersion and part immersion tracks.

In Northern Ireland, the Irish medium schools are currently hampered by a policy which dictates proof of a potential enrolment of 200 children in an urban area and 100 children in a rural area, before any grant aid can be considered. This strategy applies the same viability criteria for funding to all forms of schools, both English and Irish medium, and fails to take account of the realities of Irish medium education.

Furthermore, there is—in practice—differential access to Irish language which effectively prevents Protestants from developing a full appreciation of their heritage and makes them reluctant to send their children to all-Irish schools even when these have adopted an inter-denominational ethos and are managed by cross-community committees. Consequently, any policy concerned with the position of Irish in education in Northern Ireland needs to aim, in the first instance, at reducing these barriers.

Remedial Action

In recent times, the British government has initiated an agency known as the Ultach Trust to promote the language and indeed Irish culture in Northern Ireland. 'Ultach' is an acronym for 'Ulster Language, Traditions and Culture'. Its board of trustees is composed of both Catholics and Protestants. Representation by both groups is almost equal. This organisation has a number of objectives. Not only does it serve as an information centre for Irish language activities, it acts as a medium between Irish language activists and the British government. Furthermore, it works with the European Bureau for Lesser Used Languages.

With regard to the viability criteria of Irish medium schools, various recommendations have been made by the Ultach Trust. One of their prime concerns is that the British government should acknowledge a clear distinction between the needs of Irish-medium schools and English-medium schools and that viability criteria should be modified appropriately. Furthermore, they support the recommendation that these schools should receive seed funding in the form of a per-capita grant over a number of years, to help them meet their running costs.

In conjunction with this, the question of differential access to the Irish language needs to be addressed. This question is particularly relevant when one takes account of the fact that on various occasions in recent years, Protestant children have expressed a desire to learn the Irish language. The *Opsahl Commission* reported that

> there was a desire among both Catholic and Protestant sixth-formers at the schools' assemblies that both Irish history and Irish language be made available in all schools (Pollock 1993).

Furthermore, in a survey on social attitudes in Northern Ireland, almost a quarter of the Northern Irish Protestants agreed or strongly agreed with the statement that all secondary school pupils should have to study the Irish language and culture (Stringer and Robinson 1991).

Chris McGimpsey feels that it is imperative to persuade the state educational system to include Irish in the syllabus in those schools largely attended by Unionists. It is in this context that he has recommended the introduction of specialist peripatetic teachers without extra cost to the schools, who could assess the demand for Irish in these schools and stimulate the demand for it.

If Unionists are to come to terms with the language, a non-threatening environment is essential. Therefore, McGimpsey regards it as important that language classes are set up in loyalist areas. Development in this direction has already been noted in the *Shankill People* of 5 March 1994, which—under the headline 'Glencairn Goes Gaelic'—reported on Irish language classes being run in the estate. It ought to be stated, however, that those who attended these classes displayed courage in the face of adversity, as the *Sunday Times* reported:

> The Irish language, long regarded as a symbol of Irish nationalism and the preserve of Catholics, is finding a new following among the working-class Protestants of Belfast. Students and housewives are braving hate mail and taunts to attend language courses that have won support from senior loyalists, who see them as an important element in breaking down racial sectarianism (*Sunday Times*, 9 May 1993).

Further suggestions by the Ultach Trust to alleviate Protestant discomfort with the language include the grant aiding of Protestants and Unionists to attend summer colleges. Additionally, they feel it is vital that a campaign be mounted to increase Protestant awareness of their Gaelic culture.

CONCLUSION

Obviously, the widespread view that Irish today is the language of Catholics and Nationalists is a rather inaccurate reflection of the facts of history. Despite the current separatism, the contribution of the Protestant tradition to the fortunes of Irish are gradually being acknowledged and promoted. It is vital at this stage that the language become accessible to all Catholics and Protestants who wish to learn and speak it. The successful maintenance and promotion of Irish will largely depend on its becoming viable as a community language across the sectarian divide. History reveals that the language has already extended across the partition.

BIBLIOGRAPHY

Adams, G

1974 The 1851 Language Census in the North of Ireland, *Ulster Folklife* 20, 65-70.

Beardsmore, H

1982 *Bilingualism: Basic Principles,* Clevedon.

Blaney, R

1991 The Irish Language in County Down since 1800. In *Language and Cultural Heritage of Down District—The Connection*, Proceedings of Coiste na Gaeilge/The Irish Committee Seminar held in the Down County Museum on 27 April 1991.

Byrne, C

1993 Protestants Ignore Taunts to Learn Irish, *The Sunday Times*, 9 May.

CAJ (Committee on the Administration of Justice)

1993 *Staid agus Stádas na Gaeilge i dTuaisceart na hÉireann: The UK Government's Approach to the Irish Language in Light of the European Charter for Regional or Minority Languages*, Belfast.

Cnámh, S

1985 The Struggle in the 'Jailteacht', *An Phoblacht/Republican News*, 26 July, 9.

Council of Europe

1992 *European Charter for Regional or Minority Languages*, Strasbourg.

Davies, J

1993 *The Welsh Language*, Cardiff.

Department of Health and Social Services, Registrar General Northern Ireland

1991 *The Northern Ireland Census 1991: Summary Report*, Belfast.

Fishman, J and Terry, C
1971 The Contrastive Validity of Census Data on Bilingualism in a Puerto Rican Neighbourhood. In Fishman, J, Cooper, R, Roxanna, M *et.al.* (eds), *Bilingualism in the Barrio*, The Hague, 177-97.

Fitzgerald, G
1984 Estimates for Baronies of Minimum Level of Irish-Speaking amongst Successive Decennial Cohorts: 1771-1781 to 1861-1871, *Proceedings of the Royal Irish Academy* 84C(3), 117-55.

Foley, C
1993 Gaelscoileanna: The Rise and Rise of All-Irish Schools, *The Irish Times*, Education and Living supplement, 5 October.

Harris, W
1744 *The Ancient and Present State of the County of Down*, n.p.

Hyde, D
1986 On the Necessity for De-anglicising Ireland (1892), reprinted in Ó Conaire, B (ed.), *A Literary History of Ireland*, Dublin, 145-70.

Lepretre, M
1992 *The Catalan Language Today*, Barcelona.

MacDonagh, O
1983 *States of Mind: A Study of Anglo-Irish Conflict, 1780-1980*, London.

MacNamara, J
1977 The Irish Language and Nationalism. In Hederman, M and Kearney, R (eds), *The Crane Bag Book of Irish Studies*, Dublin, 124-8.

MacPóilín, A
n.d. *The Protestant Gaelic Tradition*, Belfast.

Mag Fhearaig, C
1994 Meánscoil Dhoire Cholm Cille—fadhb mhór airgid le sárú fós, *Anois*, 17/18 September, 5.

Maguire, G
1990 *Our Own Language: An Irish Initiative*, Clevedon.

Mason, S
1814　*A Statistical Account or Parochial Survey of Ireland drawn up from the Communications of the Clergy*, Vol. 1, Dublin.
1816　*A Statistical Account or Parochial Survey of Ireland drawn up from the Communications of the Clergy*, Vol. 2, Dublin.
1819　*A Statistical Account or Parochial Survey of Ireland drawn up from the Communications of the Clergy*, Vol. 3, Dublin.
McGimpsey, C
1992　*Irish Language and the Unionist Tradition*. Paper presented at the Ulster People's College, Belfast, 9 May.
McKee, V
1994　Politics of the Gaelic language in Northern Ireland and the Scottish Hebrides: A Focus for Contrast. In Hudson, K (ed.), *Questions of Ideology*. Occasional Papers 3, Politics Division, Business School, South Bank University, London, 34-50.
Murphy, J
n.d.　*A Brief Account of the Irish Society,* n.p.
National Library, Ireland, Ms. 13,647: Letters to Daniel Ó Connell.
Nic Craith, M
1993　*Malartú Teanga: An Ghaeilge i gCorcaigh sa Naoú hAois Déag*, Bremen.
Ó Buachalla, B
1968　*I mBéal Feirste cois Cuain*, Baile Átha Cliath.
1965　Peadar Ó Doirnín agus Lucht Scríte a Bheatha, *Studia Hibernica* 5, 123-154.
O'Byrne, C
1946　*As I Roved Out*, Dublin.
Ó Casaide, S
n.d.　*The Irish Language in Belfast and County Down A.D. 1601-1850*, Dublin.
Ó Duibhín, C
1991　*Irish in County Down since 1750*, n.p.
Ó Fiaich, T
1992　*Ón Chreagán go Ceann Dubhrann: Aistí le Tomás Ó Fiaich*, Dublin.

Ó Glaisne, R
1981 Irish and the Protestant Tradition. In Hederman, M and Kearney, R (eds), *The Crane Bag Book of Irish Studies*, Dublin, 864-75.

Ó Muirí, P
1993 Irish in Belfast, *The Irish Review* 14, 81-87.

Ó Ríordáin, J
1980 *Irish Catholics: Tradition and Transition*, Dublin.

Ó Snodaigh, P
1973 *Hidden Ulster (The Other Hidden Ireland)*, Dublin.

Ó Tuathaigh, G
1972 *Ireland before the Famine, 1798-1848*, Dublin.

Pollock, A (ed.)
1993 *A Citizen's Inquiry: The Opsahl Report on Northern Ireland*, Dublin.

Stephens, M
1976 *Linguistic Minorities in Western Europe,* Llandysul.

Stringer, P and Robinson, G (eds)
1991 *Social Attitudes in Northern Ireland*, Belfast.

Ultach Trust
1991 *Annual Report for the year '90-'91*, Belfast.
1992 *Irish-Medium Education in Northern Ireland. A Preliminary Report*, Belfast.

Outposts of the Gael:
The Decline of Gaelic in
the Great Blasket and St Kilda

JANET LEYLAND

INTRODUCTION

The following study analyses the factors involved in the decline of the Irish/Gaelic language, contextualised in a comparative study of the Great Blasket and the island of St Kilda. Although there are fundamental historical differences between Ireland and Scotland, the decline of Scottish Gaelic is comparable to that of the Irish language (Durkacz 1983), and the Highlands and Islands of Scotland share many common features with the West of Ireland. Scotland, unlike Ireland, is not homogeneously Catholic, has a diverse linguistic heritage, and Scottish Gaelic has lacked any major nationalist impetus (Hindley 1990).

The choice of the Great Blasket and St Kilda for study has an undeniably romantic appeal as 'Outposts of the Gael'. MacDonagh (1983) has acknowledged the potency of territorial imagery in relation to Ireland, 'the power of geographical imagery over men's [*sic*] minds'. However, there is much to recommend academically a comparative study of the Great Blasket and St Kilda. There are striking similarities between the two islands, in terms of Celtic language, geographical isolation, peripheral economic position and limited natural resources, and demographic factors.

Ullrich Kockel (ed.), *Landscape, Heritage and Identity: Case Studies in Irish Ethnography*, Liverpool University Press 1995, 47-92.

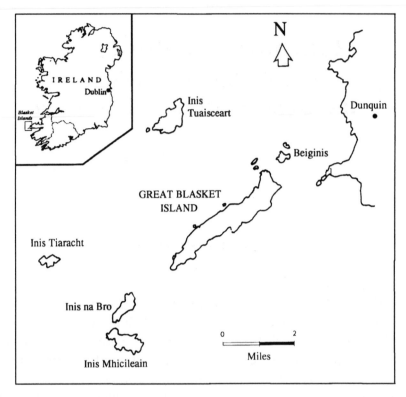

Figure 6   *The Blasket Islands*

Now uninhabited, both islands are a tangible reminder of the decline of both language and community, where a centuries-old Gaelic language and culture survived into the twentieth century.

On 29 August 1930, St Kilda was evacuated and the remaining thirty-six islanders were dispersed and resettled on the Scottish 'mainland' (Steel 1988), whilst the twenty or so remaining inhabitants of the Great Blasket abandoned their island in November 1953 and settled in Dunquin, facing their former island home.

Although, geographically, St Kilda is more remote than the Great Blasket, it should be acknowledged that a sense of isolation can be subjectively experienced out of all proportion to the actual physical distance involved. As Blasket islander Eibhlís Ní Shúilleabháin

(1992) noted: 'If it was fine and sunny on the land itself here we don't call it fine until the sea is calm'. It has been pointed out that the Blasket islanders lived with their backs to the Atlantic, looking towards the 'mainland', and therefore feeling simultaneously both close to and yet distant and separate from it.

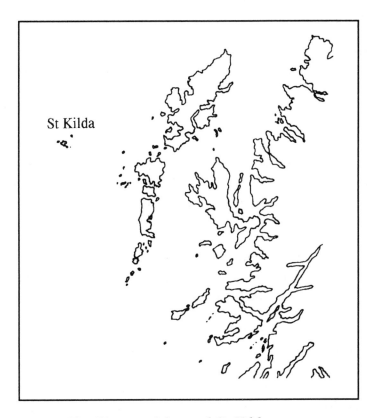

Figure 7   *The Western Isles and St Kilda*

In the case of St Kilda, it is interesting to speculate as to whether the lack of a 'mainland' vista actually further reinforced a distinct island community identity. As Cohen (1982) has pointed out, factors like peripherality and marginality are not defined by geographic terms alone, but can also be a state of mind. On both islands, the inhabitants lived in close-knit, 'Gemeinschaft'-type communities, where communal solidarity and social cohesion were prerequisites for physical and spiritual survival. St Kilda in particular can be regarded as closely approximating the attributes which formulated Redmond's ideal 'folk society', and for Redmond, there is much to be gained from studying communities 'least like our own' (*cf.* Loomis 1963).

However, there were significant differences between the Great Blasket and St Kilda. The fundamental difference was religion: the Blasket islanders were Catholic whilst the St Kildans followed the Calvinistic Protestant doctrines of the Presbyterian Free Church. Emigration patterns from both islands were also different in terms of destination and the incidence of collective migration to Australia by thirty-six St Kildans in 1852. Retrospectively, this exodus, which reduced the St Kildan community by approximately one-third, can be seen as seriously undermining the population's long-term viability.

For both islands, geographical peripheral isolation and lack of indigenous exploitable resources protected the language from erosion. However, these same factors ultimately played a major role in population decline, resulting in the abandonment of a distinct traditional way of life by both communities for whom Irish/Gaelic had been retained as the everyday vernacular.

Due to constraints of space, the depth and the variety of material presented in this study are necessarily limited. I shall begin with a brief historical analysis of language decline in Ireland and Scotland, and then identify key factors in the decline of Irish/Gaelic, analysing the impact of these factors on the Great Blasket and St Kilda from a comparative perspective.

SOURCES

Sources relating to the two islands are not directly comparable. The Blasket Islands have a rich autobiographical tradition now visually presented in the new Blasket Island Interpretative Centre. The Blasket autobiographies, written by the islanders themselves about their own lives, have an elegiac tone: an awareness that their way of life was drawing to a close. However, there is very little historical documentary material relating to the Blasket Islands. Prior to the twentieth century, very few visitors reached Dingle, let alone the outlying islands beyond, and thus reliance is placed on the work of Jane and Ray Stagles (1980), whose research on parish registers provides historical insight and confirmation of the Blasket literature.

For St Kilda, although there is little published material written by the islanders themselves, the Reverend Quine (1988) has possession of a fascinating collection of audio recordings of reminiscences by a handful of former St Kildans who left the island as children, and the diary of Alice MacLachlan, the wife of a missionary on St Kilda between 1906 and 1909. There are a plethora of books written about St Kilda by former missionaries and visitors for whom a journey to Britain's 'loneliest isle' was in itself an attraction, yet extreme caution is necessary with such accounts. It is possible to gather very different impressions about life on St Kilda from the various accounts, depending both on the outlook and occupation of the author and the time when the account was written. MacGregor (1960) sees it as important that the St Kildan community 'should not be judged by the several reports that were made (mostly with missionary zeal)' during the final decades of the nineteenth century. Indeed, these accounts often reveal more about the individual concerned than they do about St Kildan life. MacGregor recommends a study of the documentary evidence pertaining to the period 1698-1878 for a more valid evaluation. An as yet unpublished autobiography by Callum MacDonald, describing his family life, childhood and customs on the island, provides not only unique insights into the St Kildan way of life as perceived by an islander himself, but also offers a welcome counter-balance to many of the gloomier accounts, which contain impressionistic and often moralising judgements.

Except for Callum MacDonald's account, written in London in his later years, it would appear that St Kildans have not written about themselves, or their way of life. They probably did not receive the same encouragement from foreign scholars as Tomás Ó Criomhthain did, whose autobiography, *An tOileánach*, set an example for other Blasket islanders to follow.

Both island communities were effectively pre-literate until the beginning of the present century, and the fact that Irish/Gaelic culture was based on oral tradition has severely limited the potential for language retention and the preservation of a written literary heritage. In the case of St Kilda, little remains of vernacular poetry and verse which were actively discouraged by the puritanical Free Church missionaries (*cf.* Maclean 1977).

LANGUAGE DECLINE IN IRELAND AND SCOTLAND

It must be stressed that the changing fortunes of the Irish/Gaelic language have always been an integral part of broader changes and conflict in Irish and Scottish political, economic and cultural life. No study of language decline can be made without an historical appreciation of the decline of Irish/Gaelic in a wider context. In Scotland, the replacement of Gaelic by English was seen as vital '[i]n order to improve and civilise the Highlands', and as early as 1752, following his tour of Scotland, Daniel Defoe observed that 'in a few years, Ignorance, Popery and the Irish language will be utterly extirpated' (quoted in Withers 1988).

In the Scottish Highlands, economic integration and political assimilation fundamentally affected not only the Gaelic language and culture, but led to the disintegration of the whole structure of traditional Gaelic society and culture. Anglicisation was seen as a crucial first phase in the transformation of Highland Scotland towards 'an English way of life' where the adoption of English cultural values 'as the yardstick of social status had an important bearing on the Gaelic language and on those Gaelic cultural forms that were the vehicle for the language' (Withers 1984).

In both Ireland and Scotland, political integration with England resulted in English becoming virtually the sole language of law, administration, literacy and commerce, while Gaelic became associated with poverty and ignorance (MacDonagh 1983). More crucially, Irish/Gaelic became seen as an obstacle to political, cultural and economic assimilation, and only when 'English had replaced Gaelic would the Highlands be civilised, loyal and industrious' (Withers 1988). As late as 1871, a report by the Secretary of State, R. Assheton Cross, summarised the political establishment's attitude towards the Gaelic language thus:

> The Gaelic language ... decidedly stands in the way of the civilisation of the natives making use of it ... It ought, therefore, to cease to be taught in all our national schools: and as we are one people we should have but *one* language (quoted in Withers 1984; orig. emphasis).

It must be emphasised that there is no one single 'cause' of what Hindley (1990) pessimistically refers to as the 'death' of the Irish language. It has been suggested that the context in which English was sought as a second language, rather than the later abandoning of Irish once bilingualism was achieved, would be a more fruitful area of analysis (*op.cit.*). Most factors in the decline of the Irish/ Gaelic language are inter-related, and often secondary effects of historical, political, economic and cultural conflicts between Anglo-Saxon and Celtic Britain. Incipient rebellion in both Ireland and Scotland exacerbated linguistic and cultural conflicts, and it is noteworthy that anglicisation, rather than military subjugation, was thought to be the long-term solution to the problem (Durkacz 1983).

The decline of Irish/Gaelic and the insidious permeation of the English language should be regarded as two inter-linked processes which pre-dated legislative union with England, both in the case of

Ireland and Scotland. For MacDonagh (1983), the main reason for the ascendancy of English and the contraction of Gaelic was pragmatic and simply 'to improve one's lot' as English became increasingly essential both for emigration and social advancement at home. Moreover, the decline of the Irish/Gaelic language needs to be examined in conjunction with the spread of English. From the eighteenth century, agrarian secret societies had recognised the need for English, not only to write threatening letters to landlords but in order to understand legal documents and covenants. Wall (1969) suggests that in this respect, Irish agrarian societies were better prepared than the Scottish Highlanders whose lack of knowledge of English 'left them at the mercy of their landlords when they were cleared out from their crofts in their thousands between 1745 and 1845'.

By the end of the eighteenth century, Irish/Gaelic had become indelibly associated with poverty, illiteracy and ignorance. As the Highlands and Islands were subjected to 'improvement', and Ireland to 'modernisation', the Irish/Gaelic language became associated with not just political and social but also 'economic backwardness' (Durkacz 1983). The acquisition of English, as the dominant language of commerce and utility, came to be seen as the key to economic prosperity. Moreover the popular association of Gaelic with Jacobitism in Scotland, Irish/Gaelic with Catholicism, barbarity and political disaffection, and the converse association of English with loyalty, Protestantism and civilisation in both Scotland and Ireland, played a major role in language decline and a significant part in fostering antipathy to those who spoke it. Furthermore, a Highland/Lowland divide existed in Scotland, which held meaning far beyond that of a geographical boundary, and was referred to by Highlanders as 'Mi-run mor nan Gall', that is, 'the Lowlander's great ill will' (Prebble 1970).

In 1891, An Comunn Gaidhealach was founded in Scotland, but, unlike its Irish counterpart, remained non-political in the absence of any significant separatist/nationalist movement. Conradh na Gaeilge, founded in 1893 with the objective of reviving the Irish language and promoting traditional Irish culture, ironically had little success in the Irish-speaking areas. Ineffective against the tide of emigration, Conradh na Gaeilge found little favour with people who saw Irish as a badge of poverty and a social handicap which they were anxious to lose, and mistrusted the motives of Gaelic Leaguers who they suspected to care more for the language than the people (Thomson 1982).

Prior to the emergence of twentieth century nationalism, successive Irish political leaders had unquestioningly accepted that the political future of Ireland would be an English-speaking one. The politician Daniel O'Connell, although himself a native Irish-speaker from Kerry, explicitly rejected the language, declaring that he 'could witness without a sigh, the gradual disuse of Irish' (quoted in Corkery 1968), which, Corkery argues, must have been translated by the Irish people as 'keep Irish from the children'. It was therefore not surprising that Irish parents assumed that their children would 'enjoy advantages as English-speaking rather than Irish-speaking emigrants' (Lee 1989). The participation of the Irish people in popular politics and national struggle also hastened the displacement of Irish by English, as mass constitutional rallies and the production of nationalist literature spread the English language.

Nevertheless, the existence of Irish/Gaelic-speaking communities on the Great Blasket and St Kilda into the twentieth century exemplifies the only partial success of the policy of anglicisation. The main objective of this policy was to 'crush the way of life of the Gael', and although not totally successful, particularly in remote areas, Gaelic culture was damaged (Steel 1988). In the twentieth century, the majority of islanders on the Great Blasket and St Kilda (with the exception of some elderly inhabitants) had acquired sufficient English to be regarded as bilingual, but yet Irish/Gaelic remained as the language of the hearth and the community.

Janet Leyland

A COMPARATIVE ANALYSIS OF
THE TWO CASE STUDIES

There are significant parallels in the decline of the Celtic languages in both Ireland and Scotland, but no one single 'cause' can be identified. Instead, what happened must be understood as a complex process where many inter-related factors contributed to the abandonment of the vernacular language in favour of English. Major factors in this process were religion, attitudes towards the language, education, and emigration. Although each factor will be examined separately, their inter-relationship, and the historical fusion of religion, education and language in the context of the two case studies must be emphasised.

Religion

One fundamental difference between the Great Blasket and St Kilda was that of religious faith: the Blasket islanders were Catholic, whereas St Kildans followed the Calvinist doctrines of the Presbyterian Free Church. Furthermore, whilst the Blasket islanders had to travel to the 'mainland' for Mass, marriages, baptisms and burials, the spiritual needs of the St Kildans were accommodated by their own church on the island. St Kilda also had its own burial ground, and thus its inhabitants could spend their entire life, from the cradle to the grave, on the island. It is interesting to consider how this self-reliance may have consolidated a distinct St Kildan identity.

Many of the variances in social and cultural activities between the Blasket islanders and St Kildans can be attributed to the difference in religious faith. On St Kilda, the doctrines of the Free Church played a major part in the erosion of traditional Gaelic activities. In 1758, Macauley had written:

The power of music is felt everywhere ... [and] the St Kildans are enthusiastically fond of it, whether in the vocal or instrumental way ... I have seen them dancing to a bad violin... (quoted in Maclean 1977).

Moreover, it would appear that a variety of sporting activities, such as a form of shinty played on the beach, and cultural activities such as music, poetry, singing, dancing and story-telling were an integral part of St Kildan life until they were banned by the puritanical missionaries. Its geographical isolation left the inhabitants of St Kilda very vulnerable to the evangelising ambitions of successive Protestant missionaries who exerted considerable influence on the lives of the islanders. The Reverend Neil MacKenzie, who arrived on St Kilda in 1820 and departed about 1843, expressed satisfaction with what he saw as an improvement in moral standards among the people on the island:

They are now also more diligent, obliging, kind and attentive to duty than even last year. The everlasting talker has become comparatively taciturn. You would think that they were almost afraid to speak lest they should sin: and when they do speak, instead of ... talking of their own merits and of the wonderful things which their ancestors could do or had done, gossiping ... the chief subjects of conversation are [now] the doctrine and precepts of our most holy religion—the state of the soul... (MacKenzie 1911).

MacKenzie's journal highlights the issues of validity and reliability of sources, and the hazards of placing credence on the subjective articulations of an individual who had a vested interest in construing his influence on St Kilda as a positive factor in 'improving' moral standards and values. The rigours of religious discipline which governed the lives of the St Kildans can also be glimpsed from the brief autobiographical account written by Malcolm MacQueen, born on St Kilda in December 1828, who states that there were three separate church services on Sunday, in addition to a Sunday afternoon Bible class, whilst on four weekday evenings there was some religious group meeting in operation. It is difficult to perceive how the St Kildans managed to attend to the essential business of survival, given so many religious demands on their time. Nevertheless, Sabbath observance was carried to even greater extremes with the arrival of the Reverend John Mackay in 1865, who imposed rules forbidding the St Kildans to converse with each other from Saturday evening until Monday morning; singing or whistling was a serious sin (Maclean 1977). Until 1869, when his term on St Kilda ended, 'happiness was actively discouraged' (*op.cit.*) due to the 'bigoted impositions of the Free Church missionary...' (MacGregor 1960), with children forbidden to play games and allegedly instructed to 'carry Bibles under their arms wherever they went' (Maclean 1977).

The respective roles played by the churches in relation to the two islands were quite different, not least in terms of language. Differences in theology between Catholicism and Protestantism had significant implications for the fortunes of the language. At the heart of Protestantism lies the conviction that everyone has a right to read the Scriptures in her or his mother tongue. Hence on St Kilda, the use of Gaelic as an evangelical and spiritual medium in church services and regular weekday prayer meetings was supplemented by the practice of daily family Gaelic Bible reading in homes. The use of Gaelic as a spiritual language endorsed the status and enhanced the prestige of the language, thus helping the maintenance and transmission of Gaelic, and reinforcing its position as the everyday spoken vernacular. On the Great Blasket, however, the absence of a Bible reading tradition, and the lack of religious instruction in Irish, offered no such support for the status of Irish, with significant repercussions for language maintenance and transmission.

The Catholic Church has been widely indicted for its role in the decline of the Irish language. English-speaking priests were educated at the anglicised Maynooth College, from where they went on to minister, in many areas, to an Irish-speaking laity, conducting religious instruction in English (Lyons 1973). However, MacDonagh

(1983) sees the Church more as being a 'negative collaborator', rather than a causal factor in a process where the ascendancy of English was already well established. In his view, support from the Catholic Church for the language, where it existed, was essentially utilitarian, and MacDonagh suggests that 'the bulk of the clergy probably shared the peasant attitude that Gaelic was the badge of poverty and failure' (*op.cit.*).

Although some Catholic priests worked tirelessly for the promotion of Irish, many saw it as part of their pastoral duties to prepare the young for the inevitable emigration by giving them practice in English (*cf.* O'Leary 1987). Importantly, the priest, along with the teacher and the policeman, effectively formed a triumvirate of authority and a daily tangible focus for parental aspirations in depressed Gaeltacht areas. Similarly, on St Kilda, although power and authority over day-to-day life were vested in the male 'Parliament', comprising all adult male islanders who met each morning to decide on the day's work and activities, the missionary/ schoolmaster was a respected figure of authority who 'had the English' to deal with matters relating to life outside the island.

On both islands, denominational control over education and schooling was a significant factor in terms of external influence over what were effectively pre-capitalist and pre-literate island communities. The Catholic Church retained full control over the national schools where education was always through the medium of the English language—a policy which has been criticised as 'deliberately anti-national' (O'Leary 1987). Furthermore, it has been argued that the hierarchy of the Catholic Church pragmatically adopted a pro-English stance in order to strengthen its position within the Union (*op.cit.*).

The proselytising activities of Protestant evangelists, particularly in the Gaelic-speaking regions, have become legendary. Tomás Ó Criomhthain's (1978) reference to 'the old monastery of the Soupers' indicates a brief period of Protestant influence on the island. Although Ireland was, and still is, predominantly Catholic, evangelical Protestantism on even a small scale was regarded as a serious threat. The association of the Irish-language Bible with proselytism was expressed by Daniel O'Connell in a letter written in 1824, where he describes the distribution, by Protestants, of Biblical texts in Irish to poorer Catholics as part of a conspiracy, a 'deep-laid plan ... for a more dangerous scheme could not be devised' (quoted in Nic Craith 1993). However, proselytism had often unintended consequences in terms of promoting literacy in Irish. Muiris Ó Súilleabháin, in his autobiography *Fiche Blian ag Fás*, recalls a conversation about the proselytising activities of the 'Soupers', who were instrumental in promoting the Irish language. Muiris relates Liam Beg's opinion that the 'Soupers' were to be thanked because

> they were here in Bally-na-Ráha with their big Irish Bibles, giving half-a-crown to every man who would come and read a line or two, without lie or mockery there wasn't a man in the parish but used to be going to them every night, until they were all able to read Irish fluently (Ó Súilleabháin 1992).

In Scotland, however, divisions existed within the Protestant churches in terms of their attitudes towards the Gaelic language. There was ambivalence with regard to educational policy and practice. To the Established Church, Gaelic was synonymous with popery and rebellion, whilst Presbyterianism, with its own anti-establishment antecedents, adopted a pragmatic policy of the use of Gaelic for spiritual guidance and English for secular education.

Both islands can be regarded as intensely religious and it is clear that in both communities their instinctive faith helped to reconcile the islanders to the precariousness of their very existence. Their lives, a constant struggle for existence at the mercy of unpredictable elemental forces, their physical isolation, and the narrow margin between life and death at sea, would have been irreconcilable without some kind of religious belief, and thus faith was instinctive and reinforced bonds of social cohesion between islanders.

Moreover, on both islands, shared religious beliefs enhanced the tight-knit communal bonds of everyday life, and provided a measure of solace for inevitable tragedies. Many of the songs from St Kilda were in minor keys, 'wild and eerie ... imitating the crying of seabirds and the singing of seals' (Maclean 1977), mournful laments like this one, composed by a woman who lost all the men in her family at sea (*op.cit.*; extract):

> 'Tis a profitless journey
> That took the noble men away,
> To take our one son from me and from Donald.
>
> My son and my three brothers are gone,
> and the one son of my mother's sister,
> And, sorest tale, that will come or has come, my husband.

Attitudes Towards the Language

Parental attitudes towards the English language were a major factor in the decline of Irish/Gaelic in the two islands. However, this area has to-date received little attention, possibly due to the method-ological difficulties in quantifying and assessing the actual impact of attitudes. Census data and statistics of language decline provide very little information about attitudes towards the language, about the frequency of language use, or on aspects of language interaction, that is, with whom, and in what situational contexts Irish/Gaelic is used in preference to English.

In Ireland, even under the 'hedge school' system, schoolmasters had yielded to the popular demands for the inclusion of English to the range of subjects taught (Wall 1969). This can be seen as indicative of parental attitudes towards the instrumental acquisition of English. Moreover, there is much anecdotal evidence that children were physically chastised for speaking in Irish/Gaelic. Muiris Ó

Súilleabháin (1992) remembers a conversation with Liam Beg, who told him that at school he had a

> little board tied behind my back with these words written on it 'If you speak a word of Irish you will be beaten on back and on flank'.

Similarly, Archbishop MacHale recounted wearing a 'tally-stick' with the full consent of his non-English-speaking father, who was determined that his son should speak English at school and at home. Wall suggests that this 'type of barbarous co-operation between parents and teachers which was instigated by the parents, was continued in some of the national schools' (Wall 1969). Although Durkacz (1983) discounted the existence of a formal systematic policy of corporal punishment, anecdotal accounts by Irish, Scottish and Welsh people suggest that chastisement, both verbal and physical, was commonplace. Peter MacNab, an inhabitant of the Scottish island of Mull, recalled the headmaster of his school who said, as late as around 1914, that '[a]nybody using the Gaelic within the precincts of this school will be whipped' (quoted in Craig 1993).

It has been suggested that the fact that parents deliberately avoided speaking Irish/Gaelic to their children is also a contributory factor in the loss of the language (Ó Cuív 1969). Anecdotal evidence further suggests that the use of Irish and English varied even within families, between parents and children, with parents making conscious efforts to speak in English to those of their children whom they expected to emigrate. On both islands, it would appear that parents were keen for their children to benefit from schooling, which would open new horizons and offer wider opportunities beyond their small island communities. Miller (1985) has noted how in rural Catholic Ireland there was 'an almost mystical reverence' for education as parents anxiously sought to prepare their children for material success in a world dominated by English speakers. An amusing family scene is illuminated by Tomás Ó Criomhthain in his *An tOileánach*, whose mother, when he was a young boy, placed a peaked cap on his head, and his father joked that she had 'made a complete peeler' of him (Ó Criomhthain 1978). The ready riposte by Tomas' mother is revealing:

> Well, maybe he'll get a post yet. He's young and learning's to be got in his day, and he can stay at school till he's picked up all there is there (*op.cit.*).

Educational provision on the Great Blasket increased the opportunities whereby a bright child may improve family fortunes by joining the Gardaí (police force) or becoming a national school teacher, and at least one female school teacher, Miss Fitzgerald, a native Blasket islander, later taught at the island's national school. Muiris Ó Súilleabháin joined the Gardaí in 1927, and Eibhlís Ní Shúilleabháin's letters refer to several young Blasket Island men who also joined the service. Similarly, on St Kilda, several young men became Presbyterian missionaries/preachers.

In terms of wider prevailing nineteenth century attitudes towards the Irish people and their language, negative opinions can be identified in popular literature, such as Maria Edgeworth's novel *The Absentee*. In this novel of Anglo-Irish ascendancy life, Lady Clonbrony saw her Irish background and dialect as a distinct social handicap, and her attempts to 'look, speak, move, breathe like an Englishwoman' left her open to ridicule (Edgeworth 1976). Similarly, the impact of anglicisation on popular consciousness in Scotland can be inferred from veteran traveller James Boswell's apparent gratification when Dr Samuel Johnson complimented him on his lack of a Scottish accent (Summers 1991).

In both Ireland and Scotland, Celtic language and culture had become synonymous with poverty and ignorance. Hindley (1990) suggests that in Ireland there was a 'widespread reluctance to admit to a knowledge of Irish because it was associated with illiteracy and low social status'. Similarly, in the Highlands of Scotland, poverty and cultural disorientation led people to not only jettison their language but to 'even deny an ability to speak it' (Withers 1984).

Feelings of inferiority and shame have been reported by native speakers of Irish/Gaelic who had little or no English. Peig Sayers, a Blasket islander, wrote of her childhood when

we'd be ashamed and head-bent for not having little or no English. Small respect anyone had for us. 'The Asses of the Island', the Dingle people used to call us (Sayers 1962).

The association of Irish/Gaelic with poverty and ignorance is deep-rooted in folk sayings such as 'Irish will butter no bread' and 'Irish is tied to a donkey's tail' (*cf.* Hindley 1990). This negative characterisation is grounded in the everyday lived reality of economic deprivation and political marginalisation acutely experienced by Irish and Scottish people. It serves to rationalise ambiguous attitudes towards the abandonment of Irish/Gaelic, given that for any real economic advancement a command of English has become a necessity. By 1800, Irish had already ceased to be the language

habitually spoken in the homes of all those who had already achieved success in the world, or who aspired to improve or even maintain their position, politically, socially or economically (Wall 1969).

Mac Siomóin (1993) has argued that although the 'naire' (sense of shame) associated with the Irish language is widely documented, a further dimension should be noted, namely that of 'disdain, antipathy and contempt' towards others who still spoke it.

Attitudes towards language operate on a deeper level than an individual's superficial choice of communication medium, and language retention, usage and transmission are influenced by both rational criteria, and subjectively held perceptions and beliefs. The social morale of a language and culture, in terms of language shift, is an extremely significant, if somewhat nebulous and difficult area to measure and explore. Durkacz (1983) has suggested that the Celtic languages were, and remain, much more than a mere means of communication, and that they can be seen as vehicles for Celtic cultural and political aspirations. Furthermore, Miller (1985) has argued that language plays a 'corroborative role in the formation of a worldview'.

Insight into the attitudes inculcated by the policy of anglicisation can be gained by the documented experiences and articulated worldview of a group of some ninety Gaelic-speaking Highlanders who were cleared off their lands in Glencalvie, Ross-shire, in 1845, and sought temporary refuge in the Free Church yard. Within a week, the churchyard was empty, but some of the people had scratched their names and brief messages for posterity into the diamond-paned glass church windows, messages like:

Glencalvie people was in the church here May 24, 1845 ... Glencalvie people the wicked generation ... Glencalvie is a wilderness blow ship them to the colony (Prebble 1970).

The decision to write in English by a people dispossessed not only of their language but also their land, reflects not only their view that their language would be lost with them (*op.cit.*), but suggests that, by describing themselves as 'wicked', they had internalised negative images of themselves as a 'wicked' people, thus rationalising their experiences of brutal eviction in a time of widespread land clearances (*cf.* Craig 1993).

Ó Danachair (1969) has suggested that a pragmatic comparison between economically depressed Gaeltacht regions and an outside world perceived as materially affluent inevitably produced a psychological reaction. The essential conflict between the traditional and the modern way of life became part of changing perceptions where 'traditional' became seen as backward, old-fashioned and unworthy, whilst 'modern' life, perceived by Gaeltacht dwellers from impressions gained from summer visitors and brief contact with government or company officials, became seen as an easier, affluent and more desirable existence. It was in these inevitably pragmatic terms that Irish and Scottish parents viewed their native tongue and their children's education and future prospects.

Education

Education and the schools were important factors in the process of language decline, but, as Durkacz (1983) has observed, it is difficult to determine the degree of their influence. Educational provision came much earlier to St Kilda than to the Great Blasket, when in 1709 the Society in Scotland for the Propagating of Christian Knowledge (SSPCK) set up its first school on the island, and Alexander Buchan, a missionary, was appointed as schoolmaster. The attitude of the SSPCK towards the anglicisation and education of Gaelic-speakers is evident in a statement dated 7 June 1716:

Nothing can be more effectual for reducing these countries to order, and making them usefull [*sic*] to the Commonwealth than teaching them their duty to God, their King and Countrey [*sic*] and rooting out their Irish language (quoted in Withers 1988).

The aim of the SSPCK was to spread Protestantism through an anglicised education in the Highlands and Islands 'where Error, Idolatory, Superstition and Ignorance do most abound' (*cf.* Withers 1984). Buchan's account of his experiences on St Kilda illuminate the difficulties encountered in such an isolated outpost. Education always took second place to essential subsistence activities, which often involved the participation of all the islanders. After some fourteen years on St Kilda, Buchan had made little educational progress in a community where few adults spoke English while he was forbidden by the SSPCK to use their native tongue.

A succession of short-stay missionaries/teachers followed, several of whom may have regarded a post on St Kilda with 'more zeal than was good for them' (Steel 1988). In 1811 the Gaelic Schools Society was founded with the objective of providing itinerant teachers to enable the Highlanders to read the Scriptures in their own language. However, 'The Society' also saw a clear potential for English, believing that 'the Gaelic language is the best and easiest channel for the acquisition of the English' (Campbell 1936).

Behind this apparent paradox of using Gaelic for anglicisation was the belief that the 'Highlander who read only Gaelic considered himself half-educated and took active steps to learn English' (Durkacz 1983). On St Kilda, under the supervision of the Gaelic-speaking teacher, the number of scholars reached forty-four, and not all of them were children. The St Kildans appeared to have a great eagerness to learn, and often three generations of a family would attend. Yet by 1821, out of the one hundred or so inhabitants, only one, John Ferguson, was reputed to be able to read (Quine 1982).

In 1829, education on St Kilda passed into the hands of the Reverend Neil MacKenzie. His memoirs provide considerable insight into prevailing Calvinist doctrines at the time. MacKenzie initiated a Sabbath school, and found the St Kildans eager to learn, but English remained a language yet to be mastered. Even as late as 1877, it would appear that there was only one woman on St Kilda, a married-in incomer, who understood English (Steel 1988). After MacKenzie's departure, some ten years elapsed when there was no provision for education on St Kilda (Quine 1982). This pattern of discontinuity of education was a feature common to both islands, with a succession of teachers of varying degree and length of residency, and intervals when there was no teacher at all.

On the Great Blasket, a schoolhouse was constructed and opened in 1839 by the Dingle and Ventry Mission, who also supplied a resident Protestant teacher/Scripture reader. The brief period of Protestant influence on the Great Blasket spans from 1839 to 1850, during which time there is evidence to suggest that the O'Connor family converted to Protestantism, whilst other families pragmatically 'jumped' to avoid starvation during the worst years of the famine (Stagles and Stagles 1980). The schoolhouse became a centre for food relief when a boiler was installed around 1846/47. Apparently, food relief was given to all children regardless of religious allegiance, and in 1848 between 52 and 56 children were attending the school, whilst work relief schemes were also administered by the Mission on the Great Blasket (*op.cit.*). By 1848, however, both the school and adjoining teacher's house were in disrepair and the Mission's funds exhausted. During the same period, a number of 'providential' shipwrecks occurred, which reduced the islanders' reluctant dependence on Protestant charity (*op.cit.*). Although Tomás Ó Criomhthain, in *An tOileánach*, says that nobody actually died of starvation on the Great Blasket, a drop in population suggests otherwise.

On St Kilda, a report written in July 1841 also portrays famine conditions:

> During spring, ere the birds came, [the people] literally cleared the shore, not only of shell-fish, but even of a species of sea-weed ... Now the weather is coarse, birds cannot be found ... Sorrel boiled in water is the principal part of the food of some, and even that grass is getting scarce ... All that was near is exhausted (O'Dell and Walton 1963).

Vulnerability to famine was a periodic hazard to life on St Kilda right up until evacuation. Famine and food shortages were also recurrent features of life on the Great Blasket, although in the latter years of inhabitation, the islanders' deprivation was alleviated by the introduction of social welfare benefits.

On St Kilda, education passed into formal ecclesiastical control when the Free Church took over responsibility for education in 1846 after the Gaelic Schools Society collapsed into financial insolvency in 1843. However, no missionary/teacher was sent out to St Kilda until 1853. In Ireland, although a national system of education was established in 1831, the Blasket islanders did not benefit from educational provision until 1864, when the island's first national school opened. As Lyons (1973) noted, the original aim of these schools was (according to the Protestant Archbishop Whateley's phrase) to make every pupil into 'a happy English child'.

The first Blasket teacher was Áine Ní Dhonnchadha, who faced the unenviable task of attempting to teach the Irish-speaking island children entirely through the medium of English (Nic Craith 1988). The difficulties of implementing such a policy were appreciated by

Father Liam Mac Aogáin, manager of the Blasket school, who wrote:

> English is in truth a ... foreign language to these children—a language which they hear not a word of in their homes ... The present mode of teaching them English is like introducing a National [*sic*] school with its English books and English everything ready made into the heart of France with a view to teaching the children there English without any graduated introduction (quoted in Nic Craith 1988).

Tomás Ó Criomhthain, born in 1856, who attended the Blasket school for the first time when he was about ten years of age, describes his puzzlement at hearing the teacher 'talking some kind of gibberish' (Ó Criomhthain 1978) and his reaction to his teacher's announcement of 'Playtime': 'The word made me stare, for I hadn't the faintest idea what it meant' (*op.cit.*). However, from his description of his fellow class pupils' undisciplined rush to the door and freedom, Blasket children quickly picked up the meaning of this English word.

St Kildan children also suffered from the policy of anglicisation, as Callum MacDonald's account highlights. Born in 1908 to one of the sixteen families on St Kilda, he recalls that he found learning difficult as 'lessons were taught in English and I was only used to talking in Gaelic'. He also describes the frustrations he experienced 'thinking in Gaelic and trying, as I could only speak in Gaelic, to communicate with my teacher in English'.

Due to its remoteness, St Kilda, like the Great Blasket, did not benefit for some years after the introduction of national education legislation. A feature of the 1872 Education Act was the lack of any formal provision for Gaelic, and consequent implications for the language. This legislation ended the parochial system throughout most of Scotland, although St Kilda was deemed too remote to be immediately catered for under the Act. Therefore, discontinuity of education persisted, and in 1884 the Ladies Association of the

Highland Society provided funding for a succession of teachers to the island.

Commentators on St Kilda, for example, George Seton in 1878, endorsed the view that lack of English was the main obstacle to social and economic progress, recommending 'a systematic course of instruction in English' (Steel 1988). Sands (1878) noted the St Kildan view of 'Beurla' [i.e., English]: 'why it is like the cackle of a fulmar'. Ten years later, the situation had changed drastically. The diary by John Ross, a teacher on St Kilda, in 1889 reports good steady progress made by his fourteen pupils using English Readers. Whilst Ross acknowledged that Gaelic had remained the everyday spoken language, he reported 'the young [now] read and speak the English' and noted that 'the success of the children in mastering the English gives great satisfaction to their parents'.

On both St Kilda and the Great Blasket, English did not have any role or function within island life, other than affording limited opportunities, post 1880s, to converse with tourists and visitors. Remoteness, especially in the case of St Kilda, meant that there was little incentive to learn how to write, given that the island had virtually no communication, postal or otherwise, with the outside world between September and May the following year. On St Kilda, the language of the 'Parliament' was Gaelic, and Gaelic remained the language of both everyday secular life and spiritual salvation. On the Great Blasket, Irish continued as the language of the hearth, although trips to Dingle meant opportunities for contact with spoken English at Mass and going about business in the town.

In 1898 the proprietor of St Kilda, MacLeod, instigated the building of a new schoolhouse on the island. Previously a room in the factor's house had served as a schoolroom, and in 1902, 19 children were attending, of whom all except eight were under fourteen years. Again, similarities exist between St Kilda and the Great Blasket, in terms of young adults attending school to take advantage of educational opportunities. Tomás Ó Criomhthain states that he only left school when he was eighteen years old, and photographs of both islands' scholars show the presence of young adults. By 1906, there were twenty-two children attending school on St Kilda, taught by the missionary MacLachlan and his wife (Steel 1988).

It can be ascertained from documentary evidence that on both islands, education was sporadic, haphazard and lacking in continuity. Discontinuity on St Kilda was caused by the succession of itinerant teachers and visiting missionaries. Prior to the beginning of the twentieth century, teachers on St Kilda were usually young men whose socio-economic background and life experience must have been at total variance with that of the islanders, and George Murray's personal diary intimates something of the loneliness and isolation he experienced. On the Great Blasket, Tomás Ó Criomhthain's autobiography, *An tOileánach*, highlights the high turnover of teachers, who were in general, young women who often left the island after a short time to get married, and both islands suffered from remoteness which made it difficult to attract replacements. Both islands had lengthy spells when there was no teacher at all. The standard of education on the Great Blasket was questioned in an Inspector's Report in 1864 (Nic Craith 1988, 9*f.*), although competence of teaching cannot be fairly judged without consideration of an educational policy which dictated that Irish-speaking children be instructed entirely through the medium of English.

Moreover, even when a teacher was in residence, subsistence activities took precedence over school attendance on both islands. George Murray's diary reveals the frequency with which the school had to be closed, often at a moment's notice, when the island's children were needed for essential activities which demanded the participation of the whole population of St Kilda. The Blasket school roll, too, indicates that seasonal factors adversely affected attendance (Nic Craith 1988). The former St Kildan, Lachlan MacDonald, recounted that the teacher was not too worried about the children's education: '[I]f it was a good day at the harvesting he would have the older ones aged 10 or 12 out working the hay' (quoted in Quine 1988).

A range of other factors affected school attendance on both islands. On the Great Blasket, attendance was not compulsory until the Irish Free State was set up. Even a brief perusal of the St Kilda school log book reads more as a record of when the school was closed rather than open. The school log book started in 1900. It highlights the factors which affected attendance, but also offers insight into the difficult life experienced by the St Kildans and the time-consuming tasks essential for survival. A sample of extracts from the year 1918 are given below (quoted in Quine 1988):

January 11   intensely cold and heavy snow. No school in the afternoon

January 15   one scholar Rachel MacDonald has now been absent for over two weeks with chilblains.

January 22   still absent

March 6   every house in the island washing tweed today, scholars assisting, so no school held.

April 8   School closed for 3 weeks—bad attack of influenza

April 30   No school—people gathering birds eggs

June 24   School re-opened today. No school had been held since the island was bombarded on 15th May

July 31   No school for the last 2 days as Mrs. MacKinnon's baby is sick

August 16   No school for a week as all will be engaged in killing and salting fulmars for the winter

October 25   No school ... children bringing peats from the hill for the school fire

In 1919, there were seventeen children attending school on St Kilda, and as the population dwindled after the First World War, so too did the number of pupils. By 1926, only eight children were attending school.

Former islanders who attended the school on the Great Blasket, interviewed for the RTÉ television documentary *Oileán Eile*, recalled the attitudes of several teachers on the island towards English. One interviewee stated that one teacher, Pádraig Mac Gearailt from Tralee,

> had no interest in Irish. He said we had enough Irish already —so he taught English mostly. He said if we went abroad we'd never hear a word and we'd look foolish without English then.

Muiris Ó Súilleabháin describes how his mother died when he was a few months old, and the first four years of his life were spent on the mainland, where he knew no Irish and spoke only English. He recounts that when his widowed father came to collect him from school and take him back home to the Blasket, the schoolmistress was extremely critical of his father's decision to remove the child, arguing '... in the first place he will lose his English ... and how will he get work without the English?' (Ó Súilleabháin 1992). It is ironic that this prophesy proved incorrect since Muiris subsequently joined the Gardaí in 1927 and, after training, was posted to a Gaeltacht region, Connemara, where his fluency in Irish stood him in good stead.

Nevertheless, in the latter years on both islands, educational policy and teaching were geared towards preparing children for inevitable emigration. One of the last Blasket Island school teachers described this task in the RTÉ documentary mentioned earlier:

The hardest job in school was teaching English. I didn't want the pupils to leave without reasonable English. I knew well what was in store for them and the old Fenian sagas would not advance them when they went to America.

Similarly, education on St Kilda can be seen as preparation for life away from the island, and Steel (1988) has criticised a system of education which taught the young islanders that they had to leave the island in order to better themselves and 'undermined the struggle for survival on the island'. It is certainly a moot point that a national, standardised system of eduction fails to accommodate regional circumstances and meet localised educational needs, and in the case of a remote island community, aspects of education 'that might have improved their lot in real terms were never made available to them' (*op.cit.*).

In the winter of 1941 the Blasket Island population had dwindled, and there were only five pupils attending the island school. The school closed that Christmas, 'leaving the three poor scholars to run wild with the rabbits' (Ní Shúilleabháin 1992). The closure of the Great Blasket school sounded the death knell for future life on the island. Lack of a school meant that families with school-age children would either have to leave, or send their children to board on the mainland with friends or relatives.

Eibhlís Ní Shúilleabháin's correspondence indicates that whilst the primary reason for leaving the island was economic hardship, a significant secondary factor was the lack of a school for her daughter, Niamh, who was approaching compulsory school age (Ní Shúilleabháin 1992).

The anglicised education system and the attainment of oracy and literacy in English had significant effects on the Irish/Gaelic language, and ramifications for the long-term future of both island communities, in particular as the last generation of islanders' schooling coincided with the rapid encroachment of modernising external influences.

From Tomás Ó Criomhthain's *An tOileánach*, it is clear that, although he acquired little formal learning, especially literacy in English at school, in later life he developed an interest in An Conradh Gaeilge and the Irish language, and in a Dingle household he discovered children's books which prompted him to teach himself to read. Tomás was soon in demand reading books to other Blasket islanders, and their reaction supports the view that the spread of literacy undermined the Gaelic oral tradition. Tomás observed (Ó Criomhthain 1978) that after reading stories which were already known to the islanders, 'they lost their taste for telling them to one another when they compared them with the style the books put on them'. George Thomson (1982) suggests that within the space of a single generation, the Blasket islanders' whole outlook on life had been transformed by literacy. As Blasket island storyteller, Seán Eoin Ó Duinnshléibhe, advised Robin Flower, 'books and newspapers have driven the old stories out of my head. But maybe I'm little the worse for losing them' (Flower 1945). As Thomson (1982) observed, the Blasket islanders had discovered for themselves 'a new world of commercialised mass entertainment in which there was no place for the fireside tale'. From the chronology of the Blasket literature, and particularly from Eibhlís Ní Shúilleabháin's correspondence in English, the extent to which oracy and literacy in the English language was achieved in just one generation is clear.

Due to remoteness, climatic conditions and inaccessibility, the majority of English-speaking tourists visiting St Kilda only spent a few hours ashore. Nevertheless, the negative impact of tourism on St Kilda has been documented (Maclean 1977), and attributed as a major causal factor in undermining the traditional St Kildan way of life. In the late 1800s, relatively affluent and curious tourists, attracted by tales of a 'primitive' island community came to 'peer at the natives' with varying degrees of benevolence and eagerness to buy island produce as souvenirs. A more enlightened visitor commented in 1900: 'I do not wonder that they dislike foreigners, as so many tourists treat them as if they were wild animals at the Zoo [*sic*]' (Mitchell 1992).

By contrast, many of the seasonal visitors to the Great Blasket came in search of the Irish language, a high percentage of whom were academics and Irish professionals seeking to acquire Irish language skills, and several scholars lived amongst the islanders for intermittent periods. Ostensibly, for Blasket islanders, this contact possibly instilled some sense of pride in their heritage and retention of the Irish language, but idealism was unable to counter the harsh economics of life on the Great Blasket, and emigration to the 'New Island' was seen by Blasket islanders as the only viable option. Moreover, it is clear from Eibhlís Ní Shúilleabháin's letters, that the arrival of 'Lá Breághs' was seen as a welcome diversion from what increasingly came to be seen by the younger Blasket islanders as a poor and mundane way of life, as siblings emigrated and the community dwindled leaving an ageing and dependent population. It is clear from Eihblís Ní Shúilleabháin's correspondence in 1942, however, that her feelings about the outside, but seasonal, interest in her island home are mixed, and she notes:

> they on their holidays and they at home ... and no worry during winter or summer, would never believe the misfortune on this island ... Surely people could not live on air and sunshine (Ní Shúilleabháin 1992).

On St Kilda, another significant agent of social, linguistic, economic and cultural change was the English-speaking naval garrison stationed on the island for the duration of the First World War. Callum MacDonald records that the close relationships established with the English-speaking naval men from 1914 until their departure in 1919 improved the St Kildans' English skills. Moreover, it is obvious that the impact of this naval contingent went far beyond an improvement in the islanders' English, and life on St Kilda was irrevocably changed, as Callum himself recognised. Callum writes:

In the 4 years they had been stationed [on the island] we had come to learn of the wonderous outside world, now we were once more to return to our isolation. These men had been wonderful to us children, teaching us to speak the English language, expanding our knowledge with stories of far away places and giving us a wider perspective of the opportunities open to us elsewhere in the world.

Emigration

More than any other single factor, emigration has affected the social and economic development of both Ireland and Scotland. In Ireland during the eighteenth century, Protestant emigrants outnumbered Catholics by 'about three to one and continued to dominate the exodus until the 1830s' (Miller 1985). Pre-Famine emigration patterns differed markedly in 'size, composition and character' from post-Famine waves of emigration (*op.cit.*). Though now distanced by time, famine and emigration in Ireland has left an evocative legacy, noted by Lyons (1973) as etched ineradicably on 'the hearts and minds ... of all those generations that have lived in Ireland since those terrible years'. MacDonagh (1983) asserted that famine deaths 'must have been very largely the deaths of Irish speakers', since 'mortality was much the heaviest in the poorer and more remote regions'. Thus it can be assumed that a very high percentage of emigrants who left Ireland in the years following this cataclysmic event were Irish-speaking Catholic landless poor from the three southern provinces (Miller 1985), and this had significant implications for the future of the Irish language.

Similarly, in Scotland during the eighteenth and nineteenth centuries, successive waves of mass emigration of Gaelic-speaking Highlanders and Islanders departed to the New World and the Antipodes. Brutal evictions (*cf.* Craig 1993), and especially the 'Highland Clearances' (*cf.* Prebble 1970) following in the wake of Culloden and the military 'pacification' of the Highlands, have left an indelible mark on Scottish consciousness, a legacy which runs deeper than the overt landscape of empty glens, and is echoed in popular song lyrics, epitomised in what has become commonly regarded as the 'unofficial Scottish anthem'—*The Flower of Scotland.*

Thus, in both Ireland and Scotland, population loss through emigration, both voluntary and enforced, has played a major role in language decline. Letters and remittances sent home, providing passage-money for relatives, operated on one level. Occasional visits home by migrants who appeared well-dressed and affluent operated on another level, whilst some returning migrants spoke of their embarrassment at being ill-equipped to seek jobs with broken English. All this combined to consolidate the link between the acquisition of English, emigration and prosperity.

It has been suggested that a considerable number of people in both Ireland and Scotland contemplated emigration, but never actually went away (Hindley 1990). This raises the question of how far acceptance of emigration actually shaped attitudes and language practice, and fundamentally altered perceptions of, and value attached to, remaining at home once a pattern of emigration within families became firmly entrenched. As Aalen and Brody (1969) have stressed, emigration cannot be understood in purely economic terms.

The acquisition of English for pragmatic purposes was supported even by those who were otherwise favourably disposed towards the Irish/Gaelic language on cultural grounds. A letter written in 1862 to the Lord Advocate of Scotland represented the views of many:

> I have no prejudice against the Gaelic language ... but the most ardent lover of Gaelic cannot fail to admit that the possession of a knowledge of English is indispensable to any poor Islander who wishes to learn a trade or to earn his bread beyond the limits of his native Isle (quoted in Withers 1988).

It is evident, then, that in both Ireland and Scotland, emigration and the practice of seasonal migration, such as that on Gola island (*cf.* Aalen and Brody 1969), created an instrumental need for

English, whilst the lack of remunerative employment at home devalued the vernacular language.

On the island of St Kilda, population peaked at around 180 in 1697. The group exodus of thirty-six St Kildans to Australia in 1852 reduced the population by a third. Although the community then stabilised at around eighty or so inhabitants from the 1800s to the 1920s, the Australian emigration had serious implications for the long-term viability of St Kilda. Although the numbers of young people leaving St Kilda increased rapidly after the First World War, there is much to suggest a marked reluctance to leave the island. The departure of the Macdonald family in 1924 to the Isle of Lewis was a further demoralising blow for the dwindling community who remained. Between 1921 and 1928, the population of St Kilda rapidly declined from seventy-three to thirty-seven, and the thirty-six remaining islanders were evacuated on 29 August, 1930.

Table 2   *Population of St Kilda (Maclean 1977)*

Year	No.	Year	No.	Year	No.
1697	180	1822	108	1906	78
1730	c.30	1838	92	1910	77
1758	88	1841	105	1911	80
1764	92	1851	110	1920	73
1795	87	1861	78	1921	73
1799	100	1866	77	1928	37
1803	97	1871	71	1930	36
1810	100	1877	76	1931	0
1815	103	1884	77		

The Great Blasket population was at its peak about 1916, with around 160 inhabitants, but had fallen to 53 in 1947. Thereafter, the Blasket community declined rapidly, and between 1947 and the abandonment of the island in 1953, population had dropped to some twenty islanders.

Remittances sent back home from America became an established feature in poor Gaeltacht areas, and brought news of the outside world which fostered images of a land of easy opportunity outside Ireland. Muiris Ó Súilleabháin suggests that his decision to leave the Blasket was a difficult one, and insight into his perceptions of life in America can be gained from his musings about the allure of the 'next parish':

> [T]he New Island was before me with its fine streets and great high houses, some of them so tall that they scratched the sky; gold and silver out on the ditches and nothing to do but gather it (Ó Súilleabháin 1992).

Table 3   *Population on the Great Blasket (Census of Population)*

Year	Households	Population
1821	18	128
1841	28	153
1851	17	97
1859	18	?
1881	21	136
1901	25	145
1911	29	160
1947	15	53
1953	Island abandoned	

His comments demonstrate clearly the 'pull' factor of emigration. Letters and remittances sent home provided the economic means for brothers and sisters to emigrate, given the added 'push' factor of lack of remunerative employment prospects at home.

Muiris Ó Súilleabháin, who left the Great Blasket to join the police force in March 1927, described the extent of emigration within even his own family:

> Since the fishing was gone under foot all the young people were departing across to America, five or six of them together every year. Maura was not gone a couple of years when the passage money was sent across to Shaun. A year after that Eileen went ... My brother Michael was working for a tailor in Dingle and there was nobody left now in the house but my grandfather, my father and myself (*op.cit.*).

Thus, as Thomson (1982) observed,

> as the eastward flow of money increased, so too did the westward flow of young men and women ... drawn into the mainstream of modern society.

In the period following the Second World War, the decline of the Great Blasket community escalated. Whereas 'in the old days only those had emigrated who could not stay at home: now, only those stayed at home who could not emigrate' (*op.cit.*). It must be borne in mind, however, that emigration and acute population loss were established features of life in many poor rural areas, particularly in the West of Ireland (Brody 1974). Even after leaving the Great Blasket island, Eibhlís Ní Shúilleabháin was convinced that the future of her only daughter, Niamh, lay in America, declaring that 'parents in Ireland would be naked out only for their children go over here in time to send money' (Ní Shúilleabháin 1992).

On St Kilda, life was never to return to 'normal' after the First World War. The garrisoning on the island of an English-speaking naval contingent had brought major changes to the traditional St Kildan way of life of isolation and self-sufficiency. The naval garrison had provided opportunities for the St Kildans to undertake paid employment. It had increased communications with the outside world, and had offered opportunities for the islanders to practise their English. Especially for the younger generation, it had provided a window to the world, as Callum MacDonald's autobiographical account highlights. On both islands, isolation and remoteness had not only insulated the Irish/Gaelic language from the English-speaking world outside, but lack of contact with the outside world had fostered a strong sense of community identity and self-reliance as practical and psychological survival strategies. Maclean (1977) has suggested that the people of St Kilda had developed a 'psychology of isolationism' which enabled them to survive for centuries on the island, but which could not be adapted to withstand the increased contact with the mainland when it came. It was this closer contact with the outside world and external influences that brought about fatal changes in the outlook and structure of the community. 'St Kilda lost its self-reliance and in due course thereafter its identity' (MacGregor 1960).

The numbers of young people leaving St Kilda after the First World War increased. Particularly young male St Kildans were attracted by perceived economic opportunities in Glasgow and the shipyards (Mitchell 1992), or, as in the case of the MacDonald family, to the isles of Harris and Lewis with hopes of paid employment and a better way of life. As the twentieth century progressed, St Kilda increasingly came to be seen by the outside world as an anachronism, and an embarrassment to the standards and values of modern day life. John Gladstone, a botanist who spent three weeks on St Kilda in 1927, succinctly summarised prevailing popular opinion: 'St Kilda has failed to fit into the modern world' (Quine 1988). It has been suggested that St Kilda can be viewed as 'a perfect microcosm of the negative impact of modern civilisation on the elegiac self-sufficiency of the traditional world' (Richards 1992), an observation equally applicable to the Great Blasket.

Although the depopulation of both islands can be primarily attributed to macro factors, and in particular the peripheral economic position of remote island communities, micro factors, such as the impact of social change, loss of identity, and demoralisation also merit consideration. Maclean (1977) has noted that since no generally accepted theory exists to explain the breakdown of communities, a 'normal reaction to the process is to stress its inevitability'. The impact of increased knowledge of, and contact with, the outside world changed, for example, perceptions of what constituted basic food commodities. Shop bought bread and manufactured jam had replaced 'the pick of the strand, the hunt of the hill, the fish of the sea and the wool of the sheep' (quoted in Thomson 1982), unquestioningly accepted by previous generations of Blasket islanders. Imports into the Great Blasket and St Kilda increased, and as the relentless downward spiral of decline escalated, the islanders became materially and psychologically more dependent upon regular contact with the outside world. Aalen and Brody drew similar conclusions on the decline of Gola island where one inhabitant had declared that 'everything is handy except you have to be going in and out. That's the only bloody trouble' (Aalen and Brody 1969). Cohen (1982) suggests that peripherality and remoteness cannot be simply understood in geographical terms alone, but rather that isolation can be a state of mind where

> peripherality, marginality, can be collective self-images, informing and informed by a community's perception of its inability to affect the course of events—even to affect its own destiny.

Cohen's arguments offer some explanation for the sense of resignation and fatalism which, to the reader, comes across most strongly from the literature on both island communities. Moreover, Hindley (1990) has recollected how an old man on Arainn Mhor told him, 'half-laughing, that the only successful Gaeltacht industry would be a suitcase one', and this ready quip reflects entrenched fatalistic attitudes resulting from a long history of mass emigration.

The decline of the Irish/Gaelic language is inextricably linked to a wider process whereby the political, socio-economic and cultural dominance of English effectively devalued not only the Irish/Gaelic language, but a whole traditional way of life, with attendant consequences for the collective and individual self-identity of its speakers. Evidence by John Murdoch to the Napier Commission in 1884 highlights the degree of alienation and demoralisation experienced by Scottish crofters dispossessed not only of their language but also their land:

> When a man was convinced that his language was a barbarism, his lore as filthy rags, and the only good thing about him—his land—was, because of his general unworthiness, to go to a man of another race and another tongue, what remained that he fight for? (quoted in Withers 1984).

Given that the Celtic languages have survived in pockets located in scenic areas of outstanding natural beauty, Hindley (1990) has suggested that some kind of causal relationship exists between physical environment and language retention, while Ó Danachair (1969) has explored the impact of environment on language, and how the landscape itself can be reflected in patterns of speech. The assumed relationship between language and physical environment is a nebulous area, whilst relationships between language and social morale are imperfectly understood. How a sense of identity may be related to language and territory is an interesting area which merits further consideration.

A distinct feature of language retention, usage and transmission on both the Great Blasket and St Kilda was that of isolation of the islands to a certain extent from the corrosive impact of anglicisation. Moreover, it is clear from the literature that inhabitants of both islands had a strongly-developed spiritual and secular sense of communal identity, which shaped their views of island life, and perceptions of the outside world accordingly. In 1976, Comhairle nan Eilean, the association of islands, produced its regional report, *Aithris na Roinne*, which, ironically, was published entirely in

English! The report, outlining planning proposals for Gaelic communities in Scotland, recognised that

> the difference between the native language of the Western Isles and that of most of mainland Britain has produced a strong stimulus for islanders to develop a distinct outlook and attitude to life, as well as providing the basis for a feeling of community (James 1991).

Once populations on both islands dropped below a viable minimum, the unimaginative response of the authorities was to resettle the remnants of the island communities on the mainland. It seems somewhat ironic to compare the cost-conscious evacuation of the 36 remaining St Kildans in 1930 with the incalculable economic costs of the contemporary military occupation of St Kilda. The story of the St Kildans after evacuation and the dispersal of their community across various parts of Scotland makes sorry reading. The twenty or so inhabitants who abandoned the Great Blasket in November 1953 were resettled in the coastal hamlet of Dunquin, which faces the island, and thus many them and their descendants have been able to re-visit their former island home. Their severance may thus be regarded as less cruel than that experienced by the St Kildans. The evacuation of St Kilda has been described by Christine MacQueen, a native of the island, as 'the work of despairing Sasunnachs' (Mitchell 1992).

CONCLUSIONS

There are many similarities between the decline of the Irish/Gaelic language in Ireland and Scotland, and the comparison between the Great Blasket and St Kilda has facilitated an exploration of key factors involved in language decline, contextualised in a study of Irish/Gaelic-speaking communities. A number of conclusions can be drawn from this discussion.

Firstly, the geographic and economic peripherality of the Great Blasket and St Kilda facilitated the retention of the Irish/Gaelic language into the twentieth century in 'Outposts of the Gael'. Remoteness from the centres of power, commerce and influence insulated the Irish/Gaelic language on both islands to some extent from the corrosive impact of anglicisation and modernisation.

Secondly, geographic remoteness meant that communal solidarity and social cohesion were prerequisites for physical and psychological survival, and on both islands, 'Gemeinschaft'-type communities alleviated practical difficulties and psychological isolation, fostering a distinct island communal identity.

Thirdly, although life on the Great Blasket and St Kilda was undoubtedly hard and often precarious, their inhabitants appeared to have had a strong psychological attachment to their island home. Peig Sayers, who married into the island, said of the Great Blasket: 'There are people and they think that this island is a lonely, airy place. That is true for them, but the peace of the Lord is in it' (Sayers 1962). Similarly, Callum MacDonald, who left St Kilda with his family as a young man in 1924, and who returned several times during his life for visits to his former home, concluded an interview with Tom Steel thus: 'To me, it was peace living in St Kilda ... It was a far better place' (Mitchell 1992).

Finally, the comparative study of language decline, contextualised in the lived experiences of Irish/Gaelic-speaking communities, affords useful lessons for current minority language preservation movements in Ireland and Scotland. During the course of the present study, questions have been raised about the relationships between language, environment and a sense of identity, and this is an area which merits further research.

Today, the Great Blasket remains empty apart from seasonal visitors and summer residents attracted by the scenic splendour of the West of Ireland, and drawn by the evocative writings of former islanders. On St Kilda, due to greater inaccessibility, and to a less extensive literary heritage, there are fewer seasonal visitors, and of these the majority are workparties engaged in preservation of the former islanders' homes under the auspices of the National Trust for Scotland. St Kilda also has a permanent military presence—a rocket missile tracking station—as a grim reminder of twentieth century potential Armageddon.

The depopulated islands of the Great Blasket and St Kilda remain silent mementoes of the decline of the Irish/Gaelic language and the loss of their communities for whom Irish/Gaelic was retained as the everyday vernacular into this present century. For both island communities, their environment, cultural heritage and language combined to create a distinctive communal identity as Blasket islanders or St Kildans which enabled them to survive into the twentieth century in 'Outposts of the Gael'. It is fitting, then, that in conclusion, the words of two islanders, who both clearly recognised the uniqueness of their way of life, should be presented for reflection:

We are a poor simple people, living from hand to mouth ... We were apt and willing to live, without repining, the life the Blessed Master made for us ... I have written minutely of much that we did, for it was my wish that somewhere there should be a memorial of it all ... for the like of us will never be again (Ó Criomhthain 1978).

I trust they [our children] will be proud of their ancestry ... and know that all men are equal in the sight of God. Riches and wealth ... was never my ambition ... I still traverse in dreams, my native home, its shores and caves, the way of life that once was (MacDonald n.d.).

BIBLIOGRAPHY

Bute Collection (National Trust for Scotland), Edinburgh

MacDonald, C
n.d.   *St.Kilda — An Autobiography 1908-1979*, unpublished manuscript.
MacKenzie, N
1911   *Episode in the Life of the Reverend Neil MacKenzie At St Kilda from 1829 to 1843*, privately printed.
MacQueen, M
n.d.   *Autobiography of Malcolm MacQueen born on St Kilda, December 21st 1828*, unpublished manuscript.
Murray, G
n.d.   *Diary 1886-1887*, unpublished manuscript.
Ross, J
n.d.   *Diary 1888-1889.* unpublished manuscript.

Secondary Sources

Aalen, F and Brody, H
1969   *Gola: The Life and Last Days of an Island Community*, Cork.
Brody, H
1974   *Inishkillane: Change and Decline in the West of Ireland*, London.
Campbell, J
1936   The Gaelic Schools 1818-1825. In Mackenzie, C, Campbell, J and Borgström, C (eds), *The Book of Barra*, London, 87-97.
Cohen, A
1982   *Belonging: Identity and Social Organisation in British Rural Cultures*, Manchester.

Corkery, D
1968 *The Fortunes of the Irish Language*, Cork.
Craig, D
1993 *On The Crofters' Trail: In Search of the Clearance Highlanders*, London.
Dommen, E and Hein, P
1985 *States, Microstates and Islands*, London.
Durkacz, V
1983 *The Decline of the Celtic Languages*, Edinburgh.
Edgeworth, M
1976 *The Absentee*, London.
Flower, R
1945 *The Western Island or the Great Blasket*, Oxford.
Hindley, R
1990 *The Death of the Irish Language*, London.
Hussey, S
1904 *The Reminiscences of an Irish Land Agent*, London.
James, C
1991 What Future for Scotland's Gaelic Speaking Communities? In Williams, C (ed.), *Linguistic Minorities, Society and Territory*, Avon, 173-218.
Lee, J
1989 *Ireland 1912-1985: Politics and Society*, Cambridge.
Loomis, C
1963 *Ferdinand Tönnies: Community and Society—Gemeinschaft and Gesellschaft*, New York.
Lyons, F
1973 *Ireland since the Famine*, London.
MacDonagh, O
1983 *States of Mind: Two Centuries of Anglo-Irish Conflict 1780-1980*, London.
MacGregor, A
1931 *A Last Voyage to St Kilda: The Farthest Hebrides*, London.
MacGregor, D
1960 The Island of St Kilda, *Scottish Studies* 4/5, 1-46.

Maclean, C
1977 *Island at the Edge of the World*, Edinburgh.
Mac Siomóin, T
1993 Disappearing inside the Master, *Fortnight* 316, 17-9.
Miller, K
1985 *Emigrants and Exiles: Ireland and the Irish Exodus to North America*, Oxford.
Mitchell, W
1990 *St Kilda: A Voyage to the Edge of the World*, Oban.
1992 *Finlay MacQueen of St Kilda*, Oban.
Nic Craith, M
1988 *An tOileánach Léannta*, Dublin.
1993 *Malartú Teanga: An Ghaeilge i gCorcaigh sa Naoú hAois Déag*, Bremen.
Ní Shúilleabháin, E
1992 *Letters from the Great Blasket*, Dublin.
Ó Conluain, P
1985 *Islands and Authors*, Cork.
Ó Criomhthain, T
1978 *An tOileánach [The Islandman]*, Oxford.
O'Cuiv, B
1969 Irish in the Modern World. In Ó Cuív, B (ed.), *A View of the Irish Language*, Dublin, 122-32.
Ó Danachair, C
1969 The Gaeltacht. In Ó Cuív, B (ed.), 112-21.
O'Dell, A and Walton, K
1963 *The Highlands and Islands of Scotland*, London.
O'Donnell, P
1991 *Islanders*, Cork.
O'Leary, P
1987 *My Story: Reminiscences of a Life in Ireland from the Great Hunger to the Gaelic League*, Oxford.
Ó Súilleabháin, M
1992 *Fiche Blian ag Fás [Twenty Years A Growing]*, Oxford.

Prebble, J
1961 *Culloden*, London.
1970 *The Highland Clearances*, Harmondsworth.
Quine, D
1982 *St Kilda Revisited*, Frome.
1988 *St Kilda Portraits*, Frome.
Richards, E
1992 The Decline of St Kilda: Demography, Economy and Emigration, *Scottish Economic and Social History* 12, 55-75.
Sands, J
1878 *Out of this World or Life in St Kilda: The Farthest Hebrides*, Edinburgh.
Sayers, P
1962 *An Old Woman's Reflections: Story of a Blasket Island Storyteller*, Oxford.
Smout, T
1985 *A History of the Scottish People 1560-1830*, London.
Stack, P
1979 *Island Quest: The Inner Hebrides*, London.
Stagles, J and Stagles, R
1980 *The Blasket Islands: Next Parish America*, Dublin.
Steel, T
1988 *The Life and Death of St Kilda*, London.
Summers, G
1991 *Traditions of Scotland*, Cambridge.
Synge, J
1912 *In Wicklow and West Kerry*, Dublin.
Thompson, F
1974 *The Uists and Barra*, London.
Thomson, G
1982 *The Blasket Island That Was: The Story of a Deserted Village*, Dublin.
Wall, M
1969 The Decline of the Irish Language. In Ó Cuív, B (ed.), 81-90.

Janet Leyland

Withers, C
1984 *Gaelic in Scotland: The Geographical History of a Language*, Edinburgh.
1988 *Gaelic Scotland: The Transformation of a Culture Region*, London.

Paul Henry and Achill Island

MARY COSGROVE

INTRODUCTION

Reproductions of Paul Henry's paintings of the west of Ireland are found in many Irish homes. The idyllic, Arcadian scenes (Figure 8) create a nostalgic image of a country left behind by emigrants and city dwellers. As part of the project to demythologise Ireland's history these images are beginning to be dissected. For many, Henry's paintings represented the Free State that De Valera wished to create, and he had described in his St Patrick's Day broadcast in 1943:

A land whose countryside would be bright with cosy home-steads, whose fields and villages would be joyous with sounds of industry, the romping of sturdy children, the contests of athletic youths, the laughter of comely maidens, whose firesides would be the forums of the wisdom of serene old age.

Although there is an obvious omission of all politics in Henry's autobiography (Henry 1953), he writes nothing to dissuade the reader from the view that this indeed was his intention. It is only when one places the paintings alongside history that one is permitted an insight to the many levels at which these works may be read. In this essay, I shall read parts of Henry's book in relation

Ullrich Kockel (ed.), *Landscape, Heritage and Identity: Case Studies in Irish Ethnography*, Liverpool University Press 1995, 93-116.

to its contemporary art historical developments and in relation to historical events on Achill. The chief characters are Henry the artist, Michael Mangan, a resident of Achill, and Darrell Figgis, novelist, poet and politician.

THE ARTIST'S VISIT TO THE ISLAND

Paul Henry became curious about Achill after listening to the account of the travels there of his friend, the journalist and essayist Robert Lynd (1879-1949). Lynd had been especially impressed by the island when researching a book on Ireland. In a tone reminiscent of earlier travel books, Lynd wrote of Achill (Lynd 1909):

> Here amid the gloom and the dark wind, rises a land populous in parts with cottages as a city with human beings. It is a place of tiny dwellings and tiny farms. Out in the fields you see the women labouring and bringing wonder into the rocky darkness of the island with their heavy petticoats of red and blue that you will not surpass for colour in a Titian. The men dig the earth into strange shapes—furrows and ridges that you would conceive might be dug blindly by night. The social spirit is here, however, making continual war on the hungry bareness of things. The people delight in dancing and song and old men scrape a living from twittering fiddles on the earthen cottage floors in the evenings.

It is not difficult to see the attraction such a description would have for Henry the painter; the colours, the entertainment, labouring peasants reminiscent of the work of Millet and Van Gogh and the remoteness of the place resembling the remoteness of Gauguin's Tahiti.

In his autobiography, Henry wrote that his interest in the west of Ireland had already been raised by Synge's *Riders to the Sea* (Henry 1953):

94

There was something in Synge that appealed to me very deeply. He touched some chord which resounded as no other music ever had done.

The musical metaphor alerts the reader to the theory behind Henry's decision not only to go to Achill but to stay as long as he did. Although he says at the outset that there was 'no inner urge' (*op.cit.*), by the time he reaches his description of arriving at Achill he has advanced an argument that is based on one of the basic tenets of Post-Impressionism.

Figure 8   *Paul Henry's ' Mountains and Cottages'*

The 'deep ancestral feeling' that he claims to have experienced echoes the atavistic feelings he underwent when viewing *The Winged Victory* in the Louvre in Paris, and represents the establishment of his classical credentials. The putative familiarity of the place, of which he wrote that '[i]t was home' (Henry 1953), was not just due to the fact that his mother's relations came from nearby Connemara, but that, in viewing Achill, he recognised that he had the permission of Post-Impressionist critics and the means at his disposal to give form to the emotion aroused by the landscape (*op.cit.*):

> Everywhere I went I saw strange new beauty: in the mountains sloping on the south side towards the sea, in the setting of the villages; Keel compact and friendly, Pullough more strung out on its road which hung over the sea, Dooagh crouching by its little strand under the shadow of Croaghaun...

The strangeness of the place is part of the fascination, and although he had already expressed his dislike of tourists and his wish to distance himself from them, he shares many of their attitudes. Chiefly, he shares the sense of difference that inspired the tourism of the previous century. His observations have, at times, an almost voyeuristic tone (*op.cit.*): 'I was spying out the land, and it seemed to me exceedingly good'.

Like the tourist, he wanted to preserve the olde-world charm of the costumes and manners of the older generation on Achill, and his sadness at their passing has a hint of foreboding (*op.cit.*):

> The change, it is true, was very slight, but it was there and I was to watch with a growing uneasiness this change for the worse.

He shared the current urban fashion for living the 'simple life', and through his observations he claimed to have gained intimate information of life there (*op.cit.*):

I had gained another little bit of the secret knowledge, the knowledge that man does not live by bread alone.

His claims to having grasped such an understanding are diluted considerably by his failure to give any details of what might have sustained the islanders' hopes and political aspirations. We are left to imagine that the sustenance he is referring to is so spiritual that it is beyond description and can only be felt in emotion. His omissions are so consistent that it is doubtful that they are accidental.

Feminine Imagery

Henry portrays himself as a man caught up by a force beyond his control. Such passivity conflicts with the purposefulness of his determination to cast himself in the role of Post-Impressionist painter. As when writing about Paris, he denies himself any rational role and attributes all responsibility to his emotions (Henry 1953):

I was not actively thinking, I was not weighing any pros and cons, I was in the grip of something that could not be argued about, something that would not be denied. I wanted to stay in Achill, and whatever reason seemed to be against such a plan was swept aside by my overpowering desire.

The desire that Henry writes about has many sources and is more complex than he would have us believe. He had come to a part of Ireland which was well known for its scenic beauty. The newspaper *Today*, which he worked for in London, regularly published travel items on the area including Achill. He had contracted with the editors of *The Graphic* and *Black and White* before leaving London to send drawings from Achill for publication. His paintings were used to illustrate Robert Lynd's *Rambles in Ireland* (1912b), lending a commercial aspect to the inspiration he had received from Lynd.

Henry mentions some school-boy reading that he thinks may have helped foster his wish to live on Achill: Thoreau's *Walden*, Hugh Maxwell's *Wild Sports of the West*, and Hugh Millar's *My School and Schoolmasters*. Thoreau describes living a solitary life with nature, Maxwell writes about hunting expeditions on the Erris Peninsula in Mayo, and Millar about wild life in the Scottish Highlands.

Robert Lynd, the friend who initially aroused Henry's interest in Achill, was already a member of Sinn Féin, and some idea of the sort of pressure he may have exerted on Henry to return to Ireland can be gained from his nationalist book written three years before Henry went to Achill (Lynd 1912*a*):

The destinies of Ireland are in the hands of the free and noble men and women of Ireland whom you can persuade, but could never compel, to join you ... The Nationalists who matter to Ireland are those who serve Ireland, not because they have to, but because they see her beauty and her desolation and feel towards her as children feel towards their mother. Men and women of this sort you can always appeal to with reasonable and quiet words. They cannot help being good Irish men and women, if only some one shows them the way.

The personification of Ireland as a mother in this context is interesting in the light of Henry's concept of returning home to the land of his mother's ancestors, the 'ferocious O'Flaherties of Ballinahinch' (Henry 1953). There is a contradiction between the strangeness he found so fascinating and the familiarity he also felt (*op.cit.*):

It was strange, and apart from its loneliness, bizarre; it was troglodyte in its uncouthness, but it had an intimacy, a friendliness, a familiarity, it was the ancestral home of the tribe.

It could be argued that Henry's 'overpowering desire' is a desire to contact the maternal essence, to return to a pre-oedipal stage, to search for what Barthes (1982) called 'the feminine referent'—the sense that one has already been to a place, the familiarity that Henry writes of, has been linked by Freud to the feelings for the maternal body: 'There is no other place of which one can say with so much certainty that one has already been there' (Barthes 1982). Henry does not mention his mother, nor indeed any of his relatives. The omission of any reference to his wife, whom he married he married in London around 1903, may be on account of their bitterly disputed separation in 1929.

Henry left his mother to go to Paris and his rejection of her religion and attitudes may have created in him the need to reclaim her in some form. The reiteration of subjective feelings when confronted by the landscape of Achill permits Henry the wilful 'suspension of discourse' (Barthes 1982). His application of the techniques of Post-Impressionism to images of Achill allow for the controlled return of the Mother. His search for the secret knowledge, referred to in a conversation with George Russell as the soul of Ireland (Henry 1953), could be seen as a quest for the Real, the Mother, with all the ambiguity that relationship implies.

Henry personifies Achill, although not literally, as feminine. He refers to houses 'huddled close together as if for warmth and companionship', hears the island speaking to him, and strives to identify with its changing moods (*op.cit.*):

Keel was a village of moods and never looked the same from one day to another. When it was windless (which was seldom on that wild coast), and the sun shone and the workers were busy in the fields it lay beside the sea, calm and peaceful. It was gay and lively during spring and harvest with people going about their chores. In rain it gave one the impression of a flock of speckled hens huddled together, and during the great gales that swept over it, it cowered, the cottages crouching low among their sally gardens while the wind boomed overhead

99

and the devouring sea was at the doors snarling among the rocks.

The changing moods are a reflection of the ambiguity of the parental relationship where the mother can be kind or disturbing depending on how the child feels about itself. Henry was confronting a landscape traditionally objectified as feminine and, as such, silenced and possessed. His troglodyte reference (Henry 1953) may indicate a wish to explore pre-historical matriarchal myths in the land of Grania Uaille.

Paintings of rural life were widely accepted by artists as a valid subject in Paris during the second half of the nineteenth century. The young Henry was deeply influenced by the work of Millet and later, like Pissaro, he came to prefer his drawings of peasants. Henry was familiar with the work of Gauguin and Van Gogh, both known for their work amongst peasants. To Henry, painting peasants would have represented a respected and traditional genre. He had spent all his life previous to coming to Achill in cities—Belfast, Paris and London—apart from brief spells in Rambouillet and Surrey, and the fact that he was following a well-established route in artistic circles slightly ameliorates the incongruity of his atavistic memories of the western seaboard. Achill, unlike France and England, retained a feudal system of tenant and landlord. It presented an opportunity for Henry to experience peasant life in a way that he could not do in France or England. Like Van Gogh, he responded in an emotive way to Millet's work and wanted to live among the people of Achill to identify with the myth of the peasant-painter (*op.cit.*):

I wanted to know the people, their intimate lives, the times of seed-time and harvest. Only after I had gained such knowledge would I be able to paint the country which I had adopted. I wanted to study them, I wanted to study the lives of the people and their surroundings as closely and as single-mindedly as the French naturalist Fabre studied the insects of his devotion in the stony fields and vineyards of Provence.

Perhaps the choice of comparison is merely unfortunate, but as Henry is best known for his landscape paintings, one cannot ignore such a remark. One must turn to the paintings for evidence of his endeavours and ask if there is any sign of Henry's knowledge of the inhabitants of Achill or has he just thought of them as subjects of entomology.

The Primitive

Henry saw Achill as a place which fulfilled, in many respects, the artist's idea of a primitive source of artistic inspiration. He saw it as remote and isolated (Henry 1953):

Geographically Achill is an island, and it held all the islander's susceptibilities to the outside world although only a few hundred yards separated it from the mainland, and its current of life was entirely traditional, which separated it still further. There were many folk who had never seen a train. All these things proved attractive and satisfying to me, and the habits and ways of this remote community surrounded by savage rocks and treacherous seas, provided me with all I required as a painter.

However, he was writing about a place where all the men and young girls and boys went to Glasgow and its surrounds every year as migratory labourers. A Laird steamer went direct from Achill to Glasgow from 1910.

In Mayo, the only county in Ireland in which migratory labor was a principal factor in the economy, 14.3% of the males 20 years and upward were still seasonal migrants to England and Scotland in 1881. For some localities the proportion approached 100% (Solow 1971).

He himself had arrived at Westport by train on a line which had been constructed seven years earlier, in 1895, and the line to Clifden had been open for nine years. Only the very elderly and infirm would not have seen a train by 1912. Henry's conceived notion of remoteness was one influenced by tourist literature and ideas of urban dwellers and bourgeois artists. It suited his artistic purposes to see the island as a primitive arcadia. It provided him with a subject and gave him the opportunity to resolve the technical difficulties arising from Neo-Impressionism by developing a style suited to his new found security.

For Henry, Achill contained many 'primitive' qualities. He describes the village of Keel when he first saw it as looking like an African village, although he had never been to Africa and was dependent on images or reconstructions. He is concerned in his description to emphasise a sense of disorder and lack of planning or precision—a place which he could enter without causing any disturbance, almost as though he were unseen, looking through a telescope (Henry 1953):

> Seen from a distance it had the appearance of a Kaffir Kraal; what seemed like leaf-thatched huts were the thatched roofs of the cottages and the straw-thatched hay stacks of the community. These latter were tethered, tied first of all circularly with straw ropes (sugans), then with heavier ropes crossing the tops diagonally and weighted with large stones. There was no order of any kind. There was no street; you could wander among the houses in any direction through stone-walled bohereens, streams in wet weather, boulder-strewn like the bed of a mountain torrent, in dry.

The same quality was to be found in the disorder of the natural scenery—turbulent, treacherous seas, savage rocks and formidable mountains. 'But what attracted me above all these things was the wild beauty of the landscape' (*op.cit.*).

The people—especially the 'wild-eyed children' and the foot-loose vagrants—are not exempt from his romanticising. He castigates the young girls for discarding the clothes handed down to them by their grandparents because they are not so picturesque. Their high heels and silk stockings do not accommodate his vision of the remote arcadia. Bare-footed and bare legged, they have for him a 'wild picturesque grace'. He makes no effort to understand why they might want to change into their best clothes before they model for him.

Again it was the old people who most fulfilled his ideas of what a remote society should be like. They still dress in red petticoats and still had a graciousness of manner, he thought reminiscent of aristocracy. The difference between their considered ways and the urban values he had met with in Paris and London struck him as strange and bizarre and captivating. He describes Michael Mangan, an elderly shoe-maker and musician, thus (*op.cit.*):

> He had a long grey beard parted in the middle like the beard of God the father one sees in early Italian pictures; his long grey hair in ringlets on his shoulders, a refined, sensitive, aesthetic face, a beautifully modelled aristocratic nose, and gentle brooding grey-green eyes, the colour of the sea, under a thick thatch of eyebrow.

Mangan's face represented to him a symbol of the early Italian paintings so admired by the French artist and theoretician, Maurice Denis (1871-1943). Henry is obsessed by the man's appearance, and by the appearance of his squalor-stricken hovel. He had just arranged with Sir Horace Plunkett to repair his cottage when Mangan died. Repairs like this would have required the permission of the landlord, and in the usual case would automatically have raised the rent. He recognises Mangan's authority but supposes it to be a position peculiar to the artist, driven apart from the society by his refinement. It is only on reading Mangan's obituary in the *Mayo News* of 27 February 1915, that one learns how he was the first to establish the Land League on the island. Henry either is not aware of this or thinks it not important or relevant. He prefers the romantic image of the solitary mystic (Henry 1953):

> An artist he was, of the vague kind one meets occasionally in Ireland, inchoate and purposeless, through the lack of some guidance in early life, an imperfect education, the harsh surroundings, the indifference of one's early associates.

Mangan was a Gaelic-speaker. He supplied Henry with the place names and their English translations. Henry could not really communicate with the man in any meaningful way as Mangan seemed to be more at ease speaking Gaelic (Henry 1953):

> I asked Michael to tell me what he knew about 'Tir-na-Og' [*sic*] and where he thought it actually was. But this was too much for him and he broke into a spate of Irish, which he often did when deeply moved and where I could not follow him.

Mangan, presumably, was not inchoate regarding Gaelic, nor was he uneducated about Irish writings, as Henry deciphered the names of Yeats and Standish O'Grady and *The Annals of the Four Masters* from his 'spates'. He also held meetings in his house where current events and newspaper articles were discussed under his supervision. Nevertheless, Henry depicts a pathetic old man, isolated and neglected because of his mysterious refinement.

Henry was upset to discover that the women of the island did not want to be sketched by him and believed it was because of their superstitions and modesty. He worked furtively, often offending people. This might explain his lonely landscapes. He is disappointed that the island's inhabitants do not fully co-operate in his vision of a primitive world. Yet, when they do expose their feelings—as, for example, when protesting about a shortage of flour in the shops—he is filled with wonder (Henry 1953):

I remember at one time there was a shortage of flour, due to a miscalculation on the part of the flour merchant, and the women got so excited and worked up it required all the persuasiveness of a police inspector and several constables to protect the flour merchant. I spoke to a lot of these women myself and was astonished to see these otherwise kindly and innocent people lifting up rocks which they were prepared to hurl at the police inspector.

Henry contributes the heated feelings to the people's post-famine fear of hunger, but it must also be seen as an example of the type of relationship that existed between a shopkeeper whose customers were continually living on credit and a police force who often had to defend figures of power from the wrath of the people. To understand this, we have to look at the history of the estates on Achill.

THE LAND QUESTION ON THE ISLAND

In 1833, the Reverend Edward Nangle leased 130 acres in the north-east of Achill at £1 per annum. The moor was reclaimed, and by 1834 a house and school with a minister had been established. In 1848, after a fund-raising tour of England, an estate of 23,927 acres, three fifths of the island, was purchased from Sir Richard O'Donnell under the Encumbered Estates Act for £11,000. It yielded a rent of £1,400 per year until 1883 when it was cut by the Fair Rents Commission to £900. The Achill Mission had its own printing press and published a paper called the *Achill Missionary Herald*. The mission's aim was to convert Catholics to their beliefs, and the paper concentrated on anti-Catholic rhetoric. Long theological arguments were conducted through the paper by Nangle and the Catholic clergy. On 31 July 1837, the Reverend Connelly, parish priest on Achill, wrote in the *Herald*:

Permit me to assure you that the Catholic clergy and people of Achill are prepared for the contest, should you wish for its continuance and that they will oppose every legitimate obstacle to your proselytising scheme, supported though this may be, by the influence of a clique of paltry bigots in this neighbourhood, who want the moral courage to avow it openly and that they will not allow you or your much interested Missionaries to trample with impunity on their conscientious and religious feeling.

To which Nangle replied at great length in the issue of 19 September 1837, finishing thus:

As an Irishman I take my stand on the side of Irishmen against the intolerable tyranny which the Pope of Rome and his Janissaries, the Romish Priesthood, have usurped over the souls and bodies of my countrymen.

Although a small number of converts were made, the local people —with the encouragement of the parish priest—remained Catholics and referred to the mission as the Souper Mission because of the soup that was offered to the starving during the famine in exchange for their Catholic faith. By 1881 there were 600 tenants and they held about 2,000 acres of reclaimed land.

Plots of four acres had to support a whole family. The weather was awful: rain and storms from the Atlantic. The islanders lacked adequate boats for fishing. There was insufficient seaweed to fertilize their plots. The agent for the Mission estimated if you took two-thirds off the rest might live (Solow 1971; quoting the Bessborough Commission of 1881).

In 1891, the Congested Districts Board (CDB) was established to administer assistance to areas of exceptional poverty. According to the commissioners, a 'congested district' was one in which the rateable value was less than 30s per head of the population. Such districts were to be found in the west from Donegal to Kerry, where 500,000 people were classed as poor or destitute. Wyndham's Act of 1903 authorised the CDB to acquire estates for the purpose of enlarging holdings.

Landlords had already lost real control over their estates with the Ballot Act of 1872, depriving them of influence in parliamentary elections. In 1898, they had already lost control of local government with the establishment of elective county councils. They were increasingly ready to sell and welcomed the Wyndham Act, whereby they were paid substantially more than under previous acts. As the agreement of only three-quarters of tenants was required, the act encouraged landlords to sell complete estates. On doing so, they were given a bonus payment equal to twelve per cent of the total sale price. Legal costs were paid out of public funds, and the purchasers had an extended time in which to pay. By 1909, when the act was amended to give the CDB compulsory powers, some 270,000 estates had been sold.

The landlords of Achill had still not sold by the time Henry arrived there in 1912. A campaign of protest was under way, organised by the United Irish League (UIL), which had been founded in 1898 to re-establish the Home Rule campaign, and in 1909 had succeeded in ousting Dr Ambrose, who had been the standing MP for West Mayo for sixteen years. Mr Doris, the newly elected UIL member, was the brother of the editor of the *Mayo News*, and this paper supported tenant agitation in Mayo and Sligo. However, the priests had supported Ambrose, and they continued to oppose Doris when the All For Ireland League put up a candidate in 1910. Doris won, and tenant agitation thereafter was supported by the clergy and the UIL. Clare Island was sold in 1895 and the islands of Inisbofin and Inishark were sold to the CDB by the landlord, Mr Cyril Allies, in 1905. There were many delays involved in the sale of estates and subsequent delays for tenants in obtaining assistance.

Landlords who sold their estates for cash were obliged either to wait an indefinite time for such payment; or else, if they could not wait owing to their financial position, to accept in lieu of cash, payment or part payment in depreciated Stock. Tenants suffered loss by the delay of the Treasury in paying their landlords, as until vesting consequent on payment took place tenants could not obtain the full benefits of Land Purchase (Micks 1925).

The trustees of the Achill Mission Estate were particularly slow in coming to an agreement with the Board. As most of the land in the poorest seaboard estates in Connemara and parts of Mayo was already tenanted, it was less capable than inland estates of improvement by a re-arrangement of holdings. The corresponding lack of commercial interest encouraged an ambiguous attitude to sales among landlords and tenants. The CDB's annual report of 1909 recommended that the Board should retain the estates bought on the western seaboard in order that the people could be assisted to improve their houses, roads and local industries.

The UIL's *Mayo News* ran regular articles about the exploitation of the harvesters, using their grievances to enlist support for their Home Rule campaign.

One third of the girls are not seventeen. Some are twelve and thirteen years old ... Jostled like pigs in third-class M.C.W. Railway Company, dumped on the docks with their little bundles, exposed to the cutting remarks, the derisive jeers, the contemptuous laughter, the scorn, the disgust, not only of the ignorant, trampish mob which nearly always infests such places, but also to that of the more genteel street-goers whom partly curiosity, partly the striking scarlet petticoats of our poor bewildered girls have attracted in crowds to the spot (*Mayo News*, 8 January 1910).

After working for twelve hours, the young people slept on straw. They were paid 3d per hour or 2/6 a day. In one season—from early June to the end of October—they could save £8-10. Considering an estimated total number of 1,500-2,000 harvesters, this brought some

£18,000 to the district each year. The island was over-populated and the rents were excessive.

> At home an impoverished peasantry on an impoverished soil, the dread of eviction, the necessity to provide an honest sustenance to force the peasant from his peaceful homestead to less hospitable, even hostile shore,—above all the landlord, generally a virulent old croney encumbered by constitutional obesity must receive his relatively crushing quota (*Mayo News*, 8 January 1910).

Rent was due to be paid at the end of the season, and in November 1912 the parish priest, Fr Colleran, addressed a meeting of some five hundred tenants outside the office of the Achill Mission land agent in Dugort. He demanded that the trustees give their pledge to sell the estate to the Congested Districts Board and advised the tenants to hold back their rents until the trustees had lodged the maps of the estate with the Board. The estate trustees immediately began legal proceedings and early in the next year ejectment processes were served on tenants in three villages. The process server was attacked by a crowd of women in Keel and required police protection to escape.

> Following on the recent resolve of the tenants under the Achill Mission Trust to abstain from paying rents until the Mission had declared its willingness to sell to the Congested Districts Board, on last St. Stephen's day, amid scenes of great excitement, processes were served on a number of homes at Keel, Pollac and Duagh. The process server was Mr Patrick Lavelle of Dueega and in order to better deliver his 'Christmas cards' took a circuitous route round by Dugort. The result was that he had delivered his three processes at Keel before his mission was discovered. And by the time the horn of alarm was sounded he had got safely to the road to Pollac and Duagh. So a great army of the women of Keel laden with sods of turf and harder missiles, met him on his return. The police

were quickly summoned, and it seemed at one time there would certainly be bloodshed. Indeed there was no reason to doubt that this would certainly have been the result except that the police bethought themselves of the coastguard station that lay adjacent. Mr Lavelle was quickly housed there and the army of women and lads took it in turns to wait outside the station (*Mayo News*, 4 January 1913).

In Duagh, a free fight with the police took place when they tried to remove the server's car. The women of Achill were in the forefront of this type of confrontation because the men were in the hills and had to be summoned down. These women were hardly the shy, timorous, naive creatures that Henry describes. Such incidents occurred while Henry was there, and in the village he stayed in. He stayed at the Post Office and was aware of everything that happened. There can be no doubt that his omissions are deliberate, as these incidents provided a focus of attention for the whole island.

The following morning the whole of the district was in a state of ferment. At an early hour the band from Duagh marched to Keel with a large contingent of men. At Keel the Keel band joined them and the whole mass of men marched through Dubhoinnaille where others joined them to Dugort village. There must have been 5 or 600 men in the procession. At Dugort a large meeting was held at which Fr Egan, Mr Anthony Kilcoyne, Mr Patrick Molloy and Mr Darrell Figgis spoke (*Mayo News*, 4 January 1913).

Further meetings were held the following Sunday. Fr Colleran announced that the tenants would pay their rents as soon as the trustees made public their willingness to sell. The *Mayo News*, as expected, supported the tenants.

The tenants may be assured of one thing; unless they exert themselves on their own behalf, no other body or part will. The time has arrived when misdirected officialism must give way to a genuine endeavour to give merit where merit is due, and to extend to those most in distress, the benefits of those Acts which were primarily intended for their relief, but which, through influences we do not care to mention, have been diverted to other channels. If our tenant farmers would look to the strength of their own brawny arms, and less to uncertain forces outside, they would long ago have gone beyond that stage when active agitation is necessary to secure for them their just rights (*Mayo News*, 11 January 1913).

The 'uncertain forces' may be a reference to Horace Plunkett's co-operative movement.

At Westport Quarter Sessions on 8 January 1913, the trustees of the Achill Mission estate were named as Colonel Robert Wade-Thompson, Clarskeagh Castle; Mr Joseph Abbot, Monkstown, County Dublin; Mr Joseph Vaughan, Town Clerk, Kingstown; and Dr O'Sullivan, Bishop of Tuam. The tenants who were processed were: William E. Egan, Anthony Barrett, Patrick Fadian (Anne), Patrick O'Malley, Joseph Moran, Thomas Burke and Michael Mangan. The judge granted decrees and refused application for payment by instalments. A meeting was held at Dugort the following week attended by five hundred people at which a Tenants' Defence Fund was inaugurated.

On 1 February 1913, charges of intimidation and disturbance of the peace in December 1912 were preferred against tenants by District Inspector Adderley. Mr Barry of Westport and Castlebar defended:

Everybody in Ireland knew the privation and poverty of the people of Achill. They were in misery since their birth and had to go to the harvest fields of Scotland and England to pay the rents due to the Achill Mission. This was an unusual state of affairs in the twentieth century and the sooner that state of affairs was brought to a close the better. The people of Ireland —yes of the United Kingdom—have come to realise that the land was theirs and should be the property of the tillers of the soil, but according to Mr Grierson and the trustees of the Achill Mission it should be confined to a class who would get a rent out of it, and the tenants should remain in bondage for ever (*Mayo News*, 8 February 1913).

The first charge was dismissed and the second adjourned until the next day. A large procession took place afterwards, accompanied by loud cheers. At the second hearing, the defendants were not professionally represented as they could not afford to rehire their lawyer. Anthony Kilcoyne defending himself said:

We demand the land and the land we must have and we are prepared to continue to fight against landlordism as honestly and legally as we can. We have no desire to intimidate any man; we will fight our cause in a constitutional manner until we emancipate the people from the accursed system they have been subservient to for years (*Mayo News*, 8 March 1913).

The cases were dismissed. A large meeting was held afterwards on Fair Green at which Fr Colleran stated that there would be no rent paid until the maps were lodged with the Congested Districts Board. On 18 February, another attack by women had taken place, this time on the estate manager.

The agitation on the Achill Mission estate took an interesting turn on Tuesday. About 30 police in charge of D.I. Adderley, Newport, were escorting the agent on the estate, Mr James Grierson, J.P., from Achill Sound to his home, about nine miles away, when they were vigorously attacked by a large body of women, numbering over a couple of hundred. The women kept up a running fire of turf, mud and sand etc. at the police, who, however, took the thing good humouredly. The attack was kept up for practically the whole length of the journey though here and there the number of assailants gradually diminished. At length the police reached their destination with their charge (*Mayo News*, 22 February 1913).

Summons were issued to some of the women, but withdrawn after a promise from Fr Colleran that the violence would stop. He said later that the agitation would continue by peaceful means. It was reported that the trustees were refusing to sell and that the tenants were petitioning the Congested Districts Board to use its compulsory powers and to treat the estate separately from other estates because it had been a Trust since the famine clearances. The Board was reluctant to do so, as it was not until the Clanricarde Estate had been settled in December 1913 that the Board's right to compulsory purchase was established.

The secretary to the estate trustees, George Larkin, wrote to the *Mayo News* complaining of 'boycotting, intimidation and violence' on the island and stating that the Trust was an independent body which would not be intimidated (*Mayo News*, 29 March 1913). Anthony Kilcoyne, one of the previously charged tenants, replied, giving interesting details of tenant conditions. He wrote that tenants could not build or enlarge their dwelling house or even a cow-house without the consent of the trustees, and if permission was obtained then the rent was raised; that if a tenant kept a piece of driftwood he would be evicted or prevented from putting seed in the ground for one season. He continued:

Achill people are the most law-abiding people in all Ireland, and well the Trustees know it or the tenants would not tolerate their diabolical work. I would ask Mr. Larkin is it a crime for the unfortunate Souper Mission tenants to ask them to comply with the law that is placed on the statute book for the benefit of the tenants. Could Mr. Larkin explain why the Trustees repudiated the legal demands of their tenants. This agitation is brought about by the rents being too high and the mission not acting like human beings and they are a so-called religious body of men having an olive branch in one hand and a spear in the other (*Mayo News*, 5 April 1913).

Questions were asked in the House of Commons about boycotting in Achill. Mr Birrell, the Chief Secretary, said in reply that there were now thirty policemen on the island instead of the usual sixteen, and that the Congested Districts Board would not buy until the disturbances stopped (*Mayo News*, 3 May 1913). The situation was considered serious enough for Mr Birrell to visit Castlebar the same month.

Five per cent of the tenants on the estate were Protestants and they fully supported the rent strike. A letter signed by Protestant tenants addressed to the Congested Districts Board, asking to have their holdings included in the sale, was published in the *Mayo News*. The signatories were: Croly, Bindon Scott, Sheridan, McNally, Grey, Bourke, Ost, Atkinson, McNally, Clarke, Egan, Hennigan, Egan, Watts, McDowell, McNulty, Egan, Weddall, Atkinson, Callaghan, Lavelle, Johnson, and Hoban. Meanwhile, surrounding estates were sold off. In 1912, Lord Sligo was forced by the Tenants Advisory Committee, set up by his tenants the year before, to lodge maps and documents of his estate with the Congested Districts Board. The estate was sold in January 1914, and the tenants objected to Lord Sligo reserving fishing and shooting rights. In January 1914, the estate of General Clive at Ballycroy, comprising of 40,000 acres including 30,000 acres of mountains, was sold to the Congested Districts Board. General Clive retained 700 acres and his lodges. The tenants agreed to allow the General also to retain sporting rights in perpetuity.

It was not until two years later that agitation about the sale of the estate recommenced. This time it was led by Darrell Figgis, the local organiser of the Irish Volunteers, who had played a prominent part in the Howth gun running in July 1914. When the Volunteers split over conscription in October 1914, Figgis remained with the anti-conscriptionists, anti-Redmond group, later known as Sinn Féin. When a new agent for the Mission estate was appointed in 1915, Figgis led a deputation to let him know that three years earlier the people had voted to pay no more rent until the estate was sold. He afterwards wrote to the *Mayo News* about the hundred policemen guarding the agent when men were supposed to be at the 'front'. Fr Colleran and the local Ancient Order of Hibernians sided with Redmond and the National Volunteers and took exception to Figgis organising tenant protests. They wrote furious letters attacking him to the *Connaught Telegraph*, and condemned him as a 'blackguard, ruffian and liar'. However, Figgis had support from the islanders. He wrote to the *Mayo News*, demanding that the Congested Districts Board be made to complete the sale of the Mission estate. Fourteen days later the Board bought the estate.

CONCLUSION

Henry could not have been unaware of these proceedings. He knew the main characters and lived in a central position on the island. Papers relating to the Achill Mission are to be found among his notes in Trinity College, Dublin. His failure to include the historical events of the lives of Michael Mangan and Darrell Figgis could mislead the reader into partaking of the illusion of artistic separateness. Henry's reasons are open to interpretation. Among them we must consider his determination to fulfil the role of a serious post-impressionist painter by following artistic dictums of formal autonomy. We must also consider that perhaps there was a wish to distinguish himself from the grievous personal and political separations that had taken place between the events in question and the writing of his autobiography. The exclusion of both exposes Henry's desire to secure his Irish identity premised upon a representation of an ideal image of Ireland and himself.

BIBLIOGRAPHY

Barthes, R
1982 *Camera Lucida. Reflections on Photography*, London.

Henry, P
1953   *An Irish Portrait*, Batsford.
Lynd, R
1909   *Home Life in Ireland*, London.
1912*a* *The Ethics of Sinn Féin*, Limerick (reprinted from *The Irish Yearbook 1909*).
1912*b* *Rambles in Ireland*, London.
Micks, W
1925   *An Account of the Constitution, Administration and Dissolution of the Congested Districts Board for Ireland from 1891 to 1923*, Dublin.
Nash, C
1993   Embodying the Nation—The West of Ireland Landscape and Irish Identity. In O'Connor, B and Cronin, M (eds), *Tourism in Ireland*, Cork.
Solow, B
1971   *The Land Question and the Irish Economy 1870-1903*, Boston/Mass.

The Burning of Bridget Cleary
A Community on Guard

SHARRON FITZGERALD

INTRODUCTION

In 1895, Bridget Cleary was burned to death by her husband in the townland of Ballyvadlea, thirteen miles north of Clonmel, County Tipperary. It is the last reported case of witch burning in Europe. In the Irish context, past research has concentrated on a description of folk customs and beliefs (Ó Súilleabhain 1977; McGrath 1982).

However, my work uses much of the 'new' narrative approach to recreate an understanding of the past. It involves a contextual dimension, imitating the 'thick description' of space used by Geertz (1973). The research is thus placed firmly in the everyday lives of ordinary people, a concept which is closely associated with the *Annales* school and the notion of *mentalité* in modern social theory. This essay also builds on research done by Ginzburg (1983) and Le Roy Ladurie (1987). Ladurie looks at witchcraft in the context of social relations, a theme central to my own work. He describes the story of a young woman named Françouneto, with whom all the young men in the village fell in love, to the extent that they lost the power in their arms. A series of events ensued which resulted in the locals accusing the woman of being a witch.

Ullrich Kockel (ed.), *Landscape, Heritage and Identity: Case Studies in Irish Ethnography*, Liverpool University Press 1995, 117-34.

As in the case of Bridget Cleary, there was a strong community belief in the presence of evil and an allied attempt to do something about it. On an initial reading of the Bridget Cleary case, it is possible to say that superstition was the cause of her death. However, this would be an all too easy conclusion, emulating what Geertz (1973) calls 'thin description', or a pure description of events. Instead, what is revealed when all the superstition is 'unpacked' is a network of social relations, and ways in which these social relations combine to produce certain types of behaviour.

This essay concerns itself with a description of my fieldwork which was carried out over the space of a few days in August 1994. Furthermore, it is an account of my particular experience while in the 'field'. The account is written from the standpoint of a white Irish female concerned with feminism and geography. This, of course, will determine my perspective, and therefore may explain why certain issues are treated in a more considered way than others.

Our shared experiences are all located outside the spaces and times of the written text (Smith 1993). The meanings of these texts not only depends on what is written and who is writing, but also on how it is read. Therefore, I would like to begin by placing my work in its intellectual context.

THEORETICAL CONTEXT

The First World War publicly tested historians' claims that their practice of history was an objective, scholarly discipline based on scientific fact gathering and rigorous criticism of the evidence. Fink (1989) believes that the reason for this was that in the aftermath of the First World War, historians were enlisted to attack or support the Paris treaty, which brought insufficient peace, security and economic revival in its wake. Struck by the consequences of mass mobilisation, a small group of historians were determined to expand their discipline's range beyond its traditional preoccupation with politics, war, diplomacy and great leaders, and to transcend pure narrative with strong analytical frameworks, to make history more complex, more accurate and more 'human' (Fink 1989).

The past, it was felt, had been plundered to justify war. Not surprisingly historians, geographers and social scientists generally wanted to avoid the selective use of history by presenting a critical analysis of the past. The historians at the epicentre of this debate between the traditional paradigm—what Burke (1991) describes as 'Rankean history'—and the 'new' paradigm were those who went under the umbrella title of the *Annales*.

The theory for this new approach was developed in France and was adopted in other western countries somewhat later. Marc Bloch, Lucien Fèbvre and Fernand Braudel are widely recognised as the founding fathers of this theoretical school. The arguments that raged were a direct result of what was perceived as history's pretensions to be a science. This suggested that history could be both neutral and objective. Bloch and Fèbvre realised that it was impossible to expect history to be neutral, and that history had a tendency to be used for propaganda purposes. Instead, the *Annales* advocated the notion that they could create a kind of history that crossed all frontiers. Their intellectual agenda was to suggest new paths of research and to question past historical methods. They were in firm agreement that only by taking into account collective phenomena can the historian, geographer or the ethnographer explain the genesis and evolution of societies. In short, for the first time researchers were contemplating the lives of ordinary people as worthy of examination.

La Nouvelle Histoire

The *Annales* have been closely associated with 'La Nouvelle Histoire'. This 'new history' did not accept ideas of 'subjectivity' or 'objectivity'. Traditionally, the job of the historian was to give the facts and 'tell it as it is'. Now it was felt that this approach was somewhat unrealistic. Instead, the new history advocated the notion that no matter how hard we try to avoid the prejudices associated with colour, class, creed and gender, we cannot avoid looking at the past from a particular point of view.

Our minds do not reflect reality directly. We perceive the world only through a network of conventions, schemata and stereotypes—a network which varies from one culture to another. This new history sought to expose the limitations of the 'traditional' paradigm which tends to limit itself to examining great events and great leaders, who invariably were men.

Geertz's 'Thick Description'

Max Weber believed that people were animals suspended in webs they themselves had spun. These webs could be interpreted as ideas, superstitions, beliefs, mythologies and notions of space and place. Geertz (1973) took this idea a step further to claim that culture was indeed what constituted those webs:

> It is in understanding what ethnography is that a start can be made toward grasping what anthropological analysis amounts to as a form of knowledge.

Geertz feels that ethnography is defined by the kind of intellectual effort it is: an elaborate venture in, to borrow a notion from Ryle, 'thick description'. This concept is used as a tool to go beneath the description of events to analyse the meaning of underlying gestures. Geertz believes that culture is public because meaning is. However, Silverman (1993) believes this is not always the case. He insists that what is acted out in public may hide the true meaning.

In anthropological writing Geertz believes that what we call our data are really our constructions of other people's constructions of what they and their compatriots are up to. Analysis is wading through what Geertz describes as structures of signification. These are very often piled upon each other.

Ethnography is not about seeking to be a native:

> What it means is that descriptions of a culture must be cast in terms of the constructions we imagine these people place upon what they live through, the formulae they use to define what happens them (Geertz 1973).

This, of course, does not mean that these descriptions are definitive, but they are part of an evolving analysis. Geertz's 'thick description' indicates the importance of examining social behaviour. It is through social action that cultural forms find articulation.

As in any discourse, code does not determine conduct, and what we perceive as what was said, may not have been said at all. The point is not to describe what did or did not happen, it is to demonstrate what a piece of anthropological interpretation consists of in tracing the curve of social discourse and fixing it into an inspectable form.

Insider versus Outsider

Susan Smith's (1993) work has been useful in its analysis of the struggle between the 'insider' and the 'outsider'. Recently she has examined an annual carnival in the Scottish town of Peebles on the border of Scotland and England. Smith feels that it is at this time every year that the difference between an insider—a 'gutterbluid' —and an outsider—a 'stoorifoot'—is most acute. During the celebrations, there is a parade which usually contains a number of golliwogs as part of the spectacle. In 1991, their inclusion in the festivities was called into question. Eventually it was decided that the golliwogs were to be removed. This caused uproar within the community. The locals felt that if the golliwogs were to be removed, it should not be carried out by outsiders on the grounds of racism.

From this standpoint, the issue was not the possible offence which the golliwogs might cause, but that 'outsiders' did not respect or understand the traditions of the locals.

Susan Smith goes on to say that her perspective is limited. As a woman she sees the activities of the people of Peebles as racist. She believes that the pageant is taking place in contested space, which to her way of perceiving events is highly racist and obviously gendered.

The question is, would others agree with her perspective? Some would argue that by going into an event one is automatically changing its construction. This, I feel, is not the job of the researcher, and carries with it many moral and ethical questions. It is from this theoretical standpoint that my fieldwork was carried out.

THE NARRATIVE

I would now like to recount the events as they occurred on 14/15 March 1895 in Ballyvadlea, Co. Tipperary. There are many different versions of the story. This particular narrative has been compiled using extracts from a daily national newspaper, the *Cork Examiner*, which reported on the case in 1895.

Who was Bridget Cleary?

Bridget Cleary was a young woman of twenty-six years. She had been married for five years to Michael Cleary. They were childless. At the time of the incident, they were living with Bridget's father, Patrick Boland, in the townland of Ballyvadlea, County Tipperary.

> Mrs Cleary was of middle height, perhaps with brownish hair, blue eyes and regular features—a pretty woman. She was an industrious woman, and a real helpmate. Having been an apprentice to a dressmaker, she earned money by doing little

dressmaking jobs, and she sold fowl for profit. People speak of her as being 'a bit queer' in her ways, and this they attribute to a certain superiority over the people she came into contact with (*Cork Examiner*, 29 March 1895).

Additionally, the paper goes on to describe Michael Cleary.

Cleary her husband is a cooper. He is described as a well dressed man, with a high receding forehead. A good workman with a lucrative trade for one so remotely situated.

The Events of 14/15 March 1895

On 13 March 1895, the doctor from Fethard, Doctor Creen, was called to the Cleary home. He found Bridget Cleary suffering from slight bronchial catarrh and nervous excitement. When at the trial he was questioned about the woman's health, he replied that

she was perfectly healthy. She was of good physique and well nourished. The only thing that I can say is that she was awfully nervous (*Cork Examiner*, 6 April 1895).

When Michael Cleary felt that the doctor's medicine was not working, he set about rectifying what he believed to be a supernatural malady with a supernatural remedy.

Denis Ganey was the local 'fairy doctor' who lived on nearby Slievenamon. He was consulted by Cleary and was asked to help rid his wife of the fairy changeling.

Ganey inherited his fairy-doctoring from his father, and it had come down from sire to son for generations (*Cork Examiner*, 29 March 1895)

On the evening of 14 March, Cleary attempted to carry out an exorcism in his home with the help of a traditional potion, created by Ganey which was designed to prevent fairy abduction. This testimony, given by Bridget Cleary's first cousin Johanna Burke, tells how she perceived the events:

> On Thursday evening I went to leave some bread at the house, but I was unable to get in. I saw William Simpson and his wife coming up towards the house. Michael Cleary said he would not leave us in. I heard 'take it you witch, you bitch'. Immediately after that the door was opened by Michael Cleary and we three went in. When we went in Bridget was in bed. John Dunne, Pat Kennedy and William Kennedy held her by each shoulder, while William Kennedy was lying across the bed where her feet would be placed. Cleary then put his hand to her mouth, saying if the medicine touched the floor she could not be brought back from the fairies. She was almost smothered. Then they began to ask her who she was in the name of the Father, Son and Holy Ghost. 'Make down a good fire and we'll make her answer quick' said Dunne and caught her by the shoulders. Pat Kennedy took her by the feet and Cleary also held her and put her in front of the fire. Bridget wore only a flannelette night-dress with a calico chemise underneath. Bridget was held in over the fire, and they went on asking her who she was. Cleary then put her resting on the grate. That night I stayed with Bridget. Everybody seemed to be happy that they had gotten rid of the changeling and that Bridget was back (*Cork Examiner*, 6 April 1895).

However, Michael Cleary was not convinced, and the following morning he sent for the priest to say mass in the house. At about eight o'clock that evening, Johanna came back to the house. At this stage Bridget had been dressed and brought downstairs to join her husband for tea. Cleary cut three slices of bread for his wife to eat and insisted she do so without having something to drink.

However, Bridget could only eat two slices of bread. Johanna recalled:

He put his arm around her as if he was fond of her and said 'if you don't take it down you will go' and he threw her on the ground and forced the bit of bread into her mouth (*Cork Examiner*, 6 April 1895).

Johanna pleaded with Michael not to choke the woman but she was quickly rebuffed by the man saying 'hold you tongue, it is not Bridgie I have'. Cleary took a lighted stump and continued to ask the woman her name. He proceeded to strip her, and said that he would put his wife back to bed. Johanna goes on to describe how when her back was turned Bridget's chemise caught fire:

Michael went and got the oil and threw it upon the lower part of her body. I said not to burn her and Cleary said he would burn me also if I did not keep quiet. My mother ran down and said not to burn the poor creature, but he shoved her back saying 'hold your tongue, you will soon see her go up the chimney'. Pat Boland then came into the room and on seeing his daughter he said 'is it burning my child you are?' Cleary answered 'It is not Bridget I have' (*Cork Examiner*, 6 April 1895).

According to Johanna Burke, Cleary coerced Bridget's father to help him place the body in the fire. When the body was burned, Cleary took it from the grate and placed it face down on the kitchen floor. He then went upstairs and got an old sack bag and then placed his wife's remains in it. With the help of Johanna's eldest brother Patrick, Cleary took the body out to be buried. This is how Johanna recounts the events of the following day:

Next day Cleary was in a terrible state, and said he would do away with himself for burning his wife. He said that he would go up to the fort at Kylenagranna where she told him she would return on a white horse. So he gathered the lot of us on Sunday night, and we went with him to the fort, we did not hear or see anything, we went there for three nights and then we did not go anymore, and said that he was after killing his wife and give himself up to the police. He said it was not his wife, and that his wife would come back (*Cork Examiner*, 6 April 1895).

Eventually Michael Cleary gave himself up to the police. In all nine men and one woman were arrested. When Bridget Cleary's body was discovered about one quarter of a mile from her home,

she was buried about two feet in the dyke and her only covering was a chemise and some old bags (*Cork Examiner*, 25 March 1895).

ANALYSING FIELD EVIDENCE

The burning of Bridget Cleary by her husband in 1895 occurred in the confines of a very isolated and integrated community. Ultimately, it was the time spent 'in the field' in Ballyvadlea that gave shape to this event and created yet another narrative. It was possible to view all the related sites in detail, but also it provided reflections on local reactions to me as an outsider and as a woman.

I was curious to discover whether the story had ingrained itself in the minds of the locals. My field work involved visiting the townland of Ballyvadlea, meeting local people, and basically getting a feel for the place with a view to understanding past events. In my field journal, I recorded everything I saw, heard and thought during my stay in the area.

Researchers who work in the field frequently comment on the curiosity they arouse in the minds of the local community. This trip to Ballyvadlea was no different. In all rural communities the world over, there is an almost innate sense that if something is happening in the community, then everyone has the right to know. In small communities such as these, it is very difficult to avoid the feeling that one is intruding, and if too many questions are asked one is meddling in a past that many may yet feel ashamed of and would rather forget. Yet it was difficult to avoid the feeling that one was being given the official story—the version that was reserved for 'outsiders'. This 'outsider' status of the researcher was constantly being reinforced.

In the Field

Cloneen is a little hamlet situated at the foothills of Slievenamon. As I drove into the village on this August morning, I tried to imagine what secrets, if any, my fieldwork would reveal. The arrangement made with my field collaborator was that I would meet him at his home. This proved to be a difficult task. Finally, in sheer desperation, I relented and stopped at the local post-office cum general store to ask directions. As I entered, all eyes turned to stare at this strange woman who had literally been blown into the shop. This would not be the only time that day I would feel the focus of much attention.

My initial contact with my field collaborator was made through the Clonmel-based newspaper, *The Nationalist*. For the purpose of this essay, he shall be referred to as Mr X. However, it is possible to say that he is a native of Cloneen and has lived all of his life in the area. Currently he holds a position of relative importance in the community as a member of local government.

As soon as I had located my guide's home, my tour of the local environs began. The grave and final resting place of Bridget Cleary was where the tour commenced. This is quite a forlorn sight and is situated in the old graveyard (see Figure 9). Access to this section of the graveyard was via a boreen on the Fethard side of the village. The grave is demarcated by four stones. This is unusual because no other grave in the graveyard has the same appearance. Perhaps the nature of Bridget Cleary's death caused her grave to be marked in this fashion. This was very intriguing.

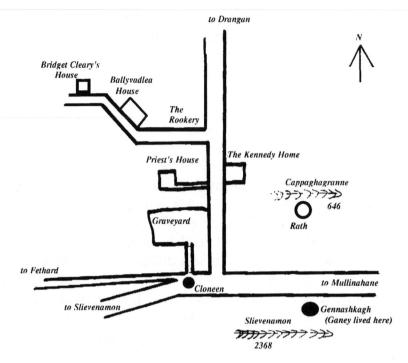

Figure 9   *The village of Ballyvadlea, Co. Tipperary; places mentioned in the text*

In *Wakeman's Handbook of Irish Antiquities*, Cooke (1903) states that people's belief in a spiritual existence was a cause of respect for the dead, which has shown itself in the countless sepulchral monuments scattered all over the world from pre-history down to the present day. The point of the exercise was not only to house the spirit fittingly, but to prevent its return to the mortal world. Therefore, there were four stones instead of one to hold the spirit in. After the trial, Michael MacCarty, a Church of Ireland clergyman, commented,

> not a single human being male or female, clerical or lay, would lend assistance to give burial to the body (MacCarty 1901).

Asking questions without wanting to appear to be aggressively seeking information is difficult at the best of times. I had many questions I wanted to ask, but I felt that I should breach my questions with some caution. At this early stage it was asked if many of the local people knew about the events of March 1895. The reply was quite adamant. Mr X said quite categorically that nobody else knew anything about the case. I found this difficult to believe. However, at this point the issue was not pressed.

The tour advanced from the graveyard back out onto the road, through the village of Cloneen and onto the Drangan road. The townland of Ballyvadlea lies on the left-hand side of the road as one travels north (see Figure 9). Along the way lie the ruins of the family home of the Kennedys, who were related to the Boland family (Figure 10).

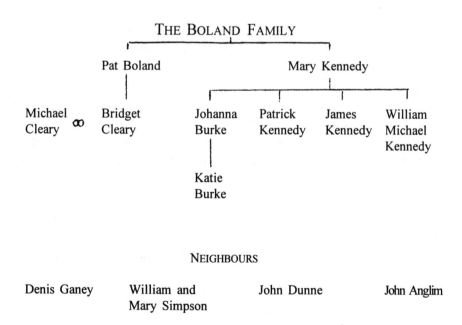

Figure 10   Family and community relationships in Ballyvadlea

On the night of the trial, the Kennedy's home was burned to the ground. Some of the locals believe that this was some kind of public display of disgust at what had happened. Others believe that the house was burned down by relations of the Kennedys in some vain attempt to win public sympathy. It is difficult to ascertain which story is accurate, as the story varies from person to person. About one hundred yards from this spot there is a T-junction on the road. This is an area locally known as the rookery. This is where Bridget Cleary was born and grew up. The local story goes, that at the time when Bridget was murdered, there used to be a rookery in this area. However, when Bridget was murdered, the birds left and never returned. It is interesting to note how this story has had an impact on every aspect of place and popular lore in the townland.

An analysis of the impact of the story necessitates sifting through what Geertz (1973) terms structures of signification. It is not so much about how important the story is to local culture, but it has more to do with what is being said about local culture in this story. The story reveals much about the local mystique or supernatural feeling that surrounded Bridget Cleary. In European folklore, the witch or wise woman often had what was termed 'familiars'. These familiars were kept as the witch's attendants, given her by the Devil or inherited from another witch. The tale almost suggests that Bridget had some supernatural power over the rooks, and that their continued existence in the area depended on Bridget being around.

Interestingly, the local map shows the rookery located on the border between the townlands of Ballyvadlea and Tullycussane. Boundaries have always been associated with instability and change. Bridget Cleary's space, therefore, occupied a zone of transition manifesting itself locally in a fear of space. This fear impinged on people's perceptions of the world around them. Additionally, it affected people's mobility to the extent that people in Ballyvadlea would not go out at night for fear of being abducted by the fairies and taken to the other world beyond their known space. At certain times of the year this fear of space was more acute. The fort on Kylenagranna hill (see Figure 9), for example, was feared by the locals. It was believed that it was dangerous to go near the fort at night for fear of being struck down by paralysis.

Turning off to the left, the road leads past Ballyvadlea House to the former home of the Clearys. The house is still in excellent condition, which came as quite a surprise as it was expected that at this stage it would be a ruin, like so many similar houses in the townland. Mr X related that nobody ever goes near the house now. It was occupied until twelve years ago by a woman by the name of Ellen Moloney, but now it is vacant. This explained its relatively good condition. Since 1895 there have been a few changes to the house. The front section has a new porch and at the gable end of the house there is a garage. It is possible to see into the downstairs kitchen. One becomes o voyeur, simply looking and imagining. The methodological implications of this are that we as ethnographers are observing. This is what Geertz (1973) referred to as constructions of other people's constructions of what they and their compatriots are up to. Therefore, the way we reconstruct what we see before us may not necessarily an accurate account.

At the back of the house there are the remains of Bridget's henhouse.

Sitting on the walls of the henhouse, Mr X asked: 'Why are you interested in this place anyway?'

In reply he was told: 'I am using this story as the basis for a much broader study on folklore and witchcraft'.

He seemed relatively satisfied with this answer. Yet again it was easy to feel that one was being 'sussed out'.

At a later stage, while the house and its immediate environs were being photographed, one of the locals came by, who shall be named Mr Y.

Mr Y asked in a good humoured but curious way: 'What are ye doing here? Are ye making a film?'

As Mr X had indicated to me that nobody ever goes near the house, it must have been blatantly obvious to Mr Y what all this activity was about. This type of statement is similar to Geertz's concept of winks and twitches. On the one level they are all the same, but at a much deeper level there is a significant difference. When he asked was a film being made he communicated a certain message. He revealed that he knew the significance of the house and was aware of the Bridget Cleary case. Having spent some time at the former Cleary home, attention was turned to other sites involved in the story. The old priest's home lies halfway between Cloneen and the Cleary home; this was the next stop.

It is necessary to walk along a mucky pathway to reach the house, which has a few adjoining outhouses. It was in one of these outhouses that Bridget Cleary's body was held during the inquest. Mr X's father was a member of the jury who was present at the inquest. This had implications for the story that was being told. Not only did he possess the local story—he also had snippets of the official story, and both were being combined to create his version of the events.

Leaving here, the next stop was the graveyard for a second visit. Through the course of conversation a few more relevant names cropped up. As already mentioned, Mr X had stated with utmost certainty that nobody else knew anything about the case. However, on this second visit to the graveyard, this time from the main Drangan road (see Figure 9), Mr X advised me that we should give the impression that we were interested in another grave altogether—the reason being that members of the fairy doctor family happened to be working in the graveyard at the time, and would not appreciate us taking photographs. This was, indeed, a delicate situation, and the implications of Mr X's request contradicted what he had told me previously. From this apparent contradiction, it became obvious that there are many levels of interaction in the community, each with its own, situationally contingent set of meanings. These interactions have a very important part to play in what Geertz describes as the informal logic of everyday life.

If nobody knew what had happened to Bridget Cleary, why was it necessary to act in this manner? The Sicilian code of 'Omerta' came to mind. This type of behaviour is culturally bound. Being an

Irish woman had its advantages in trying to see through the webs of meaning. One is relatively familiar with the way rural Irish people perceive the world around them. It was felt that the story was being suppressed and locals were ashamed of the event. Not wishing to discuss it with an outsider could be interpreted as a rejection by the locals of a way of life that to outsiders might be perceived as primitive. Silence is perhaps a reaction by the community to prevent further negative commentary on their way of life.

CONCLUSION

Many may disagree with the way I have approached this research topic. That, of course, is their prerogative. The topic is open to much debate. However, it was never my intention to cast judgement on the people of Ballyvadlea. Rather, I was trying to reconstruct the events that caused the death of a young woman in rural Ireland in 1895, and, having done this, to place this event in its wider context of social relations. My fieldwork would not have been completed without the co-operation of the people of Ballyvadlea, and I think they deserve to have their past treated in a sensitive and considered fashion.

This case offers many challenging research questions. It opens up the whole area of the position of the established church juxtaposed with folk belief. It questions the position of women in rural Irish communities and how ideas of gender are produced and reproduced through the everyday space in which we live. Finally, it uproots the mosaic of superstition, through an analysis of its content and its implications—in the past as well as the present—for the everyday lives of ordinary people.

BIBLIOGRAPHY

Burke, P
1993 *New Perspectives on Historical Writing*, Cambridge.
Cooke, J
1903 *Wakeman's Handbook of Irish Antiquities*, 3rd ed., Dublin.
The Cork Examiner 1895.
Fink, C
1989 *Marc Bloch: A Life History*, Cambridge.
Geertz, C
1973 *The Interpretation of Cultures*, Princeton.
Ginzburg, C
1983 *The Night Battles*, Oxford.
Le Roy Ladurie, E
1987 *Jasmin's Witch*, Aldershot.
MacCarty, M
1901 *Five Years in Ireland 1895-1900*, Dublin.
McGrath, T
1982 Fairy Faith and Changelings: The Burning of Bridget Cleary
     1895, *Studies*, 178-86.
Ó Súilleabhain, S
1977 *Irish Folk Customs and Beliefs*, Cork.
Silverman, E
1993 *Towards a More Description*, London.
Smith, S
1993 Bounding Space: Claiming Space and Making Place in Rural
     Scotland, *Transactions of the Institute of British
     Geographers* NS 18, 291-308.

A Landscape of Memories
Heritage and Tourism in Mayo

MOYA KNEAFSEY

INTRODUCTION

This essay is based largely on fieldwork carried out during 1989-1992 at the Institute of Irish Studies, University of Liverpool. Evidence is based on informal interviews and conversations in addition to secondary printed resources. The bulk of the text consists of a re-reading of the material collected at that time in the context of my current research into tourism, place and identity. This re-reading of those initial thoughts and observations has provoked a number of questions which relate to recent developments in the theories of place, identity and the construction of rurality. In writing this essay I have attempted to highlight some of those issues as they emerge, and to point to areas for further thought and investigation. As such, the article is tentative and exploratory in nature, and is perhaps more successful in raising questions than answering them.

The basic aim of this essay is to examine the way in which a particular aspect of the landscape is being developed as a tourist attraction in North West Mayo. In doing so I wish to show how a place has different meanings for different groups in society, and that the identity of a place is not fixed, but is composed of layers of different interpretations and relations between people, their actions,

Ullrich Kockel (ed.), *Landscape, Heritage and Identity: Case Studies in Irish Ethnography*, Liverpool University Press 1995, 135-53.

the environment and social structures. Traditionally, landscape is seen to be an intrinsic part of the identity of a place, in the sense that at a basic level, places are created when people interact with the landscape in order to live, grow crops, extract materials, and so on. At another level, the landscape is also given symbolic meanings, and is associated with historical events, myths and legends, as well as contemporary events. These symbolic meanings may be imposed by people who live on the land, and also by people from 'outside'— writers, intellectuals, poets, politicians, planners, and tourists.

The meanings imposed on a landscape by each of these groups will be different, from each other, and from the views held by the inhabitants of a particular landscape, who in turn will not present a homogeneous attitude towards their environment.

Tourism could be seen as a use of landscape as a resource. In this essay I would like to look at the case of an Interpretive Centre based on stone age remains which have been preserved by the bog for over 5,000 years. In following a little of the history of the centre it is hoped to challenge the notion that places have fixed identities, and to show that they are constructed from many layers of social relations and interpretations, which are imposed not only by those within places, but also by external influences. The aim is to begin questioning the ways in which tourism contributes to the construction of notions such as rurality and tradition.

INTERPRETATIONS OF LANDSCAPE

Landscape is being interpreted in new ways for tourism, and in Ireland we have seen a proliferation of heritage centres designed to interpret aspects of this landscape, be they archaeological, historical, ecological, botanical or mythical. The interpretation of landscapes can contribute to constructions of place and identity, acting as a powerful symbolic and cultural icon. Within the landscape are bound up the memories of the past, as Seamus Heaney (1975) evokes in his poem Belderg—named after a small town near Céide Fields:

> When he stripped off blanket bog
> The soft-piled centuries
> Fell open like a glib:
> There were the first plough-marks,
> The stone-age fields, the tomb
> Corbelled, turfed and chamnered,
> Floored with dry turf-coomb.
>
> A landscape fossilized,
> Its stone-wall patternings
> Repeated before our eyes
> In the stone walls of Mayo.

Heaney's lines capture the storative capacities of the bog, that huge wet wild landscape, which is unique in Western Europe. He is talking about stone walls and fields which were dug over 5,000 years ago, and were preserved by the bog at Céide. Today those stone walls are being re-discovered, and re-interpreted. Part of their new function is to serve as a tourist attraction for North West Mayo.

The landscape has always held a fascination for travellers and tourism, and has layers of culturally and politically significant interpretations. Catharine Nash (1993) explores the ways in which, within a colonial and neo-colonial setting, cultural nationalists celebrated the West as an archetypal Irish landscape, as 'part of an attempt to identify with a landscape which was a confirmation of cultural identity'. It was not just that the West was

> farthest from England and therefore most isolated from the cultural influences of anglicization, but that its physical landscape provided the greatest contrast to the landscape of Englishness.

She continues:

> The landscape of the West, that of mountain, bog, lake and ocean, could be contrasted to the verdant richness of the landscape of English 'south country'.

> The region came to be perceived as a pool of cultural and racial strength and beauty, in a sense 'embodying the nation'.

The bog is an intrinsic part of this landscape. Yet it is evident that the people who lived on or near the bog probably did not share the romantic views held by the writers. As O'Toole points out, in reference to Tomas O'Crohan's early twentieth century writing, 'real peasants don't spend their time lost in wonder at the beauty of the mountains' (*Irish Times*, 17 February 1993).

Some contemporary inhabitants of the West dump rusted old cars in the bog, and despise it as a wasteland, good for nothing. It is huge from the perspective of the people who live on it, whereas to outsiders, it can be seen as part of a beautiful romantic landscape, as well as being a threatened natural environment, which should be preserved as one of the last habitats of its kind in Europe. For farmers, life is a struggle against the bog which always threatens to encroach upon the small green patches of cultivated land which spread out from the farms and villages and around the feet of the hills.

The battle to tame the bog is never won, the tell-tale reeds pushing up through the sodden ground a sign that it is trying to re-claim its territory. Yet although the locals are faced with a day to day struggle against the bog, it provides them with turf for their fires and grazing for their cattle. The bog has shaped a whole way of life for generations, and is intrinsically connected with the folklore and mythology of the west.

The older people near Céide Fields can tell of how a family were once swamped by a bog burst in the locality, and in recent years the bog began to move once again, sliding down the hill side carrying with it trees and saplings, blocking the road between Ballycastle and

Belderrig, and creeping down a gully just beyond Céide to fall over
the cliffs and into the sea.

LANDSCAPE OF MEMORIES: CÉIDE FIELDS

So, what is Céide Fields? It is located in the north western corner
of County Mayo, on the edge of the sixteenth century barony of
Erris, between the two small towns of Ballycastle and Belderrig.
This is a bleak and lonely region, bounded on the north by
spectacular sea cliffs, and to the south by the empty mountains of
the Nephin Beg range.

John Brett, bishop of nearby Killala in the 1730s, described Erris
as a 'Western Siberia' (*North Mayo Historical Journal 1990-91*).
Within its borders lie some 400 square miles of blanket bog, and
beneath this bog on the cliffs at Céide lies an archaeological site of
world importance. Now into the stark horizon has been inserted a
pyramid. A seemingly empty landscape concealed stone walls which
in turn hold the story of a way of life which passed here over 5,000
years ago. Céide Fields is an evocation of Heaney's (1969) idea of
'the bog as a memory of the landscape, or as a landscape that
remembered everything that happened in it and to it'.

Inside the pyramid, the story of the stones is told, and in its
prominent location on the brow of the cliffs, it seems to emphasise
the sheer size of the landscape, and the bog that stretches on as far
as the eye can see. Although the pyramid evokes thoughts of ancient
Egypt, and serves to remind us that these stone walls are in fact
older than the pyramids, the interior is gleamingly modern, with
light, airy spaces and audio-visual display. There are collages and
paintings using the colours of the landscape—vibrant greens, blues
and browns. Thus the centre could be seen to create a particular
image of the region—as the home of an ancient civilisation, an area
of great natural beauty, and yet also a place which has not been left
behind by modernity, and which is at ease with technology, science
and progress. That is, a place which is not inhabited by 'culchies',
or country bumpkins propping up gate posts, as the stereotypical

image of the rural Irish, and perhaps especially the Mayo people, suggests.

In this sense, the centre makes a break from the usual tourist image of rural Ireland, which, as Quinn (1994) notes, is

> distinctive in its portrayal of an old-fashioned, stereotypical Irish native: a middle aged/elderly man, dressed in dark clothing, complete with hob-nailed boots and the requisite cap and stick.

The only people inside the centre are stone age ones, engaged in stone age activities such as eating, making things, cooking, and sleeping. In fact there is very little reference to neighbouring villages and people. Landscape, ancient history, botany, geology and ecology are the themes. Yet these features may contribute in subtle ways towards the moulding both of visitor perceptions of the place, and host perceptions of themselves. The image-landscape continues to be a sparsely populated one, swathed in its mysteries; here there is no reference to the problems facing rural Ireland—emigration, unemployment, decline and poverty. These are not tourist-friendly images, and they conflict with the rural idyll. It is true that the Interpretive Centre is based around stone age remains, and telling their story is what it is meant to do, but what I am suggesting is that it contributes towards a certain, selective image, which does not give much prominence to contemporary inhabitants of the area, or the living cultural practices which do exist. A coachload of foreign visitors could arrive, visit the centre in a couple of hours, climb back into the coach and then drive off up to Sligo, without coming into contact with local people, or realising some of the other features of the area. On reflection at the end of their holiday, what would they be able to say about Ballycastle and Belderrig? It is quite possible that they would not even be aware of the names of the neighbouring villages. This is an argument which could be raised against many heritage centres, by those who question the impact of tourism on rural areas (*cf.* O'Connor and Cronin 1993)

The hi-tech part of the image may be aimed as much at local people as visitors. The modern, up-beat aspect of the centre is a feature which has been emphasised, as a spur to inhabitants who in the past may have experienced a sense of alienation from Dublin, and from decision-making processes. Increasingly there are calls for more grass-roots development and community-led initiatives based on the use of landscape as a tourist resource. For instance, Feehan (1994) talks about the need for 'a blossoming of community awareness of the nature and importance of landscape heritage', and cautions that the community's sense of cultural heritage is in danger of being smothered by imposed values and well-intentioned development. Certainly, Céide Fields was seen as a focal point for a new drive towards self-development not only in the locality, but in Mayo as a whole. The idea, by now well-known, is for more 'bottom-up' development for rural areas. We are not seeing a 'death' of the rural, as the more romantic view would have us believe, but, as Kockel (1993) puts it, 'the "corpse" is pretty much alive and kicking, although it may be dancing to a rather unfamiliar tune'.

This links into important questions about the very notion of 'rurality'. As John Waters argues, '"rural Ireland" is a phrase that means whatever you want it to, depending on your perspective' (*Irish Times*, 13 June 1993). Whereas in earlier times, rural Ireland was associated with romanticism and nationalism, as mentioned earlier, in contemporary politics, 'rural' has come to be a synonym for 'conservative', 'backward' and 'reactionary', and rural Ireland is classed as a 'problem' area undergoing a 'crisis' of some kind. Anthony Cronin (1985), on the other hand, writes of a kind of nostalgia which has accompanied the move from country to town which has been a feature of Irish society over the last few decades:

The actual departure from Ballymacarbry and the slopes of Slieve Miskish was not accompanied by a movement of the heart. Far from it in fact. The rewards and comforts of the city having been accepted and its fleshpots tasted, the mental flight, as reflected in our art and literature, our songs and our imaginations, was in the reverse direction.

This nostalgia is much stronger, he argues, than that usually felt by societies in transition, and was part of a feeling that, in fact, 'the rural reality, in short, was somehow more real than the urban', and

the more rural the rurality apparently the better. When you got to the rock-bound coasts of the desolate west you encountered ... the realest thing of all.

This is a sentiment that the promotional literature for Mayo taps into, with the phrase 'Mayo naturally'. However, Cronin goes on to perpetuate the negative connotation of the rural that Waters talks about, in blaming 'backward-looking primitivism' as the 'principal cause of the failure of Free State nationalism to produce worthwhile results'.

Although it is beyond the scope of this essay to discuss Free State nationalism in relation to attitudes to the rural, the point is that place identity is a fluid, and negotiated concept, and surely one of the tasks for research within the social sciences at the moment should be to contribute towards the process of what Chris Philo (1992) has called the 're-definition of the rural'. To see how communities and individuals negotiate their own sense of identity in relation to these different visions of the rural would be a part of this research, and one way of looking at that is through tourism.

Céide Fields in Context

County Mayo is one of the least well developed counties of Ireland in terms of tourism and economic growth, and has suffered badly from severe emigration which has been more or less continuous since the Famine. A report in the *Western People* (27 March 1991) claimed that

[r]ecent figures indicate a reduction of 20% in population throughout many parts of Erris over the last five years and the enrolment at our National Schools is declining steadily.

Thus Mayo is a county facing demoralisation and de-population at a continuing rate, a situation which has been reflected in many villages dotted along the western seaboard. For instance, Ballycastle, just four miles from Céide Fields, was once a thriving little market town, and in 1836 had a chief revenue office, a police station, a petty sessions every Wednesday and six fairs a year. There was a penny post to Killala, and the parish had nine schools. Today it is a much quieter place, with the loss of many services and industries, and indeed a whole way of life. It has passed by quietly and with it the Irish language has disappeared from common use, at least in this town. However, that is not to say that this old way has not been replaced by new ways, new strategies for survival and new cultural practices. In some parts of Mayo, there does seem to be a feeling among inhabitants and policy makers, that tourism really is one of the last remaining options, and that the county must promote itself as an attractive destination. Thus tourism is one of these strategies for survival.

Tourism is a lens through which concepts such as the 'rural' are constructed, and by looking at how things such as heritage centres come into existence, we can start to unpick some of the tangled social relations which make up places, and also some of the new strategies, or different 'tunes that are being danced'. So, how did the Céide Fields Interpretive Centre come to exist and what features of the process of the construction of identity can be traced through a brief look at the story behind its development?

In the 1930s, the local national school teacher, Master Patrick Caulfield, wrote to the National Museum, telling of how local farmers had discovered stone walls beneath the bog whilst cutting turf. Decades later his son, Seamus Caulfield, an archaeologist, returned to excavate the site and found an enclosed field system a thousand years older than anything that had previously been found in Europe. He argued that only by explaining Céide Fields to everyone, could any financial gain be brought to the area. He stressed that it was necessary for the local community to take the initiative: 'The thing that struck me is that these things just don't happen. They have to be taken and made to happen' (*Western People*, 26 May 1993). To the outsider, it appears that local support has been forthcoming, with the regional newspaper doing an extraordinary job of promoting Céide Fields as holding 'immense potential for the whole of the region', with the potential to become 'the greatest theme park in Europe, if not in the world' (*Western People*, 18 July 1990). There does seem to be some conflict here between this somewhat 'Disney-esque' interpretation and Seamus Caulfield's rather more sedate ideas of incorporating archaeological research with tourism and promoting a broad development potential for the region. Indeed argument about the extent to which the centre should cater for tourists and scientists respectively was a point of discussion throughout the construction of the centre. In any case, money at least was made available, with £40,000 from the County Development Council, £40,000 from the County Council, £30,000 from the American/Ireland fund, and £50,000 from North Connacht Farmer's Co-operative.

The rest of the £2.5 million came from the government and the EC, with politicians obviously gaining political mileage out of the government's substantial contribution. The Taoiseach at that time, Charles Haughey, photographed at the site, enthused:

This ranks as one of the greatest wonders of the ancient world, I am personally attracted to this development—it's the engine of recovery for this region, and I want to see it happen (*Western People*, 25 July 1990).

In the same article, the editor comments that

[f]or the north Mayo community at large it cannot happen quickly enough: the wait has been a long and patient one, but Mr. Haughey's pledge that there will be action has made it all worthwhile.

As for the local inhabitants, the two site archaeologists I spoke to agreed that after initial scepticism, people had been generally enthusiastic. Of course there are those who are apathetic, particularly among the older generation, or in the words of one cynical observer, 'those who have enough land and enough to drink'. Another response to the developments seemed to be one of faint amusement, which goes back to the ideas mentioned earlier about differing perceptions of the bog and landscape. In the words of one archaeologist, the locals see Céide as 'strictly for the tourists', and for them there is something a little humorous in the site of tourists, archaeologists and politicians tramping around the bog in wellington boots to look at a pile of stones which their grandfathers had always known about.

The attitude of the majority is perhaps best expressed by the following quote from one inhabitant: 'It's what Ballycastle needs ... it needs something'. This is something of a contrast to the boundless enthusiasm of certain newspapers and politicians, and raises issues about people's own sense of identity in relation to place, and the accuracy of their own assessments of the future.

For instance, Céide Fields was billed as something of a panacea for North West Mayo, but it remains to be seen how many benefits local inhabitants will actually enjoy, as proponents of the centre have argued would happen.

At a local Integrated Resource Development (IRD) meeting it was hard to tell whether people really were ready, or wanted to take advantage of the Céide Fields development. For instance, one local business man, and member of the committee for promoting industry, was sceptical as to whether there would be enough tourists to justify a craft industry in Ballycastle, and there are other instances of a rather doubting attitude towards the development. Did this view express realism, pessimism, or, as some critiques suggest, a failure to realise the full opportunities offered by the project? During construction local firms were used, temporarily creating around fifty jobs in the area, and some full-time and summer jobs were created at the centre. Estimates of visitor numbers have been exceeded over the first two years of full operation, with over 50,000 visitors annually. Yet the neighbouring settlements are not equipped to deal with this number of people. Out of 1,263 planning applications in Mayo in 1989, the year that talk began in earnest about the centre, only one was for a caravan site/vehicle parking site.

Now that the centre is finished, and having enjoyed several years of attracting high numbers of visitors, one wonders if this success can be sustained. Will the novelty wear off, and will the fickle tourist move on to fresh pastures? Fintan O'Toole discusses some of these questions in relation to the controversial Mullaghmore Centre, and concludes by describing interpretive centres as 'misconceived' because

> [t]hey present the experience of a place precisely as being infinitely repeatable. They define the experience and offer it again and again, day in, day out, throughout the season. They seek to satisfy, when the quest is for a form of dissatisfaction, to offer a calculable gain, when the search is for a sense of loss. They treat tourists as rational consumers rather than what they are—consumers of the irrational (*Irish Times*, 17 February 1993).

Perceptively, he has seen that in tourism there is paradox; the aim is to produce a sense of loss, a sense of regret that we have to move on back to our everyday lives, and that this holiday experience is only a temporary fleeting moment, a reminder of the things that we are missing. The core of his argument against the centre at Mullaghmore is that it gradually reduces the power of the landscape itself to produce moments that are at odds with our everyday experience.

The more interpretive centres there are, the more potent this argument becomes, as more repeatable experiences are produced, and eventually seem to become the same, and are subsumed into everyday lives. Caulfield's response to criticisms was simple: 'there is nothing more boring than an archaeological monument which has no information or interpretation' (*Western People*, 26 May 1993). For him, the Céide Fields centre is not only a site for the interpretation of landscape and archaeology, but also a landmark for tourist development in the area, and a focus for the re-generation of Mayo. Importantly, it is also a venue 'for the ordinary people of Ireland to come and marvel at their heritage' (Kelly 1989). Thus, the centre is seen as particularly important, at least by those from the outside—as a marker of a unique identity, and a kind of confidence-booster for Mayo. As Kelly (1989) noted:

> in modern times it is considered very desirable, very prestigious, to have roots that go deep into the earth. This leaves the people of North Mayo streets—or perhaps fields is a more apt description—ahead of their competitors.

This brings in the idea that places are in competition, that they are engaged in processes of trying to label themselves, in the hope of economic gain. Yet it is not only at the local level that such projects are seen as important for morale and confidence, but at a larger scale. Céide Fields has been seen as an important national symbol, in terms of the Irish as a whole being able to say that they have roots, origins, and know where they come from. As former Taoiseach, Charles Haughey, put it:

> The whole world is tracing its roots, but while most of it is stumbling around in the dark, we in this country, have something unique ... [W]e can trace our continuity over five thousand years, and that's of phenomenal interest (quoted in *Western People*, 26 May 1993).

He also enthused: 'We are the children of the first Europeans' (*Irish Times*, 18 August 1990). Thus, in a single sentence, the Taoiseach put Ballycastle and Belderrig on the European scene and linked them with Dublin. From relative obscurity to being the home of the first people of Europe—a vast leap! The statement had, of course, political and nationalist connotations, especially with '1992' in mind, and what Shore (1993) calls the 'attempts to forge a supranational "European Identity"'. Indeed, it could be said that, as the project has developed, so has a sense of 'Mayo-ism'. The *Western People* congratulated Charles Haughey on 'remembering his Mayo roots' and Seamus Caulfield was dubbed 'Mayo Man of the Year'. Indeed, Seamus Caulfield has become something of a local hero, and the romantic story of how the son returned to realise his father's dream has a kind of homely appeal. This Mayo pride has been still further boosted by the Mayo roots of President Mary Robinson, who appears in full technicolour on the back of the latest glossy promotional material for Mayo.

The Taoiseach's visit seemed to lift Ballycastle out of obscurity, improving the status of the village and boosting morale in the surrounding area. In the words of one local, quoted in the *Western People* (25 September 1990), '[o]ur future has been secured by the Taoiseach's declaration of support here today'.

Yet for all this hype, many of the people who live near Céide, predominantly farmers and fishermen, perhaps do not attach much significance to the discovery of stones that are over five thousand years old. Perhaps this is because 'the past represented in museums and heritage industries largely serves the interests of the better educated middle classes' (Hodder 1990). Certainly, those most likely to visit the site and appreciate its historical value will probably be middle class visitors both from Ireland and abroad, and 'green tourists' attracted by the environmental package which the Interpretive Centre offers. As far as who profits from Céide Fields in a material sense, the small entrepreneurs will be the ones to take advantage of the development, that is, the shopkeepers and publicans rather than the farmers in remote cottages off the beaten track. The whole idea that there will be 'trickle down effects' is in question, and requires further research into changing attitudes towards development, entrepreneurship, and new uses of culture and landscape as resources. Hodder (1990) argues that

> subordinate groups create connections with the past and try to situate themselves in relation to their heritage in order to form an alternative identity. They want the past to tell a story about themselves which confronts the dominant ... ethic.

This begs questions about the extent to which local people assert their 'alternative identity' in view of structures in society which may constrain their actions, and about the relative influence of other groups—such as design professionals, academics, politicians and tourists—on the way in which this identity is created. One must also ask to what extent 'subordinate groups' exist or act with a common purpose, or function with any sense of collective identity or aim. It is the whole concept of 'community' which is in itself fundamental and problematic to many ideas of what rural Irish life involves.

At the most obvious level, there was a certain amount of local involvement in the centre, as was mentioned earlier in terms of funding, and a local committee was set up and local contractors were used. One of the questions which is often raised about the whole heritage industry is that of 'who decides how to interpret'. Ultimately the final decision will rest with professionals who may have different agendas depending on the perceived use of the heritage. For instance the Office of Public Works, which was in charge of building Céide, is mainly concerned with protecting and conserving environments rather than selling them as tourist attractions—a factor which affects the content and lay-out of interpretive centres.

It is notable that there has been much emphasis on the civilised and co-operative nature of the stone-age settlement, and perhaps there is a hope on the part of proponents of the heritage centre that this will somehow reflect upon the community of today. There is an image of North West Mayo as a demoralised and declining area, where relative poverty and backwardness in terms of agricultural and economic development are apparent. Yet the image of the place five thousand years ago is of rich, cultivated farmlands, a sophisticated field system, and a peaceful co-existence of people on the land. Parallels have been drawn between society then and now:

> Five thousand years later that same co-operation was evident in the area. State and semi-state companies, private investment, local and international funds were being provided to make the project happen (*Western People*, 25 August 1990).

The government at the time was publicly wholeheartedly behind the scheme, no doubt anxious to reassure the Mayo people that they have not been forgotten, and it was the Taoiseach who asked the Board of Works to take over the project and provide necessary funding when it began to look as though the EU grant would not be as substantial as expected.

CONCLUSION

I have tried to show how some social relations, on a rather general scale, have intersected in one process of the interpretation of a particular aspect of landscape in North West Mayo. The aim has been to try and illustrate the theory that place and identity are culturally constructed notions, which are open to various interpretations. Future research could aim for a more in-depth analysis of these processes, and could follow some deep changes which may be occurring in rural areas, and in their relationship with the urban. For instance, it has been argued that rural tourism can actually result in changes in culture and identity which may not be easily discernible.

Tourism involves the adoption of new signs, a language which is highly visible, and which can communicate in a short space of time a sense of identity, authenticity and difference. Research into the production of these new signs and language through interpretations of place and identity could perhaps contribute to our understanding of new relations between places, people, processes and structures as they emerge in a changing world.

The issue of place and identity is one which assumes importance in an economic order where places are marketed and where identity can become an 'added value product'. Current theories of place stress the contested nature of its construction, bringing in Foucauldian ideas of power and control, and seeing place as a structuring and mediating context for social relations. In Massey's (1994) words, space can be seen as 'stretched out social relations'. She describes the spatial as an 'ever shifting social geometry of power and signification', and argues for the concept of simultaneity, which implies the 'existence of simultaneous multiplicity of spaces'. The idea of spaces as dynamic can challenge exclusivist, or nationalist attempts to fix meanings to places, or to identify places as sites for nostalgia, with unproblematic, fixed and authentic identities, as occurs in the process of commoditisation of tourist destinations and products. Another point is that the mix of social relations which define place, stretch beyond the local, and encompass global flows of change and power. This concept is intrinsic to a study of tourism, as places are often marketed on the global scene, and both internal and external agents and structures have a role in determining how those places are to be presented and managed as tourist destinations. So work on tourism, could interrogate these ideas about place, and reveal the social contests which occur in order to label them.

ACKNOWLEDGEMENTS

I would like to thank all those who have contributed their opinions, and especially Ms Greta Byrne, archaeologist, for her help and assistance.

BIBLIOGRAPHY

Cronin, A
1985 *An Irish Eye: Viewpoints by Anthony Cronin*, Dingle.
Feehan, J
1994 Tourism, Environment and Community Development. In
    Kockel, U (ed.), 97-102.
Heaney, S
1969 *Door into the Dark*, London.
1975 *North*, London.
Hodder, I
1990 Archaeology and the Post Modern, *Anthropology Today*
    6(5), 13-5.
Kelly, S
1989 Roots that go down Very Deep, *Country Living* 4(34), 1 &
    15.
Kinnaird, V and Hall, D
1994 *Tourism: a Gender Analysis*, London.
Kockel, U
1993 *The Gentle Subversion: Informal Economy and Regional
    Development in the West of Ireland*, Bremen.
Kockel, U (ed.)
1994 *Culture, Tourism and Development: the Case of Ireland*,
    Liverpool.
O'Connor, B and Cronin, M (eds)
1993 *Tourism in Ireland. A Critical Analysis*, Cork.
Mac Eochaidh, G
1994 Tourism Development at Community Level in Dis-
    advantaged Areas. In Kockel, U (ed.), 183-8.
Massey, D
1994 *Space, Place and Gender*, Oxford.
Nash, C
1993 The West of Ireland and Irish Identity. In O'Connor, B and
    Cronin, M (eds), 86-112.

Philo, C
1992 Neglected Rural Geographies: A Review, *Journal of Rural Studies* (8)2, 193-207.
Quinn, B
1994 Images of Ireland in Europe. In Kockel, U (ed.), 61-73.
Shore, C
1993 Inventing the 'people's Europe': critical approaches to European Community 'cultural policy', *MAN* NS 28(4), 779-800.

'A Dacent and Quiet People'
Palatine Settlements in County Limerick

HERMANN RASCHE

INTRODUCTION

The attentive visitor to the little Methodist church in Ballingrane near the town of Rathkeale in Co. Limerick will notice an unusual liturgical implement hanging from the wall: a cow's horn. This used to be sounded to assemble the people working in their fields and homes when the itinerant Methodist preacher, travelling on horseback, had arrived to address the little community. They would then drop everything and make their way to the church.

The members of this colony were successors of the first settlers from the Rhenish Palatine region in Southern Germany, who had come to Ireland at the beginning of the eighteenth century and had eventually settled in County Limerick.

At that time, a war was raging between France and a European confederation which included England and many German states, and this had devastating consequences for the people of the Palatinate. French invasion troops had exhausted and bled the country dry; religious oppression and the immediate threat of further religious persecution had caused adherents to the Protestant faith to seek protection from the French Catholic army.

Ullrich Kockel (ed.), *Landscape, Heritage and Identity: Case Studies in Irish Ethnography*, Liverpool University Press 1995, 155-77.

And to worsen this calamitous situation, the winter of 1708/09 had been extremely severe; irreparable damage had been done to crops and vines. Many families had to face extreme economic hardship and were often close to starvation. The only alternative to a hopeless economic and religious situation meant leaving the Palatinate and emigrating in the hope of finding a better future. Thus a veritable mass exodus of some 13,000 refugees from the predominantly Catholic Palatinate around the towns of Landau, Speyer, Worms, Mannheim, and Heidelberg took place in 1709.

THE PLANTATION

Queen Ann, who was sympathetic to the plight of the German Protestants, invited them to England, where they were to be made 'free denizens of Britain without charge' (Hick 1989), which gave them permission to settle on British soil in England or in any other of the new colonies in North America. In fact, most of them hoped to continue on to the land of milk and honey across the Atlantic.

The English Queen facilitated their transport down the Rhine. Barges which had carried British troops to Holland for military action in the Spanish War of Succession, and were on their way back, shipped them from Rotterdam up the Thames estuary where they were encamped outside London, apparently in terrible conditions. Their reception among the ordinary folk was often downright hostile since their numbers soon made them unpopular. These German refugees were resented as unwelcome lazy intruders who had come here under false pretences—'there was no flagrant persecution in their territories' (Hayes 1937)—and only aggravated the economic hardships which the English had to suffer, too—'eating the bread out of the mouths of our own craftsmen and people' (*op.cit.*).

But the colonial enterprise to settle them in the British Carolinas failed to materialise, because funds that had been promised for such an undertaking were ultimately not forthcoming. Heated arguments were exchanged in Parliament as to the disentanglement of this problem. One obvious and rather attractive solution suggested sending the Palatines to Ireland. Thus a Government scheme was set in motion—a few hundred families were selected who should, as it said, 'strengthen and secure the Protestant cause'.

Towards the end of 1709, some 3,000 Palatines (the exact figure given is 3,073) came to Ireland through no fault of their own. Three years later, by 1712, more than half of them had already had enough of Ireland—many having complained of hostile treatment at the hands of their Catholic neighbours—and returned to London; some went on to the USA. The majority of those immigrants who stayed in Ireland were settled around the town of Rathkeale in the villages of Courtmatrix, Killiheen and Ballingrane, on property owned by Sir Thomas Southwell, a member of the Irish Parliament.

This plantation, albeit numerically not an exceptional influx, was the last of the significant historical immigrations into Ireland and constituted a specific political strategy. The settlers were received on advantageous conditions and generally given preferential treatment by colonising landlords—causing envy for a long period. Each family was granted ground for a house and garden, as well as several acres of farm land at a moderate rate (de Latocnaye n.d.). Apart from the aforementioned purpose, they were put there for obvious reasons: to bolster Protestant numbers and to bring industry to the country. Large areas of formerly cultivated rich and fertile land were still devastated and depopulated sixty years after Cromwell's invasion. The Palatines, many possessing agricultural skills and associated trades, were settled on this land in order to start its cultivation.

Those who stayed were to prove an attractive investment for Sir Thomas, but felt from the beginning resistance and hostile treatment at the hands of their indigenous Gaelic neighbours, who did not appreciate the newcomers and considered them a bulwark of Protestantism. The fact that the Palatines were soon successful in their farming methods heightened the antagonism towards them further (de Latocnaye n.d.).

Hermann Rasche

EVIDENCE OF PALATINE CULTURE IN IRELAND

The Palatines wrote very little about themselves. The few written records they did leave behind were mostly genealogical lists; the extent of documentary source-material from the insider's point of view is very scarce. Thus the images we have formed of the settlers, and the knowledge we have accumulated about their past history, are primarily based on the subjective perception provided by travellers who came to the Palatinate colonies at various periods in significant numbers. It is interesting to note that successive first-hand eye-witness accounts of those outside chroniclers in turn often seem to rely on cross-borrowings and cross-references by previous descriptions, even down to similar wordings.

From the various travel records we have a great deal of factual information and comments on all matters of daily life, including clothing and dietary habits. The Palatines were very conscious of their separate identity. Though not all the settlers had originally come from the Palatinate proper—among them were also Swabians, families from Hesse, Huguenots from various parts of Germany— the generic term 'Palatines' is very apt, for the great majority of them came from the Palatinate; different ways of life that may well have existed in the motherland were quickly assimilated into the new settlement.

Ethnic Identity

In an alien environment, they considered themselves a homogeneous ethnic group, and they were indeed perceived as such. Characteristic differences from their indigenous neighbours helped to keep them apart as a social group for a considerable time, and they continued to engage in their own specific ways of life which they had brought with them from their homeland.

The Palatines had settled in clusters, though in a relatively confined area, and had not spread out and scattered throughout the region. They were seen as possessing somewhat swarthy complexion and bearing strange sounding names, such as Bovenizer, Sparling, or Delenge. Above all they spoke a different language. German was a major symbol of cultural divergence (O'Connor 1989).

The other most decisive 'cultural marker' was their religious denomination which separated them from the native Catholic Irish, affiliating them politically very closely to the dominant Protestant class.

Life among the Palatines was organised around the core institutions of family, school and church in a rural setting. Within these confines, they were almost self-sufficient and could satisfy most of the requirements of their members.

But despite the strong cohesion of the community, a relatively constant process of change and adaptation to new demands can also be observed. Acculturation—groups of individuals with different cultures coming into continuous first-hand contact, with subsequent changes in the original cultural patterns of either or both groups—inevitably set in around the middle of the eighteenth century. The first signs of change in a more or less long drawn-out process of assimilation of one culture to another occurred relatively quickly.

The year 1760 is seen as a decisive date for the Palatine settlements by cultural historians: rates on leasehold property were drastically increased by the landlords and caused the first wave of emigration. The other great drain on the Palatine community set in during the immediate post-famine period.

But since the colonies were relatively sparsely populated, and there was almost no contact with the home country which could have provided culturally revitalising connections with forms of culture back in the motherland, the separateness was bound to be weakened in due course.

Generally speaking, the Palatines were able to uphold and keep their 'otherness', although increasingly only selected elements of their identity were transmitted to the following generations, as testified by various observers.

This process of a gradual weakening and eventual dissolution of their once distinctive identity, accompanied by loss of traditional cultural forms was of varying duration and intensity in individual settlements and only ended in the middle of the nineteenth century.

The Palatine immigrants were exposed to different influences exerted by their new environment. Although there was hardly any significant social intercourse with the native Catholic and Gaelic Irish, and equally only passing contact with the landlord class, they abandoned many cultural patterns of their home country in favour of the behavioural norms and value judgements of the Anglo-Saxon peer group. They adopted what they perceived as higher forms of civilisation of the Protestant Anglo-Irish and English over time and conformed to them and their role models, such as teachers and ministers. This 'Anglo-conformity' was, if not the expressly intended aim, then at least the consequence of a process of cultural assimilation (Renzing 1989).

Material Culture and Customs

When social customs are recorded and cited, the eye-witnesses give examples of characteristic and noticeable differences. The virtue of effective husbandry and industry is the main theme which comes out of the accounts of most visitors to the Palatine settlements, which stands in stark contrast to the perceived laziness of the Irish, as illustrated by their evident failure to utilise and commercialise the land according to English ideals (O'Connor 1989). Selective images which frequently concur with the comments of predecessor and successors are related to a value code of contrasts: better, cleaner, more efficient, but dour, compared to Irish indolence and sloth.

The eating habits of the Palatines were different. They were not as dependent on the potato as the Irish and generally enjoyed a greater variety of food items, such as cereals and pulses, bread baked with oats and wheat, and meat and poultry. They grew large quantities of cabbage for *sauerkraut*, which was the basis for their staple diet.

Like their Irish neighbours, they cultivated flax and hemp, and also developed a flourishing linen industry.

There is frequent mention of the Palatines' horticultural knowledge and their progressive farming methods, which gave higher yields. For example, the agriculturalist and veteran traveller, Arthur Young, who met the second and third generation of immigrant settlers in the mid-1770s, draws attention to the wheeled plough 'which sows the land at the same time it is ploughed' (Young 1780), allowing simultaneous drilling. From the entries in his *Tour in Ireland*, we are able to compare native Irish and Palatine agriculture.

The settlers' farmsteads appeared recognisably different in the Irish countryside. Cattle were kept in stables during the winter and fed with hay and straw. They built barns, stables and substantial out-houses for their equipment close to their homes. De Latocnaye (n.d.), a Breton soldier, who happened to come upon the colony during 1796/97, reports that the Palatine houses were surrounded by attractive kitchen and vegetable gardens, whose produce provided them with the necessary vitamins. Orchards supplied the apples for cider and fruit-wines. They were dedicated and successful bee-keepers and knew how to cure bacon and prepare delicious cakes.

The general cultivation of home decor was markedly different from the Irish surroundings, as Arthur Young (1780) points out: 'They are remarkable for their goodness and cleanliness of their houses'. He notes further that 'they appoint a burgomaster, to whom they appeal in case of all disputes', and that they preserve some of their German customs like sleeping 'between two beds', a reference to the fact that they used feather quilts instead of blankets.

De Latocnaye (n.d.) is impressed by the solidity of the furniture inside the houses and by the fact that

> their farms are certainly better cultivated than others near, and their houses, built after the fashion of their former country, are

of a comfortable character, and so clean that they look like palaces in comparison with the poor cabins of the Irish.

Similar sentiments are still expressed in the 1930s, when it is stated that 'their industry is still very remarkable' and that the solid limestone houses of the Palatines 'contrasted with the mean cabins of their crushed and rack-rented neighbours' (Hayes 1937). The poor Palatines of the early years had certainly become well off farmers!

A settlement grid pattern, resembling a typical German village plan, can only tentatively be detected in Courtmatrix: a large quadrangular square, with houses surrounding it and, later, with a Methodist chapel in the middle of it.

When de Latocnaye visited the villages near Rathkeale, he found only one man of the original colony still alive. He pointed out that until that time, they had always married among themselves, and had preserved the customs of their country, but he gave no details as to specifics. De Latocnaye notes, however, the large straw hats and short petticoat worn by Palatine women.

It can generally be observed that old customs which the Palatine settlers had brought over from the continent were disappearing fast, especially from the beginning of the nineteenth century onwards; this was often due to the influence of Protestant ministers who were all from the Anglo-Irish or the English upper classes.

Two customs which are mentioned in earlier travelogues on the Palatines have survived as linguistic forms, and were practised until fairly recently: 'Grüßenschuß', to greet the New Year with shots, and 'lighting of fockles', which is derived from the German word for torch, 'Fackel', and refers to the custom of lighting bundles of straw tied to long poles on St John's Day.

Language

Language is of pivotal importance as a cohesive factor in any culture. The early settlers spoke almost exclusively German. They had established simple colonial schools in each settlement where German was taught for the first few decades. These schools were not very well equipped, but served their purpose. O'Connor (1989) notes that

> Until at least the third generation in Ireland they remained a people set apart linguistically. In all of the Palatine settlements ... German ... remained the regular medium of communication until at least 1760.

But from 1730 onwards, Palatine children began to be sent to neighbouring English schools, where all teachers were, of course, English-speaking, and the influence of the Anglican clergy strong. After 1760, infant classes in all schools were conducted in English only. A bilingual situation had developed by that time, and

> John Wesley ... could preach in English to his new flock. The success of his missionary activities was in no small measure also due to the fact that the Palatines spoke and understood English (Hayes 1937).

Palatine identity in transition can be detected in the writings of all eighteenth century travellers. The perceptive Arthur Young (1780), for example, refers to the state of the German language 'which is declining'. The travelling preacher, Thomas Waugh, on his journey through the Palatinate around the year 1800, when halting to address the congregation after the cow's horn had been sounded to call the assembly,

> noted that the German accent still clung to the English speech of the older among them, one patriarch saying affectionately to him, 'Got pless you, my tear young mann' (Hayes 1937).

The death of the language was apparently a long drawn-out process. Similar drastic observations are made by Thomas Steele in 1824 (quoted in Renzing 1989):

There were formerly many in the settlement who spoke the German language, and there are some who speak it now, but they are very few.

The picture and its assessment is not completely uniform. The fourth generation sometimes spoke English, sometimes German at home; the following generation apparently had no German at all; by 1800, German had become almost extinct and was only heard among the very old (O'Connor 1989). Thus Hayes' (1937) statement that

[f]rom generation to generation they pursued a self-centred existence, speaking their own language, following their own native customs

must be somewhat modified.

The pressures for linguistic assimilation of a small minority living in an English-speaking context, lacking any fresh contacts with their mother-country whatsoever, could not be withstood any longer. But the colonists had accepted English willingly, for mastering it in written and oral form provided obvious advantages.

Cultural assimilation shows itself very forcefully in this respect; and with the language the Palatines and their children increasingly adopted customs, attitudes, ideals from their upper class Anglo/Irish neighbours.

A 'dearth of literature' (O'Connor 1989) has also been cited as a crucial factor militating against language survival. The accelerated loss of language can also be explained by the fact that the old Palatines used to have their Bibles buried with them. Moreover, many theological and other works were given to German troops in the Limerick area around 1798 as mementoes or as keepsakes. A lot of stories have been lost due to religious influences, including the dislike of certain stories by Protestant ministers. Five local stories were collected in 1824 by Thomas Steele, albeit only in truncated form (*cf.* Renzing 1989).

Religion and Politics

The Palatines were traditionally loyal citizens of the state because of their Protestant heritage and the favour shown them by the local landowners (Clark and Donnelly 1983). Adult males in the Palatine communities usually belonged to units of yeomanry or volunteers such as the Fusiliers and Brunswick Troupes Palatine Infantry which defended the cause of the Protestant Ascendancy with which they identified (Hayes 1937).

Generally speaking, the quiet Palatines pursuing their avocation without let or hindrance, were regarded as 'frugal, industrious, thrifty, inoffensive ... who worked their holdings undisturbed by the poorer Catholic neighbours'; in other words, they were 'dacent and quiet people who kept to themselves' (Hall and Hall 1841). But it would be an oversimplification to claim that 'even in the turbulent period of Whiteboyism they do not seem to have been molested in any way' (Hayes 1937). There were at least sporadic incidents like the one in the village of Glenisheen, inhabited almost exclusively by Palatines, which was attacked during the time of the Whiteboy unrests. Palatine tenants who had sided too militantly with Protestant upper class interests were murdered by the Whiteboys, who also destroyed three houses and set fire to another four.

Sectarian animosity towards the Palatines on account of their loyalty and obviously privileged position relative to the suppressed majority (Renzing 1989) subsided eventually. However, the resulting feeling of insecurity and a lingering mistrust vis-à-vis the potentially rebellious Irish remained strong for some time, so that quite a few emigrated (*op. cit.*).

The Palatines were Protestants, divided almost equally between adherents to Lutheranism and to Calvinism (O'Connor 1989). Thus a changeover to the denomination of their landlords constituted no problems. But the new settlers seem to have been neglected by the official Anglican Church and not really accepted by the Protestant upper classes. Therefore they turned to Methodism, which made a strong impact. Palatines quickly became the most fervent supporters of the teaching of John Wesley, who seems to have paid particular attention to his new congregation and visited them frequently.

On one of his many missionary campaigns in Ireland to spread Methodism, Wesley visited the Palatines in 1756 for the first time. It is interesting to read that during that visit Wesley complained about the drunkenness of the settlers, some of whom had quite obviously 'gone too native' for his liking. But this state of affairs was rectified swiftly. On his next visit, he recorded: 'I found much life among this plain, artless, serious people'. Wesley continued his regular periodical contacts with the colonies right up to the time of his death in 1789. In numerous entries at different intervals he recorded the religious life of these 'serious people' (Hayes 1937).

Within the Palatine groups, great power of control was exercised through Methodist religion. Its social and cultural conditioning influence was strong. It had at once a bonding effect within this minority grouping and kept them apart from the Irish who were at best indifferent, but at times hostile towards them.

Fairly strict codes of conduct due to Methodism played a major part in isolating them from the Catholic Irish and their forms of socialising and merrymaking; there was no mingling and mixing at festivals with the proverbially boisterous Irish. Different religious affiliation, of course, determined their marriage patterns. Marriages between Catholics and Protestants were practically unheard of until well towards the end of the eighteenth century. To some extent, the Palatines then did intermarry with the local Catholic population, and a number of their communities had lost their distinctiveness by the early nineteenth century, but certain others retained it (Clark and Donnelly 1983).

THE PALATINES IN 'ETHNOGRAPHIC' LITERATURE

By the time the Halls, the indefatigable travelling couple, visited the Palatine colony shortly before the Great Famine in the 1840s and became its most extensive and exhaustive chroniclers, the process of assimilation had progressed among the younger generation who 'mingle and marry with their Irish neighbours', although the records tell us that intermarriage occurred quite often with Anglo-Irish domestics and soldiers, but rarely with Catholics.

The Halls, having moved among the indigenous Irish and become accustomed to the 'brilliant smiles and hearty: God save ye kindly', and after having perhaps been conditioned by their own extrovert experience, give a most perceptive assessment of the Palatine mentality. They see the settlers as different in character and distinct in their habits and outlook from the natives. The men in Adare possess a calm temper and stern severity and are reserved, the women are perceived as sombre and unexpressive and as taciturn. Both sexes seem not actually unfriendly or unwelcoming, but ill at ease in the presence of strangers.

In fact—according to the observant Halls, who argued here along denominational lines—a veritable change of characteristic attitudes and attributes had set in with the advent of Methodism, for Wesley had admonished them to keep away from all lightness, jesting and foolish talking. Former patterns of emotional expression, amounting almost to ethnic characteristics like wit, repartee and boisterousness, had early on turned into a rather thoughtful, reserved and hesitant type of behaviour:

Them Palatines don't take on about love and fighting, and divarshin of all kind, like ourselves ... [T]hey behave mighty quiet and dacent (Hall and Hall 1841).

It is worth remembering that the Halls receive much of their information from 'Paddy'—an Irish perception of the Palatines intrudes into the Halls' image-typical comments.

The Halls' observations and descriptions—edited under the title *Sketches from Ireland*—were translated into German by V. A. Huber (1850). These sketches, and the popular folklore recorded therein, such as the tragic story of 'The Palatine's Daughter', served in turn as inspiration and source of information for *Die Pfälzer*, a play written by Paul Heyse and premiered at the Court Theatre in Munich in 1858 in the presence of the Bavarian king. Heyse, then only twenty-four years of age, was later to receive the Nobel Prize for literature. The play depicts the clash of two cultures, different modes of behaviour, divergent ideas and attitudes, and the prejudices that arise.

The Halls recorded popular folklore. Heyse used the story of 'Protestant girl falling in love with Catholic boy' as the subject for his play. The Palatines, loyal to the English crown, suffer from the attacks of the Whiteboys. Their older generation especially—as represented by the doyen of the Bodenmesser clan, Jakob, a stalwart of Palatine uprightness—look upon the Irish as lazy idlers and uncivilised Whiskey drinking rabble. The latter, in turn, see in the German settlers as land-robbing intruders propped up by English laws, and regard them as starchy, cold-blooded, stubborn, self-righteous and virtuous pale faces, lacking all vitality and poetic imagination.

Social, confessional and cultural differences seem irreconcilable, or, in the words of Old Jakob: 'Fire and water will sooner mix than a true Palatine and Irish blood'. And a true Palatine, in Jakob Bodenmesser's self-assessment, spells honourable, moderate and god-fearing. Bobenizer wants to have his only daughter Anna marry within the Palatine community; Adam Switzer has been chosen as the suitable future son-in-law. The marriage is also seen as an economic transaction, for it promises more crops and stock.

But the younger generation, represented by the daughter, tries to break this mould of frozen concepts and prejudices, this rigid dualism which is entrenched in the inherited Palatine cultural expectations and the Irish mentality, through her love for James Hennesey. She enjoys clandestine meetings with James. Nobody can later understand how Anna had managed to meet him at all, for 'they never frequented the same places of worship or of amusement' (Hall and Hall 1841). But the attempt to break free still ends tragically in the play. When Heyse wrote the play, the situation was already changing, and marriages between Catholics and Protestants were taking place more frequently.

Other travellers often concur with their predecessors in the images they produce and develop of the Palatines. Helfferich, whose work was published in 1858, has another 'Paddy' confirm the Palatine's by now proverbial orderliness, efficiency and cleanliness. He also reiterates the point made previously by the Halls, that the successors of the original colonists had

> something excessively serious, ponderous, which was possibly not so much a reflection of their nationality but their particular religious affiliation (Helfferich 1858).

A native of that area, P. W. Joyce, has also left records behind. He, too, noted down that the Palatines are reserved in their manners and hold very little intercourse with the other classes of the people.

The German ethnographer, Johann Georg Kohl, came to Ireland in 1842; he mentions the 'German settlement in Co. Limerick', but does not visit the colony, due to, as he says, pressure of time and other prior engagements. Thus we have no first-hand account by this widely-travelled and experienced German visitor. But Kohl is supplied with some information by an Irish friend, who refers to the fact that the Palatines have by now

> discarded their ... language but not their German peculiarities. One can still discern them from the rest of the people ... They are most respectable people and enjoy the reputation of being the best farmers. They are also more prosperous and much better off than their Irish neighbours (Kohl 1843).

Kohl ventures to speculate as to the causes of this situation. He reflects on their diligence, energy and industry and compares these traits favourably with an inherent idleness and slackness of the Irish.

Despite the Palatine's obvious and growing assimilation into the Anglo-Irish cultural context, various testimonies refer to a certain distinctiveness well into the nineteenth century. The picture is not always clear-cut as to its degree. It has been suggested that highly indicative shifts of some of the cultural markers occurred when the Palatines gave up their dearly held feather quilts, and when they switched from *sauerkraut* and sow's stomach and took to potatoes, butter and milk. Of more far-reaching consequence was the situation that Palatines were intermarrying with local Catholics and a number of communities were thus losing their distinctiveness.

In his stories, novels and songs, mostly set in the eighteenth century, Gerald Griffin (1803-1840) tries to recreate a Palatine experience. Griffin, who grew up in that area and got to know the Palatines well, was certainly influenced by previous perceptions of their different lifestyles and specific qualities. He incorporated non-fictional accounts into his fictional works (Griffin 1842). His images evolve around two different mentalities, the Palatines

> improving and industrious tenants—punctual ... presenting a striking contrast to the people among whom they have become naturalized—(a contrast which, perhaps, as much as any other circumstance, tends to foster the contempt with which they are regarded by the latter).

Those images from his works, in which fiction and non-fiction reinforce each other, have in turn shaped our popular notion of the Palatines. Griffin's works have been treated as a fairly reliable documentary source of information, preserving any remaining traces of the Palatines in Irish culture.

Mitchell, who was Inspector of Registration, during his wanderings through the Palatinate shortly before the turn of the last century, noticed their group solidarity: 'They still cling together like the members of a clan, and worship together' (Hayes 1937). He detects a high proportion of biblical names like Absalom, Letitia and Nehemiah and finds features still distinctly foreign. The Palatines, according to his understanding, are 'strongly built, swarthy in complexion, dark-haired and brown-eyed' (*op.cit.*). The neatness of the little flower gardens in front of their houses—some thatched, some slated, some of one storey, others of two—an orchard beside or immediately behind the house, the overall appearance of thrift and economy strike him as worth commenting on. Mitchell concludes in his assessment that the Palatines were successful in making the transition to the new Ireland.

As late as 1937, Hayes states that the Palatines 'are still a distinctive class in many ways', and that they retained

traits not only in character and temperament but in physical features; the guttural sound of their English speech in ordinary conversation is still recognizable.

The latter assertion is in contrast to earlier remarks that '[t]he last traces of German, spoken or written, even among the oldest of the present generation were gone' (Mitchell, quoted in Hayes 1937), and may be questionable.

A historian of the early Palatine emigration, the American scholar Knittle, visited the Palatines in the mid-1930s, and declared quite categorically that some of the descendants of the early emigrants had forgotten about their German origin altogether, speaking of a complete absorption, the only notable remaining difference being the denominational divide which manifested itself in a 'general lack of sympathy of Catholic for Protestant' (Knittle 1937). There is strong and conclusive evidence for assimilation which

had been delayed for about a century and a half due to the perception of one side by the other and the images each side projected. Then it came fast and with remarkable completeness as the last lingering traces of Rhineland origins faded from the memory bank and the new Ireland claimed the royal allegiance of the new Irish as well as of the old (O'Connor 1989).

Despite this evidence, Knittle, too, would still detect discipline, commitment and skill as predominant and particular features in the Palatine home and neighbourhood. In particular, he described the women of the Palatines as being as hard-working as any German *frau*, and the men as honest and scrupulous. Similar judgements of 'special characteristics' (without specifically naming and listing them) were expressed in the 1930s by Hayes who predicted:

> It is probable ... that before many decades the special characteristics of the Palatines that still remain will have completely disappeared and their community will be but a memory (Hayes 1937).

The latter part of that prognosis has not fulfilled itself—as yet. However, the Palatine community, if one may call it thus, is not very sizeable, and dwindling even further. It is fully integrated, completely absorbed in their ethnic and ecclesiastical environment. Only some of their names, which have characteristically German roots, sometimes betray their origins.

THE PALATINES TODAY

Lack of marriage opportunities among the bearers of original Palatine names was cause for an ever-contracting community:

> The cumulative figures of 59 deaths as against 13 births [from 1921 to 1980; HR] point to the poignant story of a community dying out (O'Connor 1989).

On the other hand, links with Protestant communities elsewhere in Ireland were cultivated. In other words: Palatine men were seeking wives from farther afield, and in this way, Palatine interconnections have been revived.

Due to a conjunction of circumstances, and in line with the general *Zeitgeist*, those who are left in the area remain and are increasingly conscious of their particular roots. This concern to re-discover their background, to re-emphasise their 'otherness', and the growth of a shared interest in the history and heritage of the Irish Palatines, was further emphasised by the founding of the Irish Palatine Association (IPA) and, simultaneously, the setting up of a Heritage Centre. As stated in its first *Newsletter* in 1989, the Association sees as its main aims

> stimulating and promoting awareness of the Palatine past and engendering a sense of fellowship among the Palatine people in general ... to encourage and develop a sense of identity among Palatine families and their descendants (*IPA Newsletter* 1989).

The *Newsletter*, published annually, offers a platform for stories relating to the Palatines and their descendants, information about forthcoming and recent activities, and nostalgic reminiscences about

> their glory [which] is long past and the once-manicured and lovingly cared-for fields [which] have reverted to semi-rough pasture.

The *Newsletter* thus testifies to the cultivation of images of their disciplined work ethic, their agricultural knowledge, cleanliness, resourcefulness, godliness, frugality and longevity—images that were established through centuries and linger on to our times.

In addition to the annual *Newsletter*—which, incidentally, is to be continued as a *Journal* from 1995 onwards—a news sheet is to be produced twice a year, 'to contain current news as being discussed by our committee' (*IPA News Sheet* No. 1).

Recent years have also seen the publication of two comprehensive and thorough studies of the Palatine history, one by the German scholar Rüdiger Renzing, the other by his Irish counterpart, Patrick O'Connor.

A museum, dedicated to the history and heritage of the Palatines, has been set up in the old railway station in Rathkeale—the premier town of the Irish Palatines—because of its proximity to the three parent colonies at Ballingrane, Courtmatrix and Killeheen. It was here that the largest number of Palatines were settled, and some of their descendants still reside today on their original settlements.

The museum sees its role in transmitting cultural values by trying to collect, preserve, document and interpret what is of value. Plans for further extension include an interpretative centre and research facilities with an archive and a genealogy database.

The museum's permanent exhibition is dictated, to a large extent, by what is left there to be shown and to be made accessible to the public at large. Various old portraits, family photos, surviving artefacts, tangible memorabilia treasured like priceless icons, are displayed to help to conjure up images of Palatine history. Among them are to be found: a bayonet dating back to the early 1700s, reminding museum visitors of the fact that families were issued with muskets on arrival in Ireland; the Wesleyan Hymn book 'for the people called Methodists by the Rev. John Wesley, M.A.'; account books with first entries dating back to 1799; and documents of agreement regarding business transactions.

Scarcity of tangible objects raises the important question of how representative a picture one can form in one's mind. A nineteenth century crochet-edged tray cloth and hand-embroidered tea cloth 'made from linen woven from flax grown by Palatine families' (IPA Newsletter) are on display, and are supposed to testify to the domestic industry of a Palatine woman. But how specific is such an illustrative item? Did not any Victorian lady engage in similar household tasks?

A heritage 'adventure' trail, which coincidentally links the three parent colonies with Castle Matrix, home of the Southwells, and incorporates all the ancestral homes and places, is being developed. It invites the visitor to go down memory lane, taking in the mature orchards at Killeheen, which yielded the apples for the cider press, a subterranean 'Palatine well' close by, the remains of Palatine relics in Killeheen and Courtmatrix, and remnants of the stone floor of the Methodist church in Killeheen. These are among the last material witnesses to a culture now assiduously preserved.

Part of the awareness raising activities involves taking interested parties on conducted tours, organising lectures and inviting local and national media to take cognizance of their activities. RTÉ, the national radio and television station, produced a feature on them, in which descendants were interviewed on the material culture of the Palatines.

Palatines from the Limerick region—from Rathkeale, Ballingrane, Askeaton, Kilfinane, Pallskenry—congregate annually for an open-field Methodist service in the park of Adare Manor. The 'Picknick' afterwards provides ample opportunity for chat and more serious discussion regarding match-making possibilities. A lot of the social life of the Palatines takes place within the context of the common Methodist religion, which is still a strong cultural bond and serves their identity.

The presence of the President of the Methodist Church and the German Ambassador at the foundation stone laying ceremony for the new Palatine museum building in 1991 highlighted two of the central cultural links for the Palatines. The official German representative to this country

> stressed the possible significance of roots, new contacts, discovery of family bonds, growth in tourism, ... and awareness of identity ... It would promote cohesion among the Palatines and enable completion of the heritage centre as a centrepoint in seeking a sense of identity (*IPA Newsletter* 1991).

In 1992, this renewed search for one's roots brought a party of Irish Palatine descendants and other interested members back to the ancestral German homeland where they visited the Palatine region.

Reciprocity even went so far as to bring vines from the Palatinate to be planted in Rathkeale, a climatological adventure not even the first settlers had dared to undertake!

The Irish Palatinate venture is also a welcome tourist attraction with an attractive topographical flavour—especially for German nationals. This is borne out by the first of a number of proposed reciprocal visits organised by the Palatine Association. A ten-day tour of Southwest Ireland, organised for September 1995 and 'with a special Palatine dimension', will take in the major sites with Palatine associations, as far as the Palatine settlements around Blenerville, County Kerry.

The perception of their ancestors and of themselves as a hard working, industrious and religious people is strong among the present Palatines. A self-image of one of the descendants may further illustrate this:

> The County Limerick townlands of Ballingrane, Courtmatrix and Killeheen are still homeland to the largest Palatine group. Their descendants still retain a decernable [*sic*] life style to their forebearers portrayed through honesty, tenacity, thriftyness and dedication to work maintained for the best part by a strong faith in God.

A 'dacent people', indeed!

BIBLIOGRAPHY

Clark, S and Donnelly, J
1983 *Irish Peasants - Violence and Political Unrest 1780-1914,* Dublin.

de Latocnaye, Le Chevalier
n.d.　*A Frenchman's Walk through Ireland, 1796/97*, Belfast and Dublin.

Griffin, G
1842　*Shuil Dhuv, the Coiner*, London.

Hall, S and Hall, S
1841　*Ireland: Its Scenery, Character, etc.*, London.

Hayes, R
1937　The German Colony in County Limerick, *North Munster Antiquarian Journal* 1(2), 42-53.

Helfferich, A (ed.)
1858　*Skizzen und Erzählungen aus Irland*, Berlin.

Heyse, P
1858　Die Pfälzer in Irland. In Heyse, P., *Gesammelte Werke Vol. 9: Dramen*, Berlin, 333-406.

Hick, V
1989　The Palatine Settlement in Ireland: the Early Years, *Eighteenth Century Ireland* 4, 113-28.

Huber, V
1850　*Skizzen aus Irland*, Berlin.

Keller-Hüschemenger, M
1964　*Pfälzische Emigrantengemeinden in Irland*, Berlin and Hamburg.

Knittle, W
1937　*Early Eighteenth Century Palatine Emigration*, Philadelphia.

Kohl, J
1843　*Reisen in Irland*, Dresden and Leipzig.

O'Connor, P
1989　*People Make Places: the Story of the Irish Palatines.* Newcastle West.

Renzing, R
1989　*Pfälzer in Irland*, Kaiserslautern.

Young, A
1780　*A Tour in Ireland*, London.

Counter-Urbanisation in West Cork

HEATHER HEGARTY

INTRODUCTION

West Cork has hundreds of miles of rugged coastline but relatively few beaches, many miles of winding byroads but limited main roads, a sparse population but a huge diversity of peoples. It is rugged, beautiful, and virtually unspoilt. Peripheral and coastal, situated in the extreme southwest of Ireland (Figure 11), the region may be classified as 'farm-scape' in a scapefringe model of land use classification, such as that employed by Pacione (1983). Typically, it is an agricultural area dominated by rural lifestyles, and one which plays host to counter-urban migrants. However, it is not completely without elements which usually characterise the marginal fringe. The weak primary resource base is certainly applicable; as is the high incidence of second homes in the area, particularly in recent years.

Characteristically, too, the extensive coastal area is a delicate natural environment which can easily be damaged if not properly managed. The region may also be considered one of outstanding natural beauty and where house and property prices have risen dramatically.

Ullrich Kockel (ed.), *Landscape, Heritage and Identity: Case Studies in Irish Ethnography*, Liverpool University Press 1995, 179-96.

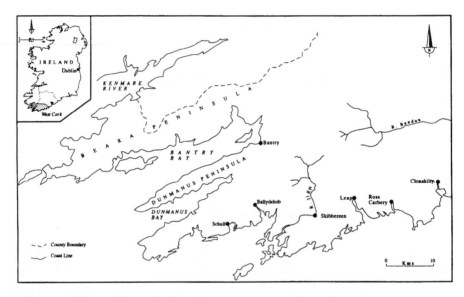

Figure 11   *West Cork; places mentioned in the text*

The focus of this essay is the counter-urban migrants to whom the region plays host. Thus the study is not concerned with forced migration, holiday or second home owners, retired people, or the more recent 'New-Age' travellers. The specific area within West Cork under review is a band stretching from Schull and Ballydehob through to Skibbereen, Leap and Rosscarbery (Figure 11).

The study is concerned with incomers who have come to West Cork since 1965. This date does not strictly mark any cut-off point, but is used because it marks the time of immigration of the earliest of the respondents of this study. It is, however, representative of the beginnings of counter-urban immigration not only in West Cork but also in Europe and America (Cloke 1985; Ogden 1985; Perry and Dean 1986).

The incomers to West Cork come from right across the globe, from America to Europe—England, Germany, the Netherlands, Switzerland, France, Spain, Sweden, even the West Indies. Those with whom this essay is concerned are permanent and settled. They are counter-urban and counter-cultural. They have left the cities unforced, and have chosen to create new lives for themselves. Their lifestyles are different or alternative to how they lived before, and different to the indigenous population. Their emphasis is on 'quality-of-life'. By and large they are very highly educated, have often sacrificed a lot in coming to West Cork, and are very hard working. Though seeking tranquillity and space and therefore living in quiet, often fairly isolated areas, they are usually no more than a few miles from the nearest town or village. They do not wish to be totally 'cut-off' or isolated and all twenty-seven interviewed for the study on which this essay is based have a telephone in their homes.

REASONS FOR MIGRATION TO WEST CORK

The reasons given by the incomers for immigrating, and more particularly for coming to West Cork, are best considered in terms of the positive and negative influences. This bears semblance to the push/pull model of motivating factors (Perry and Dean 1986; Cloke 1985), but is less deterministic.

Those negative issues which influenced the moves away from the cities may be summarised as the product of urban living and urban society. Much attention has hitherto been focused on the negative attributes of crime, unemployment, overcrowding, pollution (*cf.* Perry and Dean 1986). Amongst the lower scales of class structures such problems are rife. Crime, drugs, overcrowding and inter-racial problems are characteristic features of London's council housing developments which are largely blocks of flats. Unemployment or insufficient income from employment makes upward mobility impossible, thereby forcing people to live in very stressful conditions. This accentuates the cyclical nature of the problems.

However, the negative influences are somewhat different in the middle classes, although they too suffer the effects of pollution, noise, stress and crime. The primary concern of the middle classes is less tangible. City living virtually predetermines a ruthless drive for material success which brings about an implied need to conform to the codes, mores and dictates of society. This lifestyle, however, is too fast, competitive and aggressive in its means for the immigrants. They argue that materialism and capitalism are the driving forces of the city. Measures of materialism lead to categorisation of status in terms of wealth and, as such, it is difficult to be 'yourself'. Further, class conformity is pressured which leads to many shallow 'cliquey' social groupings. There is no 'space' to be your own person or to do your own thing.

However, socialist countries or welfare state systems do not necessarily provide the answer either. Such systems pave the way for lethargy and offer no challenge to life. In one instance, a respondent stated that if he were to leave the job he was working in, the state would provide him with 85% of his earnings which would drop to about 75% in twenty years. As Kockel (1989) observed,

> While those who emigrate from Ireland seek just this security
> in a well paid permanent job, their counterparts, equally if not
> better educated, come to Ireland for just the opposite.

The social classes are broadly reflected in the negative influences. While the issues of crime, pollution, noise etc. permeate all classes they are preponderant in the working classes. The societal issues of status, materialism, conformity etc. are expressed largely by the middle classes (and 'others'—students and artisans). These issues are therefore very significant, the working classes constituting only 15% of the respondents to this study. The social classes are taken from census categories, based on incomers' employment prior to immigrating.

The positive issues which influenced the incomers to come to, and stay in West Cork can largely be summed up in what the area is perceived as being—that is, the antithesis of city living. In short the positive influences are socio-environmental. In seeking 'space', a remote rural region was seen to epitomise this physically and psychologically. Ruggedly beautiful, scenic and green, and sparsely populated, West Cork is physically and morphologically very different from an urban area. It is conducive to artists' creativity. Further to the aesthetic quality of West Cork, the environment is good psychologically to live in. The geographical expanse of space furthered by the sea and the coast enhances the sense of freedom and space. The horizon is no longer obstructed by buildings in close proximity. This pleasant atmosphere the incomers feel is heightened by the hospitable, accepting nature of the locals, and the aggressive fast pace of life in the city is replaced by a relaxed, easy-going existence. West Cork's mixture of worlds and cultures—European, non-European and Third World (in terms of demography and infrastructure, the area shares characteristics of Third World countries)—heightens the incomers' feelings that there is room to 'be yourself' and 'do your own thing'.

Kockel (1989) asserts that most immigrants come specifically to where they want to be, but this essay argues that they know the type of place they want to go rather than the place itself. Why then do immigrants come specifically to West Cork, many of whom have no real knowledge of the area? They do so because of continuity of contact. This is fostered in various ways:

1. by knowing people already living in the area;
2. by having family roots in the area;
3. by having a specific incentive to settle in West Cork—for example inheritance of land;
4. more exceptionally through communication received by an estate agent, the immigrants generally having applied for information to any number of areas;
5. or, finally, having holidayed in West Cork gives first hand knowledge of the region.

For many, the decision to immigrate was more one of staying in West Cork, rather than consciously 'rejecting' the societies from which they came; for others, an increasing sense of alienation with their social lives led to their decision to leave and set up home in West Cork. In many cases the 'push' or negative factors were considered as such, when reflected upon having already left, rather than instigating the move in the first place. In other words, they were reasons not to go back.

The reasons for both leaving the source area and coming to somewhere like West Cork are essentially socio-environmental. The reasons for immigration only minimally took into account any economic considerations. Only 3-4% of total responses reflected any such concerns.

Cloke (1985) states that 'many people now enjoy more financial freedom to act on their preferences', and this is supported by Perry and Dean (1986). This study does not fully uphold their viewpoint. On the one, hand it does in part support the contention that only those who can afford to migrate do so—hence the lack of economic factors. As well as this, just over half of the immigrants come from middle or upper middle classes. On the other hand, however, not all were middle class and not all were earning prior to coming (students and artisans, for example, constituted 29% of those interviewed). Interestingly, some that were high earners before coming had no savings—the level of high financial security provided by the source countries probably did not necessitate saving.

This argument is evidenced by the modest and hard-working lifestyles of the immigrants on coming to West Cork. Many have sought to get away from capitalism and materialism and simply require just enough to live on. In brief, the incomers 'have taken up refuge in Ireland to do their own thing' (Kockel 1989) or to have the 'space' to be their own person. They are seeking a better 'quality-of-life'.

SOCIO-CULTURAL GEOGRAPHY

This section of the essay considers three aspects of the socio-cultural geography of the incomers once they come to West Cork. The perspective is largely as the incomers see it themselves, a more local perspective being considered in the final section of the essay. The three aspects discussed centre around how the incomers 'fit in' with the locals. The first is the process of adaptation.

'Adaptability is what is needed to succeed'—in other words, to live in West Cork as an incomer, it is necessary to be adaptable. But to adapt does not mean to become one of the locals, but to live 'quietly and not extravagantly' in conformity with them. New ideas, concepts and beliefs, if they are to be introduced at all, must be done so with subtlety and not pushed. To adapt does not mean to 'become one of' but necessitates compromise and flexibility in method and attitude.

The adaptation required by the incomers is greater than they had expected, particularly as the difference between the reality of actually living in West Cork as opposed to how they imagined it to be, becomes apparent. It is difficult to make a living in West Cork and the struggle to make ends meet is very different from what many were used to. The incomers also need to cope with the transition from being an employee to being self-employed. In effect, too, there is often a change in class status which brings about changes in priorities and values. In addition, the incomers are unprepared for the extent to which 'pull' is used in Irish society. This is almost wholly due to the extended family networking in Ireland. Even entertainment requires a conscious effort. The 'challenge to life' sought by some is readily available.

In at least one-third of cases, the initial drive to be self-sufficient was gradually abandoned as the reality of the sheer hard work and the often impracticable nature of the situation became evident. However, the desire for self-sufficiency helped integration, for more often than not the indigenous population were either called on to give, or volunteered their assistance. Interestingly, in the west of Ireland, Kockel (1991) found the opposite: that the introvert or self-sufficient behaviour of the immigrants meant that they 'hardly mixed with the local community'.

The essential medium to adaptation in West Cork is communication, which is necessitated on two levels. The first is physical. A car is required because public transport, though regular, is infrequent, and confined to the more important routeways. Thus migrants may need to learn how to drive. This was not a necessary requirement when living in the city as either walking or cycling served for shorter distances and public transport facilitated longer distances. A telephone and television are also prerequisites to avoid feeling trapped and shut off. The television has the added advantage of helping the children to learn English. The telephone is vital for those in business, and for some businesses extra telecommunication systems are essential.

Even more important, however, is the level of communication with people. This is threefold. Firstly, and perhaps most obviously, there is the need to transcend language barriers. Even with fluent English the West Cork accent is sometimes difficult to understand and needs some familiarisation. Secondly, the method of communication changes as letters and phonecalls become more necessary. Thirdly and very significantly, the incomers had to learn to communicate with more thought and care. In other words, they had to learn to 'keep their mouths shut' in order to avoid offending anyone.

This is the second dimension of the incomers' socio-cultural geography. They were not prepared for the complexity of the 'tangled web' of the extended family network in West Cork. The 'relation web' is vast, and incomers simply have to keep their 'mouths shut'. The method of communication is 'more sophisticated in the countryside'. As well as the vertical dimension or 'pecking order' in Irish society the incomers discovered a horizontal layer in which there are 'long ground disputes and interconnections'. Incomers are also drawn into things, for example contentious issues in parent/teacher meetings, because 'they can't offend a relation'.

186

They are 'often made use of in such ways'. However, this can also make them feel more isolated.

One respondent was given 'protection and initiation' through marrying a local man which led to a feeling of being part of the community, as part of a family which has always been there. People therefore know who you are and this increases your sense of identity. Others tentatively claim to belong by being able to trace ancient family roots.

Yet the immigrants do not always feel as though they truly belong in West Cork. It is as though they can claim an identity but at root level there is a realisation or acknowledgement that they are not indigenous. They lack continuity, or in other words they cannot share the past history of West Cork (nor indeed can the locals share the history of the incomers). This lack of continuity is evident for example at funerals, and also in opinions expressed by incomers where they do not wholly understand the sentimentality of the Irish in relation to such issues as colonialism.

The third aspect of this section is that of the level of acceptance of the incomers. The incomers feel that 'there is a unique phenomenon of acceptance' in West Cork, but they feel this on different levels: some feel that they are part of the community; others feel accepted as different and others recognise acceptance as not having been rejected. However, the incomers say they do not mind being different or not being totally integrated—that it is their choice. This probably reflects their desire to be their own person. There is a distance between the locals and the incomers. There is to some extent a pride in being a member of the 'blow-in' community. The fact that they 'know they are outsiders' as well as seeing themselves as 'internationalists' or 'citizens-of-the-world' illustrates that they are somehow apart. To quote one incomer, 'all foreigners are uncommon in their own culture—otherwise they wouldn't be here'. Another incomer said that 'I feel an outsider, I always am, this is my choice, this would be wherever I'd go, it is somehow a special realm'. It is questionable to what extent such statements are justifications to themselves, and if the incomers would rather be more integrated.

Lewis (1979) states that 'failure by a community to adjust fully to change can cause considerable problems of conflict and adjustment for the individual concerned'. On the whole, West Cork's role is largely passive in so far as the region has had to cope with in-migration for centuries (due both to work and invasion), and accommodates or tolerates the incomers without much resistance. Resistance occurs due to fear or suspicion or if the incomers are perceived as a threat. Sometimes anger is provoked if incomers intervene in, for example, environmental issues. On the whole, incomers readily adapt to their new socio-cultural environment and, if necessary, learn from experience (or the experience of others). Most of them have learnt not to push their ideas or values, and they do not set up business in opposition to the locals.

The main integrative forces for the incomers are work and family. Work provides direct contact with the locals, and in offering a service or commodity, the incomers are useful and therefore more accepted. Pregnancy and babies also afford common ground for conversation, and school opens up a new social arena for parents. Similarly, schooling is seen as an integrative medium by Kritzinger (1989). Clubs and committees, though requiring a more conscious effort, are also integrative agencies. Much activity revolves around committees in West Cork, but only just over one-third of incomers have ever been on a school committee. Clubs are a paradoxical issue. The incomers wish to mix with the indigenous population but ironically the clubs they join (or form) have only (if any) a minority local participation despite active encouragement by the incomers. Yet the indigenous population feel aggrieved that there are 'no locals in the local film club'. 'The social life in West Cork centres on sport' is the observation of one incomer, yet his participation is merely that of spectator if his children are involved. This is generally the case amongst the incomers.

Religion may be argued as a disintegrative force, 83% of the respondents being non-church goers. This percentage could probably be reversed for the indigenous population. Many of the incomers are confused and at a loss with regards to Catholicism; and, more practicably, 'news travels at church' both in announcements by the priest and in talking with people after church. The locals seek advice on issues from the incomers, believing that they will neither be shocked nor judgemental. West Cork provides mental freedom for the incomers but not for the locals who are 'hemmed in by the priest and mother'. Irish culture is very much focused on religion— stations, weddings and funerals being just three examples. Religion is linked closely with family, and what is untouched in rural Irish culture by religion or family is very minor. This puts the incomers in a very peripheral position.

On the basis of the findings reported in this section, 'another' culture may be argued to exist in West Cork. However, neither the locals nor the incomers readily acknowledge this, and, on the whole, the incomers do not wish to be considered as such. Furthermore, no real tensions exist between these two 'cultures'. It may even be tentatively argued that a new culture is emerging in West Cork as the area is opened up to new influences. On the other hand, there are symbolic boundaries (Cohen 1985) between the cultures. 'Cultural differences can persist despite inter-ethnic contact and interdependence' (Barth 1969). Some of the incomers have taken out Irish citizenship, but is 'Irishness' brought about by becoming an Irish citizen, is Irish culture epitomised by attending Davie Spillane concerts, or is Irishness supporting Ireland in the World Cup? Perhaps it is something more subtle: for one incomer, supporting Ireland in the World Cup was not so much nationalistic as being able to identify with the team members.

ECONOMIC ACTIVITY AND IMPACT

This final section of the essay is concerned with how the incomers make a living in West Cork and also considers some of the effects they have on the region. They are extremely entrepreneurial and self-reliant, and the many positive effects of this are evident in the community.

Initially, many of the incomers aimed at varying degrees of self-sufficiency. For those wishing to be entirely self-sufficient, anything that could not be home produced would be acquired by an exchange or barter system with neighbours. However, despite John Seymour's *Complete Book of Self-Sufficiency* (1976), the ideals were quickly recognised as being very impracticable. A few grow their own vegetables now but that is the extent of their self-sufficiency.

Notwithstanding the failure, by and large, of attempts at self-sufficiency, the incomers are highly self-motivated and have quite considerable entrepreneurial and innovative abilities, which provide them with employment. It is arguable that their high level of education is reflected in this (*cf.* Kockel 1989). The incomers make their living on activities predominantly based on craft and artisan industries. These activities range from the production of organic vegetables and produce, for sale in their own cafes; to producing stained glass, pipes or paintings, to fishing and publishing. Similarly, Kockel (1989) found 'their activities range from painting to breadmaking'.

The immigrants' economic activities centre on the 'informal economy'. The 'informal economy' here is more anthropological in meaning than its usual economic understanding which has some negative connotations. Kockel (1989) uses the term anthropo-logically, to include non-monetised exchange or bartering of goods, occupational pluralism, lack of commercialisation and market orientation, and primary goals other than utility or profit.

This is concordant with the understanding of this essay. However, a 'lack of commercialisation and market orientation' was rarely found in this case, as the incomers have considerable export-based markets as well as trying to increase their share of the home market. Informal economy is understood further as being different to the 'regular' or 'normal' economy of rural West Cork, which has its basis predominantly in farming.

Over 55% of known immigrant households are dependent on two or more incomes. With the exception of one, Kockel (1989) found this to be the case in all households in Dingle, and Kritzinger (1989) records pluriactivity in one-third of cases in a German settlement in the Pyrenees. Although Kockel (1989) also found that 'a substantial proportion of these immigrants are claiming "dole"', this is evidently not the case in the present study. Claiming dole goes against the ethics or principles of the incomers. One is 'not free of the system on the dole'. The 'system' is contrary to their concept of freedom and of space. If necessary, the dole is used, in the short term, as a stepping-stone. Further reasons supporting the contention that their incomes are rarely supplemented by the dole are as follows: they live within their means, carrying out their own house maintenance and refurbishing; cash outlays for businesses are grant aided, including IDA grants; in many cases they live in multi-income households with both partners working; they work very hard to make a living; and, their primary goals are often other than utility or profit, as they seek a less materialistic way of living. With the exception, perhaps, of those now retired, private incomes are unlikely. Savings are negligible, and whatever savings they brought with them have gone on purchasing a house. From observing their livelihoods, there is nothing to suggest they are being supported from home. In short, any such dependency would detract from their sense of space.

Even though the incomers contribute very positively in many respects to West Cork, there is in general a feeling of indifference towards them by the locals. According to one local respondent, 'the thirty or forty age group bring something to the area'; they are 'good for business'. Apart from a few such comments, the locals do not feel they need the incomers. At present, the major criticisms towards or about them concern rising property prices, to levels unaffordable to the indigenous population. This is largely attributable to second home owners and also relates to more recent phases of richer incomers who can afford to buy their 'idyllic retreat'. It is interesting to note, however, that the locals quite willingly sell property in order to make high returns.

In a region of high unemployment and emigration perhaps the incomers' greatest effect is that of creating employment. Thirty full-time Irish jobs, and at least five or six part-time ones, have been created by the incomers. What is probably just as significant is that they do not take the jobs of the locals. They generate additional income for West Cork and believe that money earned in the area should be spent in the area.

Some 90% of the incomers are entirely dependent on the local town for shopping requirements. Interestingly, they are very intolerant of second home owners who bring nothing to the region and mar the landscape with bungalows lived in for only a few months of the year.

The incomers are very concerned to protect the environment which is beautiful and relatively unspoilt, but delicate. They have learnt not to push their ideas but are very willing to give their advice and help when asked. They are

> one of the culturally and environmentally most conservative groups, because they have a dream to preserve; on the other hand they create subtle changes by trying to adapt their new environment to their personal values and ideas (Kockel 1989).

Their greatest method and greatest subtlety is by living an example. More active methods of bringing about environmental awareness include being involved in Earthwatch, hosting (with locals) a Green Environmental Weekend in Skibbereen in October, organising protests (with local participation if possible) and by writing articles to newspapers, magazines or journals.

They also propose ideas of, for example, eco-tourism, based on their overseas trading links and connections. A 'co-operative' philosophy is practised by at least one company in which they share and distribute business. This is based on a recognition of the need for top quality small diversified industry. The idea is right with regards to diversification, but where I observe the 'co-operative philosophy' to be failing is that the business being shared is not diversified enough. This is creating a dependency amongst the smaller companies. The incomers are also very involved in the West Cork Business Centre; and the West Cork Arts Centre was founded and is run by incomers. They have also established film clubs throughout the region.

There are two further significant ways in which the immigrants are of benefit to West Cork. The first is that they rejuvenate the demography of the region both in actual incoming numbers and being repopulative; and the incomers themselves are mostly young. The second effect is the quality and variety of goods which are available in supermarkets and shops. To quote again from Kockel (1989) 'the immigrants act as catalysts for innovations'. Diversity of products and hygiene at local retailers are comparable to any in the city.

Improvements in telecommunications and transport infrastructure have opened up West Cork to change. Penetration of outside beliefs and attitudes has rapidly increased over the last twenty years, and especially the last decade. This, coupled with immigration, while having many positive repercussions, has also had negative effects, leading to a 'breaking-down of society'.

On the whole, however, new life is being breathed into the community. Through the immigrants' fresh perceptions of the environment, new ways of making a living, new values, and creativity are constantly being introduced.

CONCLUSION

Dreams and perceptions of a place are often different in reality. All those interviewed, however, with only one exception, have achieved or fulfilled their dreams, albeit perhaps differently to how they thought they would. For the incomers it is often difficult to make ends meet, and there are many adaptations to be made, not least the change from being an employee to becoming self-employed. Value changes and cultural adaptations can be considerable.

There is, overall, a comfortable accord between the indigenous population and the incomers. They have 'brought something to West Cork', helping to counterbalance the outmigration of the indigenous youth and create employment. They take care to protect the environment and perhaps even more importantly help to create an awareness of it. Most of the incomers have no intention of ever moving from West Cork.

> West Cork is a land of mobile boundaries, a place whose location and character curves and shifts, depending not only on the weather, but on the different lenses and assumptions that we bring to bear on it (Smyth 1989).

The 'symbolic boundaries' (Cohen 1985) between the two groups are important in establishing where differences merge or at what level interaction occurs. Incomers are innovative and 'alternative' to the indigenous population of the area. There is a ready tolerance of foreigners in West Cork and the area has long been accommodating to incomers, yet the old indigenous 'institutions' of religion and family (for example) remain strong.

BIBLIOGRAPHY

Barth, F (ed.)
1969 *Ethnic Groups and Boundaries. The Social Organisation of Culture Differences*, London.

Cawley, M
1980 Aspects of Rural/Urban Integration in the West of Ireland, *Irish Geography* 13, 20-32.

Cloke, P
1985 Counterurbanisation: A Rural Perspective, *Geography* 70, 13-23.

Cohen, A
1985 *The Symbolic Construction of Community*, Chichester.

Curtin, C
1988 *A Geography of Beliefs in a West Limerick Rural Parish: Tournafulla/Mount Collins*, unpublished PhD-thesis, Department of Geography, University College Cork.

Dean, K
1984 The Conceptualisation of Counterurbanisation, *Area* 16(1), 9-14.

Dixon, G and Leach, B
1978 *Questionnaires and Interviews in Geographical Research.* CATMOG 18.

Horner, A and McDermott, P
1978 Aspects of Rural Renewal in Western Connemara, *Irish Geography* 11, 176-9.

Jackson, A (ed.)
1978 *Anthropology at Home*, London.

Jackson, J
1986 *Migration*, London.

Jackson, P
1983 Principles and Problems of Participant Observation, *Geografiska Annaler* 65B, 39-46.

Kockel, U
1989 Immigrants—Entrepreneurs of the Future? *Common Ground* 70, 6-8.
1991 Countercultural Migration in the West of Ireland. In King, R (ed.), *Contemporary Irish Migration*, Dublin, 70-82.

Kritzinger, S
1989 Un Exemple d'Immigration d'Alternatifs Allemands dans les
      Pyrénées Ariegeoises, *Revue Geographique des Pyrénées et
      du Sud-Ouest* 60(2), 199-222.

Lewis, G
1979 *Rural Communities*, London.
1982 *Human Migration: A Geographical Perspective*, London.

McGrath, F
1991 The Economic, Social and Cultural Impacts of Return
      Migration to Achill Island. In King, R (ed.), *Contemporary
      Irish Migration*, Dublin, 55-69.

Miller, R
1985 *Emigrants and Exiles—Ireland and the Irish Exodus to
      North America*, Oxford.

Ogden, P
1985 Counterurbanisation in France: The Results of the 1982
      Population Census, *Geography* 70, 24-35.

Oppenheim, A
1968 *Questionnaire Design and Attitude Measurement*, London.

Pacione, M
1983 *Progress in Rural Geography*, London.
1986 *Population Geography: Progress and Prospect*, London.

Perry, R and Dean, K (eds)
1986 *Counterurbanisation: International Case Studies of Socio-
      Economic Change in the Rural Areas*, Norwich.

Seymour, J
1976 *The Complete Book of Self-Sufficiency*, London.

Smyth, W
1989 The Personality of West Cork—Part I, *Chimera* 4, 93-100.

Somerville-Large, P
1985 *Cappaghglass*, London.
1991 *The Coast of West Cork*, Belfast.

Yin, R
1984 *Case Study Research: Design and Methods*, London.

German Immigrants in Ireland
A Pilot Survey

KARIN MOLDE

INTRODUCTION

Merely remembering the last holiday in Ireland and reviving pictures of the 'Emerald Isle' makes some Germans feel over the moon. Reminiscing, they drink a pint of Guinness in one of the numerous Irish pubs mushrooming all over Germany, and ecstatically jiggle their feet to the sound of the jigs and reels coming from the loudspeakers.

Ireland is a great attraction for Germans. A holiday might have been their first contact, followed by more regular visits or study courses. Census evidence shows that since Ireland joined the EC in 1973, the number of tourists as well as immigrants from Europe, and in particular from Germany, has been growing constantly. Research has always emphasised the extent of emigration from Ireland and the problems of a disadvantaged area on the fringes of Europe. Little work has been done to-date on immigration to the island. In this pilot survey, I have concentrated on German immigrants who make up a considerable proportion of the immigrant population in the Republic of Ireland.

What are the motivations for Germans to leave their highly industrialised home country? What are their hopes and aspirations?

Ullrich Kockel (ed.), *Landscape, Heritage and Identity: Case Studies in Irish Ethnography*, Liverpool University Press 1995, 197-221.

Migration research has mostly focused on economically motivated emigrants and their problems of acculturation and assimilation within the host society. I would like to concentrate on aspects of these processes with special reference to Germans who have come to Ireland looking for improvements other than necessarily in their financial situation. In times of growing violence against foreigners in Germany, I consider it important to look at Germans trying to establish themselves in a foreign country.

In this essay, I examine the extent to which German immigrants in Ireland adopt Irish lifestyles, traditions and manners, and how far they preserve their own cultural heritage in a foreign environment.

ACCULTURATION OR ASSIMILATION?

In the literature on migration, terms like integration, assimilation, adaptation, or acculturation, are often used synonymously, or at least without clear terminological distinction. For the present purpose, these terms are used as follows.

'Integration' describes the merging of different parts into a unity, in which each part, in this case the minorities and the host society, can keep their individual cultural identity. It is questionable, however, to what extent individual elements of a larger society can stay truly independent. The term 'integration', therefore, also emphasises the need to integrate, and the institutional support available to this end (Hoerder 1988).

'Assimilation' refers to a merging into the host society without reservations. The original culture is left behind, so that finally there are no noticeable differences between host society and minority (Gordon 1964).

'Adaptation' is used in the sense of fitting into the new society and bringing behaviour and moral code into line with it (Goldlust and Richmond 1990).

Finally, 'acculturation' includes traditions, morals and behavioural patterns from the original culture, the willingness to change, and the new culture with its incentives and hindrances (Hoerder 1988). Thus the intracultural socialisation which the migrants had experienced in their own culture will influence their perspective on the new culture, as well as their behaviour within that society.

The intended duration of the migration determines the motivation to understand the new culture and to acculturate. According to Hoerder (1988), only intended permanent immigration suggests a strong inclination towards acculturation. Compared to assimilation, acculturation does not imply a loss of the old culture, but the taking over of elements of the new culture and new behavioural patterns, whereas the sense of belonging to the original culture can still be maintained.

THE SURVEY

The objective of this study was to seek an understanding of complex correlations and explain their inner structures, rather than to reduce and simplify given data. Therefore, purely quantitative methods did not seem adequate. The main method used was the 'problem-centred interview' (Lamnek 1993). It combines qualitative characteristics with a loose structure and objective, so that phases of free narrative and goal-orientated questions alternate.

To take a statistically representative sample was not possible as the exact size of the German population in Ireland is not known. No system of residential registration, comparable to that in Germany, exists. The figures recorded in the census appear far too low, because many migrants do not register. The German Embassy and the Irish-German Chamber of Commerce estimate the number of more or less permanent German residents to be between 10-15,000.

For this pilot survey, I interviewed thirty-one German immigrants of the first generation. In selecting my interviewees, I tried to include a wide spectrum of socio-economic backgrounds as well as migration motives, and to divide the group as evenly as possible in terms of residence (urban/rural) and gender.

General Profile of Interviewees

At the time of immigration all but one of the interviewees were of German nationality. Only two have since become Irish citizens. One, a man, choose to do so because the Irish pay a lower price than foreigners for land in their own country. He also felt emotionally attached to his new home, where his children, who are Irish, were born. However, he was not sure whether he would have considered a change of nationality if there had not been a practical reason. The female interviewee felt emotionally more attached to Ireland than to Germany, so that for her the change of citizenship was a logical consequence.

Seventeen of the interviewees explicitly discussed changing citizenship. One woman married to an Irish partner kept both German and Irish passports, although a double nationality is rejected by the German state because of legal uncertainties. Three other women were considering a change of nationality. An emotional attachment to Ireland was important in this context, as was the rejection of political developments in Germany, especially the growing racism. Thirteen interviewees would not change their citizenship. Four of these wanted to return to Germany, whereas all the others did not consider it necessary in the face of a developing European Union.

Twelve interviewees did not explicitly mention a possible change of nationality. Half of these probably did not consider this step at all, due to their experience of isolation within the local community, or their own uncertainty about returning to Germany (see below). Two people have been living in Ireland only since 1990 and 1992, respectively, and it would probably be too early for them to think about it.

Not all of the migrants are clearly informed which elections they are entitled to vote in. To be allowed a vote only in community elections and elections for the European Parliament does not seem to be a problem for most of them.

The interviewees came to Ireland between 1953 and 1992. The majority moved in the 1970s and 1980s (Figure 12).

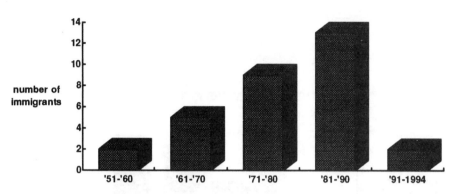

YEAR OF IMMIGRATION

Figure 12   *Interviewed immigrants by year of migration*

The age at the time of migration ranges from 19 to 53 years; the majority having emigrated between 21 and 30 years (Figure 13).

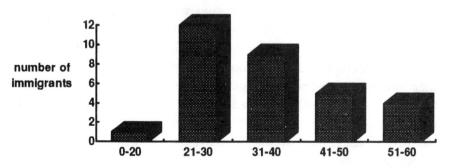

AGE OF THE INTERVIEWEES AT TIME OF IMMIGRATION

Figure 13   *Age of interviewees at time of migration*

Corresponding with year and age of migration, at the time of the survey those questioned were between thirty and seventy-nine years old, the majority being between forty and sixty years (Figure 14).

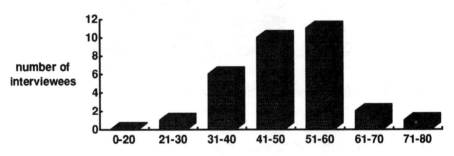

AGE OF THE INTERVIEWEES AT TIME OF SURVEY

Figure 14   *Age of interviewees at time of the survey*

Nearly half of the immigrants (fourteen) were already married to or lived in a stable relationship with a German partner in Germany and migrated as a couple. Four of these relationships came to an end in Ireland; three of the individuals involved started a new partnership (one with an English partner and two with other Germans, whom they had met in Ireland). Seven of the German women married, or lived with, an Irish partner, two couples having already lived together in Germany and one couple in the United States. For the other four interviewees, marriage was the reason for the migration. One of these relationships ended and the interviewee still lives on her own in Ireland. In one case, the woman met her German partner, who had already been living in the island, during a holiday and decided to move.

Noticeable is the relatively large proportion of immigrants with an academic qualification. Only nine out of the thirty-one questioned trained for a technical job or gained a qualification in commerce. Looking at migrants' occupations, only nine of them had a full-time position. Of these, four were involved in teaching German, two men were working as managing directors of German companies, another male interviewee was a psychologist, and one couple was working for the Lutheran community in Dublin.

Five interviewees, mostly women, were self-employed: one was running a restaurant, one organising exchanges for pupils between Germany and Ireland, and another one had a toy-shop. A couple had started a hostel with restaurant. Two of the self-employed did supplementary work for financial support.

Six of the immigrants—including two of the couples—who were working a farm added that they also did a range of other jobs, like teaching German or painting, translations, the renting of a holiday home, or running a hardware shop.

A large number of people (eleven out of thirty-one) were quite obviously occupied with different jobs, including seasonal work and casual labour. Only two of the interviewees had already worked on the same basis in Germany. Again, teaching German provided a major source of income. Other examples were the production and sale of bread, cheese and vegetables; cleaning or sales jobs; writing articles or columns for local newspapers; photography; electrical and repair work; painting jobs; or social work. All migrants had to rely on more than one income source, and these sources were all relatively irregular. Only two of the interviewees claimed the 'dole'. In a society with a high rate of unemployment, this sort of informal labour is likely to increase. Moreover, many immigrants hoped to escape a rigidly organised routine in Germany, preferring the loose structure of informal labour (*cf.* Kockel 1993).

Motivation

The aspirations people have can influence the acculturation process, because they determine attitudes towards and behaviour in the new society. The predominant feelings and attitudes the immigrants have towards Germany may determine the feelings and attitudes they will have towards Ireland.

Gender-specific differences in the motivations could be noticed. For women, partnership and/or marriage was the most frequently given reason for migration. In second place came the wish to leave Germany (for political and/or personal reasons) as well as the desire to live in a relatively unspoilt environment without industrial activities, nuclear plants or pollution.

For men, partnership was (with one exception) irrelevant. Instead, ecological reasons were the first motive, followed by a desire to organise their work more independently, freely and creatively. A third reason for migration was, comparable to that of the females, the rejection of Germany.

Indirectly, another motive could well have played a part in the decision to migrate. Three males and three females had suffered a separation before leaving Germany. Such a turning point can, as four of the interviewees mentioned explicitly, give the impulse for either realising ideas that were hitherto kept silent, or open the way for a new start in another country.

Economic considerations did not influence the migration decision, so that the financial situation of the interviewees in Germany can be ignored as a motive in the present study. The hope for a financially more secure life was not connected with the migration; in fact, the opposite appeared to be the case (see below).

For seven immigrants, Ireland was not the only country they had considered for a new home. But after they had received information about different places, they chose Ireland, either because it came closest to their aspirations, or because unexpected professional or private opportunities arose. Most of the interviewees (nineteen out of thirty-one) had come to know Ireland through various holidays or study visits, and thus their decision could develop over a period of time. Some of the migrants met their future partner on these occasions, and often private contacts did exist before immigration. Half of the immigrants (sixteen out of thirty-one) came to Ireland hoping to stay forever; twelve of these were living with a partner. For seven people, the question of how long the would stay in Ireland was left open. Another five interviewees wanted to stay for between one and five years, two until retirement. One person did not want to stay at all.

At the time of the interviews, only four people knew that they would return to Germany, including those who wanted to stay until retirement or not at all, whereas two interviewees were unsure whether they would return or not. For the majority, however, Ireland—planned or unplanned—had become the permanent home, which they did not want to leave (twenty-five out of thirty-one).

Language, Customs and Traditions

The first point of contact with a foreign culture is language. Although Irish is officially the first language in Ireland, in practice English is necessary for daily communication. Language acquisition is the first step in the acculturation process, and this was achieved by most of those questioned without major problems. With a broad, basic knowledge of English, acquired at school and/or university as well as through professional or further education, they all felt relatively fluent at the time of immigration. Misunderstandings, due to the Irish accent or the idiomatic particularities of Hiberno-English—which is influenced in its grammatical forms and phrasals by the Irish language—could soon be overcome.

A lack of language knowledge was neither a reason for missing social contacts nor a barrier for entering work situations. On the other hand, a lack of social involvement and a withdrawal from social life into a private sphere can hinder the development of language competence, and thus prove an obstacle to subsequent steps in the acculturation process; this appeared to have happened in three cases.

With regard to the language spoken at home, English, German and bilingualism (English and German) are found in roughly equal proportions. If the partner is German, the language spoken at home will also be German, but where the partner is Irish, either both will speak only English, or the German person will talk German to the children. In only one case had the Irish partner learned German and used it as much as English in conversation with his partner.

Even where English was the language of the home, a loss of German did not occur among the immigrants. The only problem mentioned was the development of 'diglossia'—a mixture of German and English which the migrants would often speak with other Germans: English words, which are declined the German way, would be dropped into an otherwise German text. This phenomenon was described by the migrants as a result of idleness and lack of concentration, rather than any actual loss of language competence.

The knowledge of Irish should not be overrated as a measure of the degree of acculturation, as it has become largely irrelevant for daily communication, although it is still required for entry to certain positions, for example in the civil service. At the same time, an interest in Irish is part of an expression of interest in Irish culture and history in general. About one-third of the male and two-thirds of the female interviewees showed great interest in Irish. Literature and culture were the focal points, whereas communication in the language played only a minor role. One-third of the females had at some stage attended classes to learn Irish, but a self-confessed lack of discipline had made most of them stop again. The immigrants found it rather disappointing rarely to have a chance to practise the language.

On a different level than that of practical competence, language is often described as being an important part of the original culture and identity. English might be spoken fluently, and might even be 'automatised' and, to a certain degree, internalised. One woman, who had been living in Ireland for twenty-four years, explained that emotional matters, being close to her heart, could be expressed more easily in English. Another woman, who composed poetry in English, described a similar feeling, regarding English as corresponding with the contemporary focal point of her life in Ireland. This did not result in a loss of German, however, and the adoption of English can therefore be considered as adaptation to the English-speaking environment.

Although the interviewees overcame practical language problems very easily, on a different level language can be the topic of discussion as well as an expression of cultural identity and identification. Significantly, the interviewees considering the German language as part of their identity always combined this belief with an interest in Irish language, which then was seen as a possibility to get an insight into Irish culture.

Another measure for the degree of acculturation is the adoption of new customs and traditions. To what extent are old traditions kept in the new culture, and to what extent are they left behind or mixed with elements of the new culture?

Planning, preparing and celebrating festivities plays a big role in active community life, and therefore can be a connecting link between people of different cultures. Christmas as a traditional family and religious feast is important both in Germany and Ireland. Ten out of thirteen women, as well as the four couples, kept the German tradition of Christmas Eve and combined it with the Irish Christmas Day. Advent does not play a big role in Irish life, but German customs like the advent's wreath are kept by ten females, the four couples, and two of the men.

Four out of ten male interviewees would usually spend Christmas in Germany. Another three said they ignored the festivities. Two of the males rejected a combination of German and Irish traditions. In one case the Irish wife did not like a mixing of customs, and her husband did not wish to impose on her. Another interviewee felt so rooted in German culture that he could not imagine adopting foreign traditions.

At Easter, eight of the women, three of the couples, and two of the men would still have an Easter tree (a few branches decorated with painted eggs), and for children Easter eggs would be hidden in the garden.

It is obvious that women in particular keep old German traditions, even if they combine them with Irish ones. This seems to be a result of the traditional role division, which leaves the woman to the domestic work like preparing feasts and food or decorating rooms. Hence she is able to assert her influence and keep the traditions she thinks important.

As music plays an important role in Irish everyday life, I wanted to know whether the immigrants appreciate traditional Irish music and take part in this aspect of cultural life. About half of the men and women liked Irish music and went to musical events. For three of the interviewees, Irish music was part of the attraction when they chose Ireland as their destination. The spontaneous and lively atmosphere that is created by music in Irish pubs was very popular among the interviewees.

Another major part of Irish culture is religion. As the influence of the Catholic Church on Irish politics is still considered relatively strong, half of the women but only one man openly rejected the institution of the Church. At the same time, they emphasised that they did not feel any negative influence on their personal daily life, neither by the institution nor by the Irish members of their local community. The tolerance of the Irish concerning religion and privacy was strongly admired by the migrants. They mentioned that they never felt under any pressure in creating their own lifestyle. Nevertheless, at a more abstract level, both men and women were critical of the influence of the Catholic Church on education, family and women's issues, and would hold the Church responsible for conservative and repressive tendencies in the state.

Although many of the women rejected the Catholic Church, they would often take part in social events organised by the local parish as part of religious as well as general social life. One-third of the women occasionally took part in a religious service, although not necessarily a Catholic one. Another third would take part in the organisation of the annual Christmas Sale which is run by the German school and the Lutheran Church in Dublin. Participation in a church choir was another example for women's involvement in the religious life of their community.

Funerals and wakes are major social events in the more rural areas; three of the male and three of the female migrants regularly took part in these. Furthermore, two of the women were actively involved in the 'stations'—religious services organised in the private home of one of the community members.

As religious discussions are held publicly and intensely due to, or indeed in spite of the accelerating secularisation process, three of the migrants said that religious questions had gained more relevance in their lives since they moved to Ireland. They felt that this was an enrichment and an extra facet of their spiritual search.

Again, the migrants emphasised that nobody felt under pressure to conform, but participation was seen as an expression of good neighbourly feelings and a sense of community.

With regard to the religious life of German immigrants in Ireland, one fact seems interesting. Women appear much more consistent in openly rejecting the institutional church and hierarchy. They are, of course, more directly confronted with women's or family issues like abortion or divorce, and they are conscious of the fact that they live in a society in which traditional role divisions are barely beginning to break up. Perhaps this is why the German Lutheran Church is so popular. It is often described as being ecumenical and progressive, and also seems to be a place for meeting other German immigrants. One of the social functions of the German Lutheran Church is the strengthening of a sense of belonging among the immigrants and the identification with their original culture. The pastor organises services in different parts of Ireland, which were mentioned by two of the immigrants living on the west coast.

The great tolerance of the Irish people concerning religious life and, equally important, the respect for individuality in general, are admired and rated highly by the migrants. On the other hand, one should not ignore a fact that might also play a significant role in shaping this perception of the host society. Germans, like other immigrants or 'blow-ins' from other parts of Ireland, have a peripheral position within their local community. This gives them greater freedom than members of the native society, who have been integrated for generations. Some interviewees called this a 'fool's freedom', allowing them to avoid the more constricting traditions.

That it is still possible for 'blow-ins' to participate in local social rituals is proved by migrants' participation in wakes and stations. This requires a high degree of cultural adaptation from both the immigrants, and members of the indigenous community, who allow a stranger to gain an insight and partake in very intimate spheres.

Social Networks

An important measure of acculturation is integration into the social networks of the host society. As a first factor determining access to social networks, geographical segregation can be an expression of separation along ethnic lines, or it can show social class differences. Accordingly, the residential area and the living conditions can be a measure for the acculturation process.

None of the interviewees live in a 'German' environment. The number of immigrants is too small to create ghettos, although there are areas that attract a relatively higher number of Germans than others, such as the counties of Dublin, Cork and Kerry.

Owner-occupancy is far more common in Ireland than in most other European countries, and among the immigrants, too, the number who owned their home was found to be considerably higher than the number of people renting accommodation (twenty-five, compared to three). One of the couples was living in a house provided by the Lutheran community in Dublin, and all interviewees living in Dublin resided south of the river Liffey, which is the more privileged area of the city.

In the following discussion of social networks, I want to make a distinction* between a circle of 'acquaintances' and a group of closer 'friends'. 'Acquaintances' were described as a group of mixed nationalities in which the Irish were in the majority, or as a German-Irish circle where other nationalities were missing.

Friendships are much more difficult to create. Although five of the eight females living in cities had German and Irish friends, other nationalities were rarely mentioned. Women living in rural areas had exclusively Irish friends. Significantly, a relatively high proportion of immigrants—more than one-third—were without closer personal contacts. Although this was not always explicitly stated, it became readily apparent from the interviews.

The men appeared to be even slower in making friends than the women. Only four out of ten had friends, and these friends were, with one exception, Irish. Of the four couples, only one had friendship contacts outside the immediate family ties.

That women find it easier to make friends is not all that unusual (*cf.* Miller 1986; Valtin and Fatke 1988). Private circles and mutual aid groups, as well as community events like a wake, tend to foster more intimate contacts and demand a high degree of openness. The men's favourite place for socialising, the pub, often only allows informal acquaintances and superficial conversations, the result being a smaller number of more intimate friends.

Both men and women, including those who had made no friends in Ireland, maintained contact with friends in Germany. This is a

---

* Editor's note:
The distinction is an important one in German culture. An 'acquaintance' is merely anybody one happens to know; 'friend' designates someone with whom one has a close relationship involving trust and loyalty, unlike in English, where the label is used more indiscriminately. Germans can get rather annoyed when somebody they barely know, and perhaps even strongly dislike, is described by an English-speaker as their 'friend'.

211

sign of the relevance of emotional support that is still sought —often even after many years—from that source.

Social life in Ireland mostly takes place in public places, and for this reason is often described as being non-committal. To a certain degree, the interviewees found this vitalising and refreshing, but at the same time the difficulty in making friends was frequently highlighted. This form of social life might have its explanation in still fairly rigidly structured family ties. The Irish (extended) family still offers support and security, and there is little need to fulfil these emotional needs outside the family. In Germany, a strong culture of friendship could develop in most parts of society, which might be a compensation and substitute for much looser family bonds.

The observations concerning the formation of friendship ties do not suggest that the migrants' own nationality is of any real relevance for the choice of their friends. Shared interests and harmonising life expectations seem much more important. Hence the number of German friends identified by the interviewees is roughly the same as the number of Irish friends.

Secondary social contacts can be described by the activities in which the interviewees participate. A great variety were named, including visiting pubs and cultural events, informal neighbourhood contacts and mutual aid groups or groups sharing a certain interest—such as literature circles, meditation groups, or groups of young mothers—as well as political initiatives. Private circles were initiated more often by women than by men, whereas the men tended to go to pubs more often than the women.

Naturally, differences in social life could be noticed with people living in cities, compared to those in the country. In the rural areas, contacts with the neighbourhood played a much bigger role, while city people tended to prefer cultural events, or participation in political initiatives. Private circles and dinner-parties also seemed to be more popular among city people. Clubs requiring commitment to regular participation were quite unpopular in general, although men showed a slightly stronger interest.

Facilities in the city, the variety of cultural events and a better public transport system offer an infrastructure that makes a certain form of social life possible. In the country, neighbourly contacts and events organised by the community or the church are usually more important, and often provide the only opportunity for social contact. Seven of the thirty-one migrants interviewed, mostly from the city, took part in political initiatives, preferably in the area of women's or environmental issues. To be thus politically involved was a form of identification with Ireland, and gave a high motivation to play an active part in society.

One man and one woman, who live alone in rural areas, withdrew from social life. They were keeping contact neither with German nor with Irish people, so that the only communication taking place was on a very informal and irregular level with neighbours. One of them being unemployed and the other retired, they also had no contact with colleagues.

Furthermore, one married interviewee and two of the couples led very secluded and withdrawn lives. The only contacts, other than with family members, were in one case with neighbours, and in another with a private meditation group. These migrants would rarely go to the pub. Both couples seemed to be fully occupied with their working life, running a hostel with restaurant and a farm. In all three cases, this withdrawal was a conscious decision and does not, therefore, necessarily suggest a lack of adaptation to Irish life. However, the identification with their German origin was particularly strong in these cases.

Contentment and Identification with Ireland

The contentment of immigrants with their lives is first and foremost influenced by the fulfilment of the hopes attached to migration; secondly, by the official migration policies of the immigration country; and thirdly, by prevailing stereotypes, which could be expressed through prejudice and discrimination. For migration within member states of the European Union, there are no legal obstacles, so that this aspect does not need to be considered here.

With one exception, none of the interviewees felt that they had experienced discrimination in Ireland. The stereotypical image of 'the German' has usually two different components. One consists of the militaristic Prussian, and the Nazi. The immigrants find it disturbing that some Irish people express a kind of admiration for Hitler, a phenomenon that can be understood as a consequence of Ireland's long colonial history, the historical focus of which has always been England. Thus whoever was an 'enemy of England' was supported simply for being just that. At school, the children of migrants were often confronted with prejudices like this. However, a third of the interviewees did not regard this as a serious matter, describing it as rather unreflected and insensitive.

The second stereotype of 'the German' involves different virtues connected with work: discipline, diligence, punctuality, cleanliness, order and ambition as well as technical know-how and a talent for organisation. A positive consequence of a German work ethic would be the creation of jobs in Ireland by German companies. While this stereotype is mostly positive, a certain ambivalence can be felt. It is a mixture of admiration and, at the same time, mockery.

Explicitly negative prejudices are rarely mentioned. The German is regarded as lacking a sense of humour; he likes to lecture about things he believes he knows; and he tends to take over, or at least dominate, organisations. Generally speaking, such prejudices did not create any discrimination.

The immigrants did not always have explicit aims when moving to Ireland. Furthermore, most of the interviewees were well established in Ireland at the time of the research, so that their motivations of long ago were forgotten, and things were taken for granted as they were. The conditions determining everyday life had become more relevant, and the degree of migrants' identification with Ireland can therefore be used as a measure for contentment.

All except two of the personal relationships which motivated a move to Ireland have lasted. People seeking a more creative work-life have found this—as managing director of a German company, by being self-employed, or by working their farm. Being relatively free, both professionally and individually, is appreciated very much.

Being close to nature and its rhythms was a migration motive for one-third of the interviewees, and remains an important aspect of their daily lives.

Only six out of thirteen women, and two of the couples, explicitly talked about their contentment. They expressed a sense of 'home', built around family and friends, the Irish mentality, landscape and cultural life. For one woman, the reason for her contentment seemed to be the sense of distance from Germany. While still in Germany, she had lived there in anger and aggression against contemporary political developments, whereas her feelings at the time when she was interviewed were more optimistic. It is important to note that she was no longer politically involved in any movement, as she had been in Germany.

Emotional loyalty towards, and identification with Ireland among the migrants reveals a high degree of acculturation. The immigrants all seem to identify with Irish popular culture and daily life to a high degree.

Two-thirds of the immigrants admired the Irish for their humanity (*Menschlichkeit*), and virtues such as friendliness, warm-heartedness, helpfulness, understanding, tolerance, and a sense of tact were rated highly. About half of the interviewees praised the easy-going lifestyle. Half of the men, a third of the women, and three of the four couples remarked that they felt a greater sense of responsibility and initiative. This has to be seen in connection with the high motivation of the men in particular to shape their work-life more independently, and the fact that the couples need a high degree of initiative of their own to run a hostel or a farm.

It was interesting to see that some men favoured a certain degree of casualness; this corresponds with the informal contacts they have instead of committed friendships (see above).

With regard to the migrants' view of the host society, negative images did not seem very relevant. Stereotypical characteristics of the Irish, like unreliability, unpunctuality, and difficulty in creating closer contacts, had to be disregarded in the context of everyday life and were easily forgotten in comparison to very cordial neighbourly co-operation.

All the above statements describe Irish everyday life: relationships, the organisation of work, and private life. Only very few migrants mentioned things they liked about Irish public life, especially the perceived lack of bureaucracy, and the absence of any strong class consciousness. On the other hand, half of the men and a third of the women noted the lack of environmental awareness in Ireland, and more than a third of the female migrants criticised women's and family politics.

Most of the interviewees seemed to identify to a high degree with Irish everyday life and the humane manners of the Irish. Friendly and cordial contacts on an informal level can, as two of the couples emphasised, diminish the need for close friendships, since a feeling of security and homeliness is always present. The easy-going life-style concerning daily work as well as the long-term organisation of one's life and life expectations has its reassuring effects. Manners that are judged negatively can then be accepted, and the immigrants learn to adapt to them.

The migration motive seemed to play a strong and influential role in the migrants' identification with Ireland. One woman and two of the couples, who lived rather secluded lives, did not criticise Irish public life, but experienced ordinary, everyday life as problematic. Clearly, personal freedom was important, while societal and political conditions were considered as peripheral. In general, however, the immigrants emphasised their newly-found individual freedom. One has to ask to what extent this freedom can be interpreted as a result of characteristically Irish conditions. One-fifth of the interviewees declared that they felt a greater sense of freedom because they had escaped rigid patterns of relationships and behaviour, and only now were they able to break down old role structures. Furthermore, they enjoyed a certain 'fool's freedom' in Ireland, a freedom which they did not exploit, but tried to make the most of. Considering this, the new individual freedom is clearly a result of leaving old structures, rather than a consequence of immersion into the new culture.

Two couples and four single people mentioned a certain sense of 'otherness'. This corresponds with their intention not to stay in the island permanently, but only until retirement. These interviewees probably had no strong aspirations to integrate into, and identify with mainstream Irish society. Those leading a rather withdrawn life also reported feeling like strangers.

None of the interviewees seemed to identify with Irish public life to any great extent, which might explain the lack of interest among the migrants in claiming a right to vote in general elections. As noted earlier, the question of Irish citizenship and the right to vote were only of peripheral significance.

CONCLUSIONS

More than half of the interviewees gave an explicit self-assessment concerning their position in the Irish environment. They did not use terms like 'acculturation' or the like, but 'acceptance', 'tolerance' and 'integration'. Three women and two men, who were living in rural areas, felt accepted by their neighbours or other members of the local community, although one man thought that, as a stranger, he would be excluded from certain aspects of community life. He was living near the Irish border and noted that conversations about the political situation were taboo.

The term 'acceptance' can be interpreted in a variety of ways. It could be an excluding acceptance—a mere tolerance of strangers. On the other hand, it might be the acceptance of the immigrant as part of the Irish community, therefore tending to be more inclusive and integrative. This was the case with two of the women, who both seem to have found their place in a closely-knit social network and have also reached a high degree of acculturation. One man, who has been living in Ireland since 1966, felt particularly well integrated. He was living and working in an exclusively Irish environment. The building and day-to-day working of his farm in collaboration with Irish neighbours had accelerated the acculturation process.

One man and one woman—both married to an Irish partner—felt excluded from the family network, and unable to cross certain social boundaries. This furthered a sense of 'otherness' and strengthened the emotional attachment to Germany and the wish to return, which, in turn, hindered full integration into the Irish 'clan'.

The sense of 'otherness' was shared by those who did not intend to stay permanently in Ireland, and also by those leading more isolated lives. They believed that they would never fully understand the Irish mentality, or that they would never become truly integrated because of their different background. In fact, they did not wish to 'become Irish', and stressed the cultural differences. One interesting case, a managing director in an industrial company, saw himself as some sort of development worker, creating jobs and promoting the German work ethic in Ireland. His self-confidence was nurtured by a sense of hierarchy and mission, rather than by a position in Irish society which defines itself by the social standards of human conduct.

Some of the women married to Irish partners gave the impression of being very well integrated, albeit in a somewhat taken-for-granted way: it goes without saying that they feel a part of Irish mainstream society. Being part of Irish society does not, of course, imply complete assimilation. The immigrants, in certain aspects, still identify, at least to some extent, with their original culture. Gordon (1964) describes the assimilation process as a development of slow change. He distinguishes between 'intrinsic' and 'extrinsic traits or cultural patterns'. Intrinsic traits are 'essential and vital ingredients of the group's cultural heritage, and derive ... from that heritage'

(Gordon 1964). Examples of this include religious beliefs and practices, ethical values, native language and a sense of a common past. Extrinsic traits or patterns 'tend to be products of the historical vicissitudes of a group's adjustment to its local environment' (*op.cit.*). Here dress, manner, patterns of emotional expression, and minor oddities in pronouncing and inflecting one's language serve as examples.

This distinction could also be noticed among the German migrants. Language competence was not seen as a problem, while the mother tongue—on a more abstract level—was a characteristic of cultural heritage and identity. Certain Irish customs were taken up, but those German customs which are considered important are kept alive, and often combined with Irish ones.

The Germans adapt to a different way of communication, social life and manner. Thus the extrinsic patterns do not seem to differ any more—or only very little—from those of the host society. The Germans 'get on in the country'.

The intrinsic culture will only change very slowly. The difference is expressed by identification with Irish everyday life and popular culture, while the public life, especially its religious and political hierarchy, is strongly criticised, and nobody seems to identify with the institutionalised Irish values represented by those authorities.

Of course, this does not mean that German migrants follow current German moral values, whatever they might be. I would suggest that those questioned occupy a marginal position without any clear-cut identification with either Germany or Ireland.

The desire to leave Germany was one main reason for coming to Ireland. Nevertheless, the interviewees did not try to forget their cultural background. Only two of those asked openly and directly rejected Germany, but even in those cases it could be argued that, because of their particularly strong emotional opposition to German political and everyday culture, their German background is relevant. Their identity could be called an 'anti-identity', that is, an identity determined by what they reject, rather than what they accept.

Prejudice and discrimination do not seem to have made life difficult for the immigrants; conflicts between themselves and locals did not seem to be worth mentioning. One reason could be a high degree of acculturation, which could be observed in most cases.

Another factor could be the characteristically introvert lifestyle of many immigrants committed to self-sufficient farming or other self-employed work (*cf.* Kockel 1993), who would rarely mix with the locals. In their lifestyle they do not provide a target for conflict, although a certain resentment of such 'anti-social' behaviour can be noticed among the Irish. Another reason for the low level of conflict could be the ability of immigrants to revive local traditions as they try to reactivate Irish crafts (*op.cit.*).

In ethnic terms, Ireland still is a very homogeneous society, and has not experienced a high influx of economically motivated migrants. Certain problems arising out of the contact between immigrants and host society, and which have their roots in an economic hierarchy in which the minority is kept at the bottom, have not yet surfaced. As a classical emigration country with a geographical position on the fringes of Europe, Ireland attracts a different type of immigrant, who often has a strong sense of idealism. They tend not to aspire to enhanced financial security, but instead to greater independence at the personal level. To gain this personal independence, a great effort has to be made, and a high degree of responsibility has to be taken. For many of those questioned, the price they have had to pay for a less rigidly organised working life is financial insecurity and the need to depend on more than one income source. Their working life has to be permanently re-organised. This observation contradicts the widespread view of the 'drop-out' leaving the responsibilities and demands of life behind—the term 'drop-ins' might be a rather more accurate description of these migrants. There was also little evidence of a romantic fascination with Celtic mysteries.

The present pilot study should be seen as an attempt to illuminate one 'hidden' aspect of Irish life. The limited amount of data only allows suggestions, and in selecting my interviewees, certain aspects of migration, or types of immigrants, might have been ignored. Still, I hope to have encouraged a different viewpoint on Irish migration. While the large-scale emigration from Ireland has attracted a wide range of research projects, immigration to the island has remained virtually unexplored.

BIBLIOGRAPHY

Goldlust, J and Richmond, A
1990 A Multivariate Model of Immigrant Adaptation. In Koch-Kraft, A (ed.), *Deutsche in Kanada. Einwanderung und Adaption*, Bochum.

Gordon, M
1964 *Assimilation in American Life*, New York.

Hoerder, D
1988 Zur Akkulturation von Arbeitsmigranten. In Hoerder, D and Knauf, D (eds), *Einwandererland USA, Gastarbeiterland BRD*, Hamburg.

Kockel, U
1993 *The Gentle Subversion. Informal Economy and Regional Development in the West of Ireland*, Bremen.

Lamnek, S
1993 *Qualitative Sozialforschung*, Weinheim.

Miller, S
1986 *Männerfreundschaft*, München.

Schulz, B
1993 Noch kann Irland Unternehmen mit Steueranreizen locken. *Frankfurter Allgemeine Zeitung*, 1 June.

Valtin, R and Fatke, R
1988 Wozu man Freunde braucht, *Psychologie heute*, April, 22.

Ethnicity in the 1990s
Contemporary Irish Migrants in London

MARY KELLS

How relevant is 'ethnicity' in today's world? As barriers, both physical and psychological, are breaking down and European unity approaches, will individual ethnic identities become an anachronism in a European Union? Looking through anthropological lenses at a particular group of contemporary Irish immigrants in London, I argue that ethnicity remains important, but complex. I begin by considering previous ethnicity studies, and definitions of ethnicity.

EXISTING STUDIES

For a long time, ethnicity studies have focused on 'assimilation' and the 'interested' character of ethnicity. Glazer and Moynihan (1981) refer to the movement 'from an emphasis on culture, language, religion as such' to the interests of the group members, noting the peculiar efficacy of the ethnic group today as a focus for gaining advantage. Emphasis has also been on inter-group conflict. My own emphasis is somewhat different. I have found assimilation less relevant than more partial integration, and 'interested' ethnicity uncompelling. It is time now to dissect these terms.

Ullrich Kockel (ed.), *Landscape, Heritage and Identity: Case Studies in Irish Ethnography*, Liverpool University Press 1995, 223-36.

Mary Kells

DEFINITIONS

Anthropological definitions of 'ethnicity' vary according to ontological outlook, that is, opinions of the nature of individual-social interaction. Factors such as conflict or stability, and subjective or objective emphases differ. Parkin (in Cohen 1974) stresses conflict in ethnic situations. Barth (1969) suggests ethnic groups are 'organisational vessels' whose content is subjective and variable. Their objective existence is thus rounded out by subjective control of individual members. Schildkrout (in Cohen 1974) considers the 'culturally accepted principle of differentiation' per se as more important than its content, which helps explain ethnicity's persistence where cultural distinctiveness has been lost. Cohen (1974), finally, suggests that ethnic symbols develop from subjective and individual to objective and collective.

For the present purpose, I define ethnicity as the articulation of a common identity based on shared cultural heritage, as perceived by those sharing this background and also by those who perceive themselves to be outside it. This may be an organisational focus in situations of conflict, and its content or resonance may vary according to circumstances, for example, of threat. This definition acknowledges the possibility of differences of opinion: if, for example, an outside group considers you as part of a distinct ethnic group (in this case, Irish), this is part of the reality, as is your opinion that you are not (if, for example, you consider yourself British). The subjective content of the cultural heritage may vary but the concept of some commonality is vital, and gives objective standing also.

'Assimilation', next, describes the blending into the receiving society and is the traditional alternative to ethnic distinctiveness in the literature. Richmond (1969) notes the expectation that migrants would almost disappear into the majority population. Recent theory has rejected previous assumptions of inevitability. Brown (1970) notes that immigrants themselves rarely speak of 'the merging of parts into a single whole'. Rex and Moore (1967) point out that the host society is not a unitary thing to be assimilated into, that relationships between immigrants and others can vary along several axes, and that the immigrant, furthermore, is not just moving between cultures, but trying to find an alternative to both. Assimilation begins to seem inappropriate as much because of the perception of its increasing factual irrelevance in a new situation as because of the theory's internal inadequacies. The new (post-1914) migrant, Richmond (1969) points out is highly qualified and mobile, experiencing neither anomie nor assimilation, but a new process of adaptation. Implications of this include the transforming of the returned migrant from failure to the successful executor of a short term plan. My rejection of 'assimilation' is thus part of a recent theoretical movement dealing with the complexities of a new situation.

THE CASE STUDY

The focus of my own current research is on concepts of identity among young, middle class Irish immigrants to London in the past decade. The 1980s-90s is the third major wave of Irish migration to England, the others being 1820-1910 and 1940-50. Because of its anthropological orientation, it is a qualitative and small-scale study, aiming for depth rather than numerical breadth. I have around 50 informants I can see regularly, many more whom I have seen more sporadically, and I have gathered impressionistic information from attending Irish gatherings. My informants derive from personal contacts and Irish groups and venues. Let me describe the current setting in which they find themselves.

British society today is much less homogeneous than during the 1950s, when signs such as 'No Irish, no Coloureds, No Dogs' were acceptable. In today's racially mixed environment, such blatant discrimination is unacceptable. In certain boroughs, positive discrimination is practised for ethnic minorities. Thus, ethnic origin may in certain circumstances aid one or satisfy 'interested' ends, certainly more so than in the 1950s. Paradoxically, it is also easier for the Irish emigre to blend into this setting: s/he is white, English-speaking and not visibly distinctive as are Afro-Caribbean and Asian neighbours. I stress choice here in keeping with my stress on the subjective content of ethnicity. The middle class status of my informants increases their choices as greater education/skill increase their control over their self-presentation, their job status and their prestige. Goffman (1956) uses the metaphor of the stage to express how the individual may manipulate her/his image in social interaction. Choice is of course limited by class and locality, but my informants still have much greater scope than the migrants of the 1950s, when discrimination was so much more blatant.

Social intercourse is like a performance in which each tries to present a staged drama of the self they wish to reveal. In his terms, these migrants have many props with which to produce a convincing performance of themselves as they wish to be perceived. As Europe unites, there is, arguably, an additional incentive (or justification) for playing down a specifically Irish identity. In this situation, what does this group think of being Irish?

Very generally, my findings suggest that being Irish is important for my informants. Perhaps it could be argued that my own Irishness influenced my findings in that people might have been more inclined to emphasise their own Irishness to me than otherwise. This is interesting in itself and fits with my definition of ethnicity as situational and flexible, where there are different emphases on its importance at different times. However, I should also add that my conclusions are based not only on what people say, but also on what they do (with the help of their giving me activity diaries, for example). Thus I feel I go beyond simply what my informants might think I want to hear. Of course, the whole issue of insider/outsider research deserves a more detailed treatment than is possible here. Perhaps the bottom line is that to consider being Irish as irrelevant would involve denying, first of all, formative experiences and educations which are rooted in locality, and, secondly, shared cultural history (part of the cultural heritage which is the basis of ethnic identity according to my definition). That 'history' is not a unitary, objective reality should be particularly obvious in Northern Ireland, where nationalist and unionist versions vie for supremacy, but Irish histories still differ from English. The meaning of this to my informants varies. Some nationalists, for example, find that Irish/English historical conflict obstructs current interaction with English people. Others find it less or differently significant. However, at the very least, a denial of Irishness seems to entail a suppression of personal history which appears undesirable for most informants.

Of course, one cannot simply say that 'being Irish' is important and leave it at that. The content of Irishness varies between and within individuals. Irishness can entail group attendance, either to do 'Irish' things with Irish people, or simply to meet other Irish. One woman described being Irish as being familiar with 'the Irish customs and the language and traditions'. Or it can entail a particular political stance, though for my informants this is quite a problematic topic, eliciting ambivalence rather than revolutionary zeal. Thirdly, for many, Irishness is seen instead as a personal thing, entailing distinctive attitudes and dispositions. These are interior; exterior mixing with other Irish is seen as unessential.

There is a high level of ambivalence and contradictions regarding the importance of Irish things within individuals. For example, saying that Irish background is unimportant yet frequenting Irish venues, reading Irish papers etc.; or stating its importance yet acting on it little. Far from playing down such dissonance, I would like to highlight it. It illustrates the complex and subjective nature of ethnic identification (and indeed of 'being') and this deserves stress. Holy and Stuchlik (1983) look at precisely this issue of inconsistency. They suggest that 'reality' is divided into levels of actions, norms and representations with different behaviour appropriate for each. Thus, apparent inconsistency can simply be a misreading, a failure to identify two types of situation, for example. However, to some extent, it is not necessary to explain away every inconsistency: people deal in contextual selection, and Amina Mama (1989) suggests that the unitary self is anyway a Western myth based on political hegemony. Given these caveats, and while the reasons behind consistency may be as interesting as those for inconsistency, it is worth considering the contradictions. Of course, the inadequacies of research may be partly responsible: talking to me about Irishness can be very artificial, separating it from the rest of one's person. This aside, contradictions can reveal cross-cutting currents, the tension between fitting into British society and remaining separate both appealing within one person at different times. The question remains, is Irishness important to today's migrants?

From the research I have carried out so far, I suggest that there is a new form of Irishness in London. New self-conscious groups aid the welfare of Irish people and celebrate their shared culture. In the 1940s and 1950s, there were county associations but not the same plethora of groups and formalised gatherings as today. Not only are the welfare-based, working class-oriented groups new, springing from an environment in which it can be advantageous to claim aid along lines of ethnic identity, but there are also new middle class groupings evolving, concerned with 'culture' rather than subsistence, and these are my focus. By culture, I refer to Irish traditional and modern music, literary works and also non-Irish intellectual and aesthetic concerns. These groups are not all a post-1950s phenomenon, but they have multiplied greatly in the past decade. Aras na Ngael in Kilburn is one venue for Irish activities (Irish dancing, language, sport, study), attracting cross-London support, though also the hostility of Irish welfare workers who see their clients' basic needs as more essential than cultural trimmings. Other groups exist for Irish people to meet without necessarily doing 'Irish' things, for example, the London Irish Network, formed in the late 1980s. It describes itself as an 'organisation of people of all ages, who are keen to ... engage in a greater range of social activities', ranging from 'houseparties and visits to wine bars, to cultural events such as the theatre and cinema, to more active events such as dancing, rambling and sports'. One committee member suggested its attraction to be that of doing things with people you had something in common with. It is a small but enthusiastic, middle class apolitical group.

Such groups validate a sense of Irishness contrasting with the negative stereotype of the drunken, violent, labouring Irish migrant. They perhaps represent a reclaiming of Irishness as something positive and acceptable for middle class people. They are not interest groups for claiming resources, but nor are they as anti-interest as forty years ago. Glazer and Moynihan (1981) suggest that ethnicity outdoes class by having an 'affective' as well as an interested appeal. By this they mean an appeal to the emotions. Kilson (in Glazer and Moynihan 1981) suggests ethnicity's affective appeal to be that of traditional values in the midst of sharp, societal shifts. If the shift towards a more homogeneous European identity is seen as threatening, the recourse to ethnic particularity could be an escape route. However, I think this is less the case than simply the particularity of shared cultural history and upbringing being seen as inescapable and fundamental to my informants' personhood.

Some of my informants also attend political groups. These are interest groups in one sense, but also rather more, in that they can include an expressive kind of politics which relates to identity. They tend to be concerned with general Irish welfare and rights rather than partition. For example, one woman told me of the 'Irish Emigrants' Voice' she attends, which works for votes for Irish migrants in Irish elections, and the 'Irish Teachers' Voice', promoting the equal status of Irish teachers (a clear response to perceived discrimination). On the whole, though, my middle class informants are wary of Irish political and especially border issues. They may have strong opinions, but voice them carefully and tend to avoid activism. Quite a number of nationalists have expressed unease about republicanism, and about Irish political groups over here. One informant, though strongly anti-partition, said she would 'never' support political groups here as they were all full of IRA supporters. She expressed shock at the increased IRA support in London compared to Eire. Protestant informants have also commented that political extremism could be greater here than in Northern Ireland. My informants usually dissociate themselves from 'extremism', defining it as violence and sectarianism, but can be ambivalent. One informant attending a Troops Out march told me that she wanted to go because she felt that the troops' presence in Northern Ireland should not become accepted, that it was intended to be temporary, and this should not be forgotten; that she felt uneasy with republican associations, but also with the many 'trendy left-wing', non-Irish people marching; for them, it was just another left-wing cause, whereas the Irish whom it affected were more apathetic. This represents a complicated set of feelings about Irish political protest. One Protestant Unionist complained of people equating his Irish accent with support for a United Ireland. He referred to a taxi driver criticising Mrs Thatcher and saying she should leave Ireland. His attitude is to agree for the sake of a quiet life.

Middle class Irish identity does not hinge on group membership, however. Many of my informants stress the importance of their Irish background to me, yet attend no Irish groups. These people stress character differences as essential. Irish people are seen positively as friendly, good 'crack' (fun), open, warm, straightforward, imaginative, spontaneous, informal and unpretentious; negatively, as moody, drunken and volatile, untrustworthy and sexist. English people are regarded as reserved, condescending, cold, arrogant, cautious, touchy, distant, easily offended; but also 'decent' if you break through the reserve, and reliable. Ethnic heritage here bequeaths attitudes and dispositions as much as being 'about' cultural traditions or politics. Some feel political history may affect national and also individual psyches, with the English having the security of coming from a nation previously possessing a powerful empire, whereas Irish experience is of invasion and domination. Among other character-comments, some women talked of Irish people, especially men, having stronger feelings than the English but less capacity to express them.

Various people distinguished between 'real' and counterfeit Irishness. Thus an objective, 'true' category of 'Irishness' is perceived, with not all subjective content valid. What is valid of course varies according to individuals. Here is Holy and Stuchlik's (1983) realm of ideal or 'normative' behaviours - what Irishness should be like. Even this is not unitary. For some, 'real-ness' can refer to religion: Northern Protestants tend to speak of Catholic Irish as 'the real' or 'the true Irish'. Catholics in turn frequently consider Protestants to be what the Unionists profess them to be— British, not Irish. Conversely, it can refer to class: one informant told me in Biddy Mulligan's (an Irish pub in Kilburn) that here were 'the real Irish', that is, 'working class people'. Or generations: one man called second generation political activists exploitatively, not 'authentically Irish'. Another group called them 'plastic Paddies'. One woman complained the Irish language had been 'hijacked' for political ends, and people talked of being 'more Irish' since they came to London when they merely meant more 'anti-English'. There is considerable antagonism towards political exploitation of 'Irishness' evident. Second generation Irish often stress political, specifically nationalist views as essential criteria for 'being' Irish, whereas my middle class, first generation informants would underplay/reject this and often reject second generation Irishness too. British and Irish identifications are seen as separate but not necessarily antagonistic. In general, politics and second generation Irish tend to be more 'out' than 'in' whereas Catholic and working class Irish are more 'in' than 'out', notions needing more investigation among my informants.

Having examined their views of Irishness, now let me look at what 'integration' means to my informants. Assimilation was never suggested by them, but integration, or adapting without losing one's Irish identity, was important to many. One man described those who 'refuse' to integrate as 'savages' and 'uncivilised', believing that

231

'when in Rome...'. This is extreme, but many felt that it was unfairly difficult to have both English and Irish friends. Declan spoke of wanting to integrate with his English accountancy work mates and also keep his Irish 'identity' and associate with Irish friends; of how he was laughed at for talking with Irish friends in the pub, when drinking with fellow accountants. Of course, class enters here, as his Irish friends were labourers. John, in London for ten years, said that he started to 'integrate' after three years. A turning point was returning from a holiday abroad and feeling he was 'home'. Integrating for him is 'knowing what makes people tick', mixing with different classes of English, not presenting oneself as 'the Paddy', starting 'where they're at, not where you're at'. He considers it 'unprofessional' to 'play the Irish card' in his business, criticising the 'over-familiarity' of those Irish who try to manipulate him by emphasising shared origin. Fitting in and respecting 'their' (British) norms is important, but retaining the 'very important' and 'very powerful' Irish part of him is too. Partly, he suggested, it is impossible to escape it, due to others' attitudes. This picture is still far from the complete absorption of assimilation theory.

Others' attitudes are indeed essential (see my definition of ethnicity). The negative side is the prejudice Irish people - including my middle class informants - face, precluding full acceptance. For some women, this was bound up with sexual discrimination. Many vacillated on the issue, describing discrimination yet playing it down. This may indicate the distinction between what should and what does happen. Integration is on several levels. Middle class attitudes to Kilburn or other Irish localities are of distaste, so residential integration is preferred. Work environment tends to be mixed, unless in the building trade, or with an Irish concern, such as an Irish newspaper. Leisure is variable: some informants mix more in Irish circles than others. Those who don't often maintain the importance of their Irish identity to them, whereas those who do may claim Irishness is unimportant to them. Those Protestants who consider themselves British first, Northern Irish second, tend to feel less desire to maintain an Irish identity, and are more disposed, theoretically at least, to integrate into British society. Similar mixing with 'home' friends occurs though - usually other Northern Irish Protestants.

Thus, the Irish jig seems to be numerous variations on a theme. Alternative themes - class, gender and sexuality, for example - may undercut whatever shared ethnicity there is. For some women, gender may mean more than ethnicity. For others, the two may inter-relate in a sense of double oppression. Within Irish women's groups, there is a potentially antagonistic split between heterosexual and lesbian women. Regarding class, middle and working class Irish socialise more rigidly apart than in Ireland. Middle class Irish Balls organised to fund working class Irish welfare organisations hint more at patron-client than kindred relations.

Other divisions militating against a united Irishness include origin in Ireland. Southerners tend to see the North as 'other' and vice versa. My informants resent being asked about happenings in the 'other' portion of Ireland, stressing that they don't come from there. For the Protestant Northern Irish, the North/South divide is fundamental. Southerners speak of variation within Eire.

'Northerners' have been characterised to me as being outspoken and blunt; Cork people as evasive; Dubliners, superior-acting. Regional stereotypes of some kind are known to most informants. And then there is religion, which on one level unites, with many informants seeing Irish spirituality as very distinct from English secularisation, and on another, of course, divides, with Protestant and Catholic Northern Irish identities meaning very different things and frequently remaining antipathetic in London. Opinions also vary over time. One informant said that since obtaining his present job, he no longer criticises the oppression of Catholics in Northern Ireland as it feels inappropriate to his new responsibilities. Another spoke of increased awareness of oppression the longer she stayed here, especially regarding the PTA (Prevention of Terrorism Act) and travelling between Ireland and England. 'It's got to the stage where I'm terrified to go home now', she said. Others indicate increasing awareness of the pervasiveness and subtlety and of prejudice.

CONCLUSIONS

My informants have many things to say about being Irish, often contradictory. As I am in the middle of my research, this is far from a finished account. I would conclude, though, that 'being Irish' is problematic and thought-provoking, in Ireland and in London, and that most informants consider it important to retain an Irish identity or indeed that it is inescapable. In keeping with my definition of ethnicity, the content of 'being Irish' varies between individuals and is partially shaped by others' attitudes. Interaction with other groups, although important, was not my specific focus. In Glazer and Moynihan's (1981) terms, the value of the middle class identity would seem to be 'affective' rather than 'interested', though it is clearly not against the interests of my informants as much as in the 1950s. Complete assimilation is not on the menu, though some form of integration with continued Irish identification, is. Irishness entailing the embracing of the Irish enclave is rejected. It is paradoxical that my informants tend to react against imposed forms of Irishness, stressing instead what is important to them, individually, yet they proffer an opposition of real-versus-artificial which would suggest a unitary form of Irishness. I would suggest that such talk is a shorthand for something rather more complicated, with 'real' indicating those who carry the cultural standard highest in some way, who embody the unspoilt traditionalism that is seen as most purely Irish. For many, their vision of Irishness is what it is all about, and the rest are simply wrong.

Of course, Irishness is not necessarily the overwhelming criterion of self. One woman, asked about her sense of herself, spoke in terms of her job and what she wanted to do with her life. Others speak passionately about other issues, from the National Film Theatre to horse racing. Yet for Joan—with her Irish Teachers Association and Irish Emigrants Voice meetings, with her passion for teaching the Irish language and for introducing mixed-race children to the value of the Irish Centre in Kilburn, her Irish dancing, buying of Irish papers, socialising with Irish in Irish places—being Irish is a much greater thing. For Eleanor—who attends Irish and non-Irish poetry writing and other groups, who works in a non-Irish environment and feels that she is considered 'odd' because of her Irishness and her gender in a position of responsibility—being Irish is a big part of her life, but along with other big things, like gender and literary aspirations. She talks about being Irish, constantly compares Irish, English and American attitudes and behaviour, reads Irish authors and papers and revels in the 'crack' in Irish pubs.

The content and significance of Irishness are not uniform, but the awareness that there is such a thing as Irish identity to be claimed or rejected is more so. It is not going to disappear because Europe is suddenly in the forefront, unless it was never important. My impression is that being Irish is important to many people, explicitly, and to those who say it is not, there is often more ambivalence than they are aware of, as they reveal attitudes which contradict their stated indifference. Part of this is being reminded of being Irish by non-Irish or feeling it distinctly at times of high media attention on Northern Ireland. Part of it is also the strong affective appeal of ethnic identity which will ensure that changes affecting its value for satisfying interest will not bring about its demise. The European identity is a larger identity than the Irish one. In certain circumstances, it may become more relevant—though at present, I find little focus on it—just as in some circumstances the fact that one is from Ireland is more relevant than the fact that one is from County Tipperary. In another circumstance, the specific town or street will be more appropriate. Place of birth is important to people: we like to place others to help us understand them—and indeed to understand ourselves. As such, ethnicity, in the sense of place of origin, will perhaps always be inescapable.

BIBLIOGRAPHY

Barth, F (ed.)
1969 *Ethnic Groups and Boundaries: The Social Organisation of Culture Differences*, London.
Brown, J
1970 *The Un-Melting Pot: An English Town and its Immigrants*, London.
Cohen, A (ed.)
1974 *Urban Ethnicity*, London.
Glazer, N and Moynihan, D (eds)
1981 *Ethnicity: Theory and Experience*, Cambridge/Mass.
Goffman, E
1956 *The Presentation of Self in Everyday Life*, University of Edinburgh Social Sciences Research Centre.
Holy, L and Stuchlik, M
1983 *Actions, Norms and Representations: Foundations of Anthropological Enquiry*, Cambridge.
Mama, A
1989 *Race, Identity and Subjectivity*. Paper read at the Centre for Extra-Mural Studies, Birbeck College, London, 12 June.
Rex, J and Moore, R
1967 *Race, Community and Conflict*, London.
Richmond, A
1969 Sociology of Migration in Industrial and Post-Industrial Societies. In Jackson, J (ed.), *Migration*, Cambridge.

'The West is Learning, the North is War'
Reflections on Irish Identity

ULLRICH KOCKEL

Consider the following characterisation of the provinces of Ireland (adapted from Rees and Rees 1961):

The East (Leinster) -
> supplies, splendour, abundance, good custom, good manners, wealth, householding; PROSPERITY

The South (Munster) -
> fairs, reavers, musicianship, melody, minstrelry, fidchell-playing, retinue; MUSIC

The West (Connacht) -
> teaching, judgement, chronicles, stories, histories, science, eloquence; LEARNING

The North (Ulster) -
> contentions, rough places, strifes, haughtiness, pride, assaults, conflicts; WAR

Ullrich Kockel (ed.), *Landscape, Heritage and Identity: Case Studies in Irish Ethnography*, Liverpool University Press 1995, 237-58.

Contemporary Ireland in a nutshell, so to speak: administered from the East, where the Dublin conurbation accumulates most of the wealth generated in the other regions, while the South abounds with local music festivals, the West remains the stronghold of Gaelic culture whence it is supposed to emanate and spread throughout the island, and the North shows but little sign of reconciliation.

Only, the original text cited here was written in Middle Irish, and relates information which Fintan son of Bóchra obtained from a supernatural being called Trefuilngid Tre-eochair during the reign of Diarmait son of Cerball, AD 545-565 (*cf.* Rees and Rees 1961).

Could such apparent continuity be interpreted as an indicator of the strength of Irish cultural identity? Whatever our answer to this question, it is certainly noteworthy that Ireland seems to have preserved the ancient (Indo-European), symbolic division of her national territory according to castes (Figure 15) more clearly than any other European country, and one might well ask why this should be so.

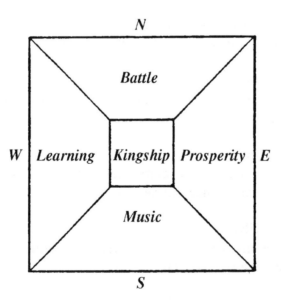

Figure 15   *Symbolic territories (after Rees and Rees 1961)*

Another ancient division of the island is also of (perhaps even greater) interest here: that into 'Conn's Half', comprising the aristocratic West and North, and 'Mug's Half', the East and South, which was regarded as socially inferior.

This division is replicated in the contemporary debate over Irish identity, where the South is usually subsumed under 'the West', while the East is only considered relevant in relation to the North. Irish identity seems to be a matter to be decided within, or at least with almost exclusive reference to, the ancient aristocratic provinces. Hence the two main strands of the debate which I want to review here might be seen as a re-enactment of the CúChulainn-Cycle, which

> commemorates the struggle between the two aristocratic provinces of Connacht and Ulster, in which the protagonists are Queen Medb of Connacht on the one hand, and King Conchobar and his nephew CúChulainn on the other (Rees and Rees 1961).

The object of this mythical struggle was sovereignty, and one may ponder the intriguing detail that the learned, priestly province is symbolised by a Queen whose desertion of her first husband, the (Warrior) King, against his will is said to have caused the outbreak of open hostilities.

IDENTITY AS PROBLEMATIC

Despite the rather inflationary use of the term 'identity' in recent years, its disparate connotations are held together by a common core: the implication of order and security in the face of change (*cf.* Bausinger 1978). This implicit continuity does not resemble a static environment, but rather some kind of stable frame of reference within changing constellations of the social world. The resurgence of regionalism in Europe since the 1960s has been interpreted in this light (*cf.* Gerdes 1980) as an attempt by certain groups to withdraw from an increasingly complex social reality, or to hold on to utopian ideals where everyday practice offered little scope for their immediate realisation. In particular the Left, thrown into disorientation and deprived of their theoretical certainties by the events which followed the years of students' unrest, cultivated their 'withdrawal symptoms', the so-called 'new irrationality', into a fashionable 'progressive regionalism'. It is significant in this context that identity only becomes an issue for extensive debate when it is no longer self-evident; the term assumes an emphatic note which adequately reflects its utopian content, but might nevertheless fail to relate its subject to the historical reality which constitutes the situational frame of reference (*cf.* Bausinger 1978). Where such social movements invoke 'tradition' or, more generally, 'the common past' as an example of coherently fulfilled identity, it becomes highly questionable whether this identity is not merely a projection of the utopian potentialities of thought into the descriptions of past life-worlds which inform such movements (*op.cit.*).

Such assessments of social movements, however, often appear to betray a disenchantment of their proponents with the reality of social change—a disenchantment which, in its very essence, is hardly different from the seemingly irrational, utopian pseudo-identification for which they criticise the disoriented Left. These critics regard attempts to increase opportunities for identification as valuable only if they conform to their more or less materialist prejudice of history, consequently denying historicity to any development which does not fit the pattern. However, if history is interpreted as a creative, indeterminate process rather than as a unilinear, predetermined path, attention can be focused on the 'transformation of the world into home' (Bloch 1959: 'Umbau der Welt zur Heimat')* - hence on the process of individual and

---

240

collective identity formation through the interplay between the cultural practices of everyday life, and the hegemonial structures of the respective society. It is in the light of this perspective that I want to discuss the current debate over Irish identity, and its cultural and societal basis.

Since the advent of modernity during the 1960s, 'Irishness' has died numerous clamorous (glamorous?) deaths as a new identity was fabricated: that of

> a European and technological Ireland, embarrassed at its nationalist past and frantically trying to show our EEC 'partners' that we are as sophisticated as they are (Kirby 1988).

'The shamrock lies a-mourning in its grave', sing the Wolfetones. And every time its executioners turn their back on the corpse, it pops up again (in a different guise), ready to haunt us until we put it down once more; yet we are never quite sure what exactly it is the corpse is up to. Let's face it, the Irish are, as one informant put it during an interview, 'exactly the same as everybody else—we are no different from anybody else in Europe'.

But are they really? And if not, who or what are they? It is of little consolation that they themselves don't really know. Strangely, other nations with a comparable history, for instance the Finns, don't seem to have this problem. Even the Swedish minority in Finland is in no doubt as to who they are. Could it be that this is a first clue? That part of being 'Irish' includes not knowing what 'being Irish' means? And could this have something to do with the fact that few European nations could match the percentage of residents (in both parts of Ireland) who were born, or at least spent a large proportion of their lives abroad, in a different cultural environment? Could it also have to do with the fact that, rather than being caught between two very different cultures (like Finland is), Ireland has been culturally and politically sandwiched—as an alien, Catholic corn—between the two strongholds of 'the Protestant Ethic and the

Spirit of Capitalism', who, each in its own (quiet?), way have been trying to dominate it, using its people as living examples of obedient compliance with this modern religion called economics? *An Spailpín Fánach*, the migrant labourer, as the ultimate expression of Irish identity? Much of recent Irish literature points in that direction. But this might simply be an attempt to come to grips with a reality that has been forced upon the people of Ireland.

At the more 'scholarly' level, a number of strands can be distinguished in the debate. The following discussion concentrates mainly on the postmodernist, and on the rather more mystically inclined 'New Age' versions, although reference will also be made to the conservative nationalists and the 'liberation theologians', where their visions show considerable overlap with the first two strands.

THE DEBATE IN IRELAND *

Three issues dominate the debate over Irish identity in Ireland. Firstly, the presumed transition from a traditional to a modern society, as in Frank Barry's 'Between Tradition and Modernity: Cultural Values and the Problems of Irish Society', or Eamon O'Flaherty's 'Atavism and Innovation: Reflections on Culture and Nationality in Ireland', both in a 1988 issue of the *Irish Review* (*cf.* also Gibbons 1988). Secondly, there is the 'Northern Question', which runs as an underlying theme through much of Richard Kearney's writing in recent years, but also features (for obvious reasons) as the main focus of the discussion on 'Who are the Irish?' in the Winter 1988 edition of the Jesuit journal *Studies*. Cutting across these two issues is a third one, which questions the major institutions of 'Irishness' from a slightly different angle: the critique of the Catholic Church and the Irish language organisations from

---

* Part of this passage on the identity debate in Ireland has previously appeared in a book on the West of Ireland (Kockel 1993, 34-35).

within. For obvious reasons, members of these institutions are reluctant to deny their own institution its legitimacy, as many of the other participants in the debate would tend to do; instead, they are trying to redefine their role as one which is still relevant for the Ireland of today, in order to demonstrate that they have not lost touch with what it means to be 'Irish'.

Up until recently, to be 'Irish' was supposed to mean: to be Catholic, (possibly) Gaelic, poor, and rural. Needless to say, this imagery was forged by Protestants with little Gaelic, but usually well-off and, of course, urban. To be Irish also meant to be from the West. There has been a certain myth of the 'Wild West' attached to the area west of the Shannon (*cf.* Gibbons 1984). It has been a romantic myth, most eloquently promoted by the Gaelic Revival since the latter part of the nineteenth century, which found its political expression in de Valera's rural idyll. Up until 1958, this idyll virtually stifled modernisation, and it has consequently come under attack for its negative effects on development. Brunt (1988) notes the debt crisis of the 1980s as an indirect consequence of the idyll, because after 1958, rapid modernisation was achieved mostly through increasing dependence on foreign capital and exchequer borrowing.

From a very different perspective, the debate about Irish identity, notably in journals like *The Crane Bag*, has criticised the idyll. This critique, championed in particular by the philosopher Richard Kearney, interprets tradition as an ambivalent concept, and is thus very much in tune with recent anthropological and sociological writing on Ireland (Hechter 1975; Bax 1977; Simms 1981; McCullagh 1984; Shanklin 1985; Kockel 1993). One point of departure for the debate has been the uncritical adoption of imported technological and economic values under the flag of modernisation (*cf.* Pratschke 1985). As Desmond Fennell put it:

The trouble with ... imported things in our life is not that they are there, but that they are there in alien, undigested form, like chunks of undigested food lying heavily on our stomach . (Fennell 1984, 47; emphasis removed).

The other starting point for this debate is the frequently noted, gross inconsistency in the behaviour of the old mythologisers, few of whom were actually living their rural idyll because, as one critic puts it,

[t]he gaelicism of the countryside was too Gaelic ... [t]he tradition ... too traditional; [t]he anomie of the countryside was too anomic ... [and its] lunacy ... too lunatic (Sheeran 1987).

The central issue of this debate is thus the reinterpretation of tradition. Against the old mythologisers, it is held that they created a static, conservative imagery which portrayed a communal, essentially rural Ireland in need of preservation against Yeats's 'filthy modern tide'. Hence an artificial antagonism was created, between tradition and modernity, which could only lead to a sweeping rejection of the former, once the flood-gates had been opened for the latter.

The current debate seeks to transcend this antagonism; Kearney (1986) summarises the rationalist, postmodernist project with reference to Marcuse's dictum that authentic utopias must be grounded in recollection, which facilitates interpretation of the past as an enabling force for the future: 'Our task is to discriminate between those national myths which incarcerate and those which emancipate'.

The postmodernist emancipation is qualitatively different from that advocated, for instance, by Witoszek and Sheeran (1985):

The ... debate on tradition is an abortion debate. The Irish girl has been raped by the Englishman. She already hates the child in her womb ... [but] ... to abort might endanger her own life ... [Nobody] ... knows what to do with the baby. Our tradition is a mongrel birth; we aspire, however, to purity of lineage or, failing that, to immaculate conception. But the child is there, red hair and all, and won't go away.

Here Kearney and the rationalists are accused of a double sin: valuing Irish tradition only in so far as it contributes to their post-modernist project, and seeking a purely and genuinely Irish tradition only. By contrast, Sheeran and other mystics argue for, in the first place, positive recognition of all tradition regardless of its contribution to (post-) modernity, and, secondly, acknowledgement of its racial impurity. From this perspective, the reconsideration of tradition is more intuitive than rationalist, and leads with a certain, expectable inevitability to the postulate of Ireland as a vanguard of a New Age (*cf.* Sheeran 1987). Not surprisingly, the debate, during 1988-89, caught on in *Common Ground*, a journal for alternative lifestyles, which is also the main networking organ of the—largely immigrant—counterculture. This extension of the debate continues, and seems even to reinforce the distinction between a rationalist, urban, secular, socialist strand which coincides with the Irish utopia of postmodernity, and the rural, mystical, (eco-)conservative strand, largely represented in the immigrant Irish utopia of a New Age. There may well be some significance in the fact that Pat Sheeran is writing in the West, at University College Galway, where from the higher floors of the Arts Building, one has (on a good day) a rather nice view of the New Age region around Galway Bay, which almost coincides with the Celtic Twilight region of W. B. Yeats and Lady Gregory, while Richard Kearney's location in Dublin 4, or Luke Gibbons' position close to the urban dereliction on Dublin's northside convey a very different image of Ireland. Which is, of course, not to say that either of these images is any more or less real, accurate or whatever than any of the others.

It seems that the debate has three geographical foci: the North, the West, and Dublin. One may excuse the postmodernists for—at least apparently—thinking that to be Irish means having grown up in a Dublin slum and hating the Americans more than the British while admiring the Germans and the Japanese. Nobody else in this debate seems to like Dublin—at least nobody talks about it, except the postmodernists. And the North?

Ullrich Kockel

THE NORTH IS WAR

The 'Northern Question' is of particular significance in any contemporary discussion of Irish identity, because it was the escalation of social and political tensions in Northern Ireland since 1968 which caused national identity to re-emerge as an issue after it had temporarily become a non-issue with the abandonment of de Valera's idyll (*cf.* Ó Tuathaigh 1986). Since then, the 'Irish struggle in the North' has, at numerous meetings of national liberation movements of Western Europe, Asia and the Middle East, 'provided the link and the sense of common cause' (Fennell 1984); in their evaluation of this development, the conservative nationalists consonate with the postmodernists when they emphasise the experience of decolonisation as one aspect of identity, the recognition of which would enable Ireland to take its proper place on the international stage (*cf.* Fennell 1984; Kearney 1986), although they differ in their location of this place. Whereas the nationalists suggest association with the young nation states of the Third World, the postmodernists would like to see Ireland in the vanguard of a post-nationalist world of cultural pluralism. And yet the actuality of contemporary Ireland seems different. The majority in the South tend to identify themselves with Europe, and the more advanced nations within the EC/EU in particular, rather than with the Third World, while the situation in the North casts a dark shadow on the postmodernist hope for a happily pluralistic Ireland—a goal which appears unattainable as long as the population is divided into two communities, one of which does not care much for being 'Irish':

> Unlike all other groups in the history of Ireland, be they the Gaels, the Celts, the Vikings, the Normans, the Old English, the Anglo-Irish and so on, the one group that failed to be absorbed into the melting pot of Irishness, is the Northern Unionist community (Maginnes 1988).

In principle, this lack of integration might not seem a great problem: why should it not be possible for two separate nations to

246

coexist in the island? The difficulty arises from the postmodernist project of creating one Ireland where both cultures coexist as one nation (*cf.* Kearney 1986). On the one hand, postmodernism advocates a cultural diversity transcending the nation state, while on the other hand the unity of all Ireland as a goal of identity formation is taken for granted. The lead singer of U2, 'Bono', once said in an interview with Richard Kearney that 'if war in Northern Ireland is what it means to be Irish then we must redefine Irishness' (Hewson 1988).

But must we really? Has not war characterised the North for some fourteen centuries or more, according to Trefuilngid? The postmodernists realise that Irishness cannot be defined for the entire island unless Irish society has come to terms with the problem of violence in the North. To simply redefine Irishness so that it excludes those who are involved in violence does not solve the problem. On the other hand, the all-inclusive project of the postmodernists is likely to alienate the Ulster Protestant community to whom it might well appear as yet another plot to subject them to Rome Rule. However, recent ethnographic research on the everyday re-construction of Protestant identity, and on ways in which communities deal differently with political violence suggests opportunities for change.

Graham McFarlane's (1989) ethnographic work in the village of Ballycuan shows that sectarian divides are neither inevitable, nor working 'automatically'. Instead, recourse to such divides can be situationally conditioned, and the necessary decisions are reached through an intricate web of communicative processes which serve to determine whether or not enacting the divide is appropriate to a given situation. It seems that there are situations in which sectarian behaviour is regarded as socially justifiable, and acceptable across the divide, while other situations hold no such justification. The working of everyday identity formation has hardly been researched in the context of Northern Ireland, and McFarlane rightly calls for more local studies as a complement, rather than a mere adjunct to 'armchair theorising'.

247

Joan Vincent (1989), in her ethnographic study of two border parishes in County Fermanagh, demonstrates how variations in local knowledge and perception of the historical past may be analysed in an attempt to explain differences in contemporary patterns of political violence. Again, with reference to the non-sectarian tradition which exists in the County, the author's analysis suggests that in everyday practice, sectarianism may be less entrenched than a distanced observer might think. This is not to say that sectarianism does not exist, or that—as a social force—it is negligible. However, Vincent's work points in the same direction as the study of Ballycuan, namely that the divide is not a static feature of local culture, but something which is situationally contingent, and re-created according to circumstances.

Postmodernists greatly value localised knowledge and situational adaptivity (*cf.* Docherty 1988), and thus this view of the North should appeal to them. The problem with both studies, from the perspective of 'normal' social science, is that they have pilot character: not enough work of a compatible nature exists to-date which would allow a critical evaluation of the hypotheses regarding social reality in the North which could be derived from them. Thus it would be too early for the postmodernists to rejoice that their new paradigm had been supported.

On the other hand, the postmodern paradigm as I understand it does not strictly conform to the convention of hypothesis testing, and some conjectures with regard to what Kearney calls 'Ireland's post-modern project' may therefore be in order here. Given that 'the North is War', and also that sectarian divides are not permanent trenches and walls, but rather situationally contingent implements of ordering the social life-world at the local level, a dual strategy is required. Firstly, all parties involved in the conflict ought to come to terms with the fact that this conflict forms part of the local cultural pattern, and seek ways of channelling it into non-violent forms of expression while, at the same time, maintaining identity at the personal as well as at the communal level; secondly, with the success of this process depending to a large degree on situational conditions of the respective communities, a radically decentralised mode of decision making would be required in which universals, the classical output of 'normal' social science, would seem quite out of place as an information input. While the latter would be well in tune with postmodernist postulates, the former poses a great challenge to received ways of perceiving the North, and hence to cultural and social research, regardless of any specific paradigm.

The idea that 'the North is War' with or without the British Army, the IRA or their Loyalist and other counterparts might suggest resignation; but all I am trying to say is that perhaps the roots of the conflict lie in aspects of the regional culture nobody has yet looked at in this context. The postmodernists in Ireland expect much of a European Union in which the nation state would make way for a 'radical pluralism and regionalism' (Kearney 1988), and Europe might indeed open up new possibilities for reconciliation; but while it is far from certain that Europe will develop in the way the postmodernists hope for, there is also to-date on their part a lack of practical vision which goes beyond the regionalist rhetoric. The meddling-through strategy may be postmodern, and highly useful in Academia, but it has no great record of achievement in the North, either way.

THE WEST IS LEARNING

The West is a different matter altogether; pilgrims of alternative life-style (some in hippy dress, some, at least mentally, in blackshirt outfit) flock towards the magical land West of the Shannon, anxious to become even more 'Irish' than the Irish themselves, disturbing the locals by setting up independent schools where Irish and German are taught as first languages, instead of English. Together with returned migrants and people from the eastern counties, they conjure up a new version of 'Irishness' which puzzles almost everybody except Sheeran (1987), and I take his point that if the old woman from Feakle from whom Lady Gregory collected herbal lore had been a Hopi rather than an Irish peasant, Lady Gregory's folkloristic collections might well have become cult books of the New Age movement. Sheeran (1988a) relates the Irish sense of place to the Otherworld, and hence it is hardly surprising that the West, where Ireland is supposed to be most Irish, should attract 'hordes of hippie [*sic*] farmers, bio-dynamic agriculturalists, sea gipsies, artists and meditators' (Sheeran 1987).

The West, as I said earlier, has been thoroughly demythologised over the past twenty years or so. Today the old images serve merely to attract tourists and foreign investors (*cf.* Gibbons 1988). And Sheeran (1988b) mourns:

> Can anything be salvaged, any value, meaning or project from the dereliction of the myth of the West? A culture bereft of its sustaining myths and legitimizing fables loses meaning and identity.

In his manuscript, Sheeran (1987) examines this problematic at length, but unfortunately the published version quoted above does not reproduce his argument in full. It is interesting that the passages which have been omitted in the latter version are precisely those which offer a new identity for the West, one which seems rather different from, but is in fact quite similar to the original 'myth'.

In the heyday of this myth, the West as repository of Gaelicism was assigned a specific educational role: to preserve the language in its Gaeltacht areas, to teach it in Irish Colleges, and to generally foster Irish culture. During the 1960s and 1970s, a number of anthropologists and other social scientists ventured to show how socially rotten 'traditional' Ireland, i.e. the West was, and the previously venerable region sank into ridicule as the rural backwater of Irish modernity. However, at the same time the new myth of the West was already in the making. And again this myth has something to do with learning.

Since the late 1960s, an increasing number of counter-culturally inclined immigrants have settled on the west coast. Ireland seems to them a country with a peculiar spiritual quality and, moreover, a special task in the spiritual transformation towards a New Age. Not only are (real or imaginary) Celtic traditions part of the New Age iconography (*cf.* Kockel 1995), but the contemporary everyday life of people in the West is idealised. For many, mostly young people from the Continent, but also from further afield, the West of Ireland has taken the place of the American West as the land of unlimited opportunity. It is difficult to estimate the number of temporary migrants who try to settle in the West, but the number of those who stay is still impressive enough, and their impact on the local communities in which they settle is, at least qualitatively, substantial (*cf.* Kockel 1989; 1991; 1993). The debate in *Common Ground*, mentioned earlier, shows clearly that the vision of Ireland as a vanguard of a New Age is not limited to immigrant counter-culture, but has a basis in the native population as well. Not surprisingly, allegations of neo-colonialism have played an important part in this debate, since the original initiative in this movement had been taken by the immigrants. Meanwhile, however, the majority of people involved in the movement are either Irish-born, or at least of Irish descent. Regardless of their origin, they try to root their movement, ideologically as well as practically, in some legitimising notion of Irishness which would set them apart from the Old Age. At the spiritual level, a rather indiscriminate globalism prevails which leads to theories like that of the mystic Poynder, who sees Sligo as the Centre of the Light Star of the British Isles and expounds an Irish genealogy which goes back to Atlantis via the Pharaos. He may or may not be right, but his 'evidence' is rather shaky.

At the more practical level, the New Age movement maintains that the West is a region where things are done differently from the way they are done everywhere else in the developed world, and—by implication—better. While the latter assertion is difficult to establish at this stage, there is considerable empirical support for the former.

The regional economy of the West is characterised by a high degree of informality, with a high incidence of forms of production and exchange which, for better or worse, defy the 'natural laws' of 'the

251

Market' just as much as they circumvent state planning (Kockel 1993). Occupational pluralism, as a traditional form of work organisation, has in many local communities proved a fairly efficient way of managing low rates of formal employment; 'casual companies' take this principle to the level of team work and the division of labour, where companies are not registered and wound up in the usual way, but formed and dissolved according to circumstances; non-monetary transactions play a major role in the economic life of the region; 'gombeen'-relationships persist or have been resurrected, adapted to the changed social and economic circumstances of local communities; at the more formal level, co-operative initiatives have spread widely since the 1960s. Although it is difficult to put exact figures on these phenomena, partly because of a lack of suitable indicators which could be quantified, their contribution to regional development can be regarded as substantial. These forms of economic activity and organisation resemble very closely what think-tanks of the New Age movement, like TOES or the Fritz-Schumacher-Foundation, have been trying to develop. It seems as if, at least in this respect and within the New Age movement, the West might well be able to resume its ancient role as the seat of learning. One noteworthy aspect of this resurgence is that it has found geographical expression in concentrations at places which will delight every pilgrim of the New Age: Fennell (1987) already noted the emergence of a new, coherent cultural region in the northwest—Lough Key Country—which also includes the mythical grave of Queen Medb; the second major concentration which is shaping a new region can be found around Galway Bay, with Lady Gregory's Coole Park almost at its centre.

IRISHNESS AND EUROPEAN ETHNOLOGY

One aspect of 'Irishness' which emerges from all strands of the current debate is the view expressed by Foster (1988), and summarised in the same issue of *Studies* by Maginness (1988). It appears that 'Irishness is something essentially political, rather than an ethnic or cultural question'. Not as if the idea were new: Weisweiler (1943) made the same point at a time when there was very little doubt about what 'Irishness' meant. Moreover, he—and many Continental observers after him, from Heinrich Böll to Alfred Andersch—claimed that to be 'Irish' meant: to be a rebel, often without a cause. The unruly, anti-authoritarian underdog—not in the sense of the boisterous drunkenness of the 'stage-Irish', but in a much more subtle, subversively quiet way. James Dean might well be a better personification of 'Irishness' than John Wayne—he stands for a very different myth.

We are left with a rather peculiar situation: There are two Irish provinces—at the same time European regions—which are generally regarded as highly problematic in most respects: politically divided, economically underdeveloped, socially deprived. Yet there are two emerging paradigms for whose proponents these provinces, and in consequence of their own reasoning, Ireland as a whole, seems to be a potential vanguard for something, or at least further advanced than most other European countries on the way to a breakdown of the nation state (*cf.* Kearney 1988).

The debate over Irish identity is part of this ideological crisis, but it may also be part of its resolution. And this is the challenge which the debate constitutes for the European ethnologist. It is a manifold challenge, and only its main aspects can be outlined here.

Initial research, albeit directed at different sets of hypotheses, has already supported some of the claims raised by the various parties to this debate; these claims should therefore be taken as working hypothesis, and further research along quite conventional lines should be undertaken in order to submit them to a proper test. In a more experimental fashion, the postmodernist and New Age projects may be treated as such, examined for their practical implications, and research be undertaken into the necessary strategies for implementation as indicated above, in the discussion of the North. The difficulty with these suggestions might be that neither project can be treated with the established methods of 'normal' social science; this, however, does not imply the inevitable need to adopt some sort of postmodern or New Age methodology (in so far as it exists).

The main difference between the postmodernist and the New Age strand of the Irish debate seems to be that the former are still in search of 'Irishness' while the latter claim to have already, however intuitively, found it. This may well be a result of their different paradigms. The ideal of cultural pluralism seems to be more readily accommodated within the universally relativistic holism of the New Age than by the rationalistically differentiating holism of the postmodernists, whose attempt to distinguish clearly and *a priori* between 'liberating myths' and 'incarcerating' ones demands a level of presumably scientific objectivity—with its correlate of political and cultural intolerance—which contradicts their very project. Are the postmodernists merely trying to be academically respectable (quite an honourable, if slightly misguided pursuit), or are they actually following Bono's suggestion to try and define away the more unpleasant aspects of 'Irishness', instead of coming to terms with them?

The nature of the New Age movement, and the contradictions in which the postmodernists in Ireland are caught up, make it obvious that in either case 'Irishness' is being fabricated (as indeed it always has been), rather than rediscovered. But whereas the New Agers in the West have fabricated a relatively continuous, unbroken identity, the postmodernists in their debate on the North apparently seek to discontinue everyday 'Irishness', trying to replace it with something more elaborate and, presumably, heroic. Research in the West of Ireland (Kockel 1993) has shown how everyday cultural practice has successfully steered the region around institutional barriers imposed by the hegemony of industrial capitalism and state planning which constitutes the Irish version of the mixed economy, and how this process has helped in the (however unintentional) formation of an identity highly compatible (for better or worse) with New Age values. The postmodernist project seems much harder to accomplish, perhaps because while the New Age movement in the West has long proceeded to action, the postmodernists are still talking...

There are at least two common themes in both strands of the debate which point beyond Ireland and 'Irishness' to wider issues: the decline of the logocentric world view, and the breakdown of the nation state. On both counts, the proponents of the debate claim that Ireland could serve as an example for the wider world. However, the construction of a coherent 'non-logocentric' worldview, and of a viable alternative to the nation state, will require extensive theoretical work.

A further challenge in the debate as reviewed here is that of unravelling the symbolism hidden in the debate. At the start of this essay, reference was made to the dispute between Queen Medb and King Conchobar. In the present context, this mythical dispute could be interpreted in at least two ways. Firstly, the New Age Movement emphasises the Feminine, while the postmodernists, although not explicitly condoning Masculine values, by virtue of their urban, secular, rationalist orientation more or less place themselves in that 'corner'. The struggle between Medb and Conchobar was a struggle over sovereignty, and this, precisely, seems to be the hidden agenda of the current debate. If, therefore, 'Irishness' and the future of Ireland are to be decided not in prosperous Leinster, but in backward Connacht and divided Ulster, then the perspective of much of our contemporary research on Ireland, and the type of questions asked by ethnographers, ought to be thoroughly revised.

In this essay, New Age and postmodernity have been presented as rival paradigms, and it may seem that the eventual 'victory' of one over the other is what is at stake here. There is, however, another possibility, and here European ethnology might meet its greatest challenge, but may also be able to make perhaps its most valuable contribution. In my introduction, I made no mention of Meath, the fifth of Ireland's four ancient provinces, the Centre, which represented, for example, stewardship, dignity, stability, supports, renown—values associated with Kingship. The Centre was supposed to hold the parts together, to invest identity in the whole.

Today, the West may still be learning and the North war, the East prosperity and the South music—but what, and where, is today the Centre that holds...?

BIBLIOGRAPHY

Bausinger, H
1978 Identität. In Bausinger, H, Jeggle, U, Korff, G and Scharfe, M, *Grundzüge der Volkskunde*, Darmstadt, 204-63.
Bax, M
1977 *Harpstrings and Confessions: An Anthropological Study of Politics in Rural Ireland*, Assen.
Bloch, E
1959 *Das Prinzip Hoffnung*, Frankfurt/Main.
Brody, H
1973 *Inishkillane. Change and Decline in the West of Ireland*, London.
Brunt, B
1988 *The Republic of Ireland*, London.
Common Ground. A Journal for Alternative Living
1988 issues April/May, June/July, August/September.
Curtin, C and Wilson T (eds)
1989 *Ireland from Below: Social Change and Local Communities*, Galway.
Docherty, T
1988 Passages to Postmodernism. In Kearney, R (ed.), 268-75.
Fennell, D
1984 *The State of the Nation: Ireland since the Sixties*, Dublin.
1987 *A Connacht Journey*, Dublin.
Foster, J
1988 Who are the Irish? *Studies*, Winter, 403-16.

Gerdes, D
1980 *Aufstand der Provinz: Regionalismus in Westeuropa*, Frankfurt/Main.

Gibbons, L
1984 Synge, Country and Western: the Myth of the West in Irish and American Culture. In Curtin, C, Kelly, M and O'Dowd, L (eds), *Culture and Ideology in Ireland*, Galway, 1-19.
1988 Coming out of Hibernation? The Myth of Modernity in Irish Culture. In Kearney, R (ed.), 205-18.

Hechter, M.
1975 *Internal Colonialism. The Celtic Fringe in British National Development, 1536-1966*, London.

Hewson, P
1988 The White Nigger. In Kearney, R (ed.), 188-91.

Kearney, R
1986 Using Tradition as a Force for the Future, *The Irish Times*, 4 November, 5.

Kearney, R (ed.)
1985 *The Irish Mind. Exploring Intellectual Traditions*, Dublin.
1988 *Across the Frontiers: Ireland in the 1990s. Cultural—Political—Economic*, Dublin.

Kirby, P
1988 *Has Ireland a Future?* Cork.

Kockel, U
1989 Immigrants - Entrepreneurs of the Future? *Common Ground* 70, 6-8.
1991 Countercultural Immigrants in the West of Ireland. In King, R (ed.), *Contemporary Irish Migration*, Dublin, 71-83.
1993 *The Gentle Subversion. Informal Economy and Regional Development in the West of Ireland*, Bremen.
1995 The Celtic Quest: Beuys as Hero and Hedge School Master. In Thistlewood, D (ed.), *Joseph Beuys—Diverging Critiques*, Liverpool, IN PRESS.

Maginnes, A
1988 Who are the Irish? *Studies*, Winter, 417-21.

McCullagh, C
1984 Entrepreneurship and Development: an Alternative Perspective, *Economic and Social Review* 15, 109-24.

McFarlane, G
1989 Dimensions of Protestantism: The Working of Protestant Identity in a Northern Irish Village. In Curtin, C and Wilson, T (eds), 23-45.

Ó Tuathaigh, G (ed.)
1986 *Community, Culture, and Conflict: Aspects of the Irish Experience*, Galway.

Pratschke, J
1985 Economic Philosophy and Ideology in Ireland, *Studies*, Summer, 145-54.

Rees, A and Rees, B
1961 *Celtic Heritage: Ancient Tradition in Ireland and Wales*, London.

Shanklin, E
1985 *Donegal's Changing Traditions*, New York.

Sheeran, P
1987 *The Idiocy of Irish Rural Life Reviewed*, xeroxed typescript.
1988a Genius Fabulae: The Irish Sense of Place, *Irish University Review* 18(2), 191-206.
1988b The Idiocy of Irish Rural Life Reviewed, *The Irish Review* 5, 27-33.

Simms, D
1981 *Tourism, Entrepreneurs, and Change in Soutwest Ireland*, PhD-thesis, SUNY at Albany.

Weisweiler, J
1943 *Heimat und Herrschaft. Wirkung und Ursprung eines irischen Mythus*, Halle.

Vincent, J
1989 Local Knowledge and Political Violence in County Fermanagh. In Curtin, C and Wilson, T (eds), 92-108.

Witoszek, N and Sheeran, P
1985 From Explanation to Intervention, *The Crane Bag* 9, 83-6.

Appendix

The Culture and Tourism Research Unit at the Institute of Irish Studies, University of Liverpool

The *Culture and Tourism Research Unit* originated from an interdisciplinary research programme on European regional development, initiated in 1990, which focuses on questions of development and change in peripheral regions of Europe from a comparative perspective, promoting experience exchange between these regions. A range of projects carried out under the programme investigate key issues in Irish development within the context of the current restructuring of the economic, political and social organisation of Europe: the Single Market, the opening-up of Eastern Europe, and the creation of a united Germany as the major economic power in Europe.

MAIN ACTIVITIES OF THE UNIT

In summer 1992, the *Culture and Tourism Research Unit* was established to provide an interdisciplinary forum and institutional focus for research on certain key issues identified within this research programme, in particular the management of 'cultural resources' as part of strategies of endogenous regional development.

Development of courses in cultural resource management

With support from the *UFC/HEFC Continuing Vocational Education Development Fund*, and in co-operation with the *European Centre for Traditional and Regional Cultures* and the *European Society for Irish Studies*, a range of innovative short courses are being developed. The courses provide professional training in the management of cultural resources, and can be credited towards an academic and/or professional qualification. They will also be available as a distance learning package.

Ullrich Kockel (ed.), *Landscape, Heritage and Identity: Case Studies in Irish Ethnography*, Liverpool University Press 1995, 259-61.

The courses are grouped into five separate units, covering the theory and methods of representing regional culture; legal and socio-economic aspects of cultural resource development; and case studies focusing on aspects of material and non-material regional culture. The testing of course materials commenced in summer 1993, and the first intake of students is anticipated for 1995. The distance learning programme will be offered through regional and national tuition centres across Europe.

Cultural tourism and local entrepreneurship

This project, with support from the *European Society for Irish Studies* and the *Economic and Social Research Council*, examines different structures of, and region-specific approaches to innovative development programmes in Ireland, comparing their experience to that of programmes in other parts of Europe. It investigates the contribution of these programmes to the growth of entrepreneurial culture in peripheral regions, seeking to find suitable ways of improving existing programmes, and to identify vital components of possible alternative strategies.

Ethnic nationalism, language and identity

With support from the *EC Commission*, a pilot study was carried out, in 1990/91, of political culture in three European border regions (Ulster, Euskadi and Schleswig) and its implications for European Unity. Following this study, several issues are currently being followed up.

The effects of the changing territorial and political relevance of borders for regional, national and supra-national government need to be better understood. The purely economic perception of borders as barriers to trade appears to be a rather one-eyed view. In the light of the opening of the internal borders within the European Union, their conceptualisation as 'central places' may well yield new insights into processes of regional development. Cultural territories often do not coincide with the territories of nation states; hence cultural regions frequently cut across national boundaries. This constitutes a major challenge for cultural policy, at the national as well as the supra-national level.

Regional and minority languages play a significant role in the formation of ethnic identities, and there has been a resurgence of lesser used languages over recent years. However, the function and experience of

260

ethnic language schools varies greatly between different regions. Comparative research on language use and ethnic schooling seeks to provide insights into problem aspects of ethnicity with a view to social cohesion, and its relevance extends beyond existing frontier regions, into all areas with multi-cultural societies.

Other projects

There are a number of smaller projects carried out under the auspices of the Unit. Members of the Unit are involved in studies on the socio-cultural impacts of economic restructuring in peripheral maritime regions; evaluative research on 'tourist trail' projects linking the North of Ireland with the North of England and the Southwest of Scotland; and comparative work on emigration from marginal rural areas. The Unit has carried out consultancy assignments for organisations in the public, private and voluntary sectors.

Membership of the Unit

The Unit brings together staff and postgraduate students from a range of departments within the University of Liverpool. During its first two years, it has developed extensive networks at the local, national and European level, reaching from the West of Ireland to Estonia and Slovenia. The work of the Unit is led by Dr Ullrich Kockel (Irish Studies) in collaboration with Dr Máiréad Nic Craith (Irish Studies) and Dr Dominic Keown (Hispanic Studies). There are a number of associated researchers in the Institute of Irish Studies, the Departments of Geography and History, and the University's Centre for Manx Studies. External members of the Unit come from the City of Liverpool's Department of Adult Education, from University College Cork (Ireland), the universities of Joensuu (Finland), Tartu (Estonia) and Tübingen (Germany), as well as from independent research institutes, such as ECTARC (Wales), and from research users in the public, private and voluntary sectors. For further details on the work of the Unit, please write to:

Culture and Tourism Unit, Institute of Irish Studies,
University of Liverpool, P.O.Box 147,
Liverpool, England, L69 3BX.

LIVERPOOL STUDIES IN EUROPEAN REGIONAL CULTURES

Forthcoming:

Borderline Cases:
The Ethnic Frontiers of European Integration
by **Ullrich Kockel**

ISBN 0-85323-520-1

The book considers the question of ethnic boundaries in the context of European integration. It compares three regions in the EU where state boundaries divide ethnic regions, examining the implications of political culture in these regions for European unity, and assessing the significance of the integration process at the local and regional level. This analysis is then placed in a wider context of ethnonationalism in Europe, East and West. In conclusion, the book draws parallels between border conflicts and the ethnic 'frontiers' which are emerging as a result of labour mobility, and discusses the significance of these phenomena in terms of European policy.

Contents: